MANNERS, CUSTOMS, AND OBSERVANCES

MANNERS, CUSTOMS, AND OBSERVANCES

THEIR ORIGIN AND SIGNIFICATION

BY

LEOPOLD WAGNER

AUTHOR OF
"NAMES: AND THEIR MEANING," "MORE ABOUT NAMES,"
ETC., ETC.

LONDON
WILLIAM HEINEMANN
1894

REPUBLISHED BY GALE RESEARCH COMPANY, BOOK TOWER, DETROIT, 1968

Library of Congress Card Catalog Number: 68–22059

PREFACE

ALL that need be said by way of preface to the following pages, is to lay stress upon the great pains which have been taken to ensure accuracy. The innumerable books consulted to this end have not involved half so much time and patience as the journeys undertaken for the purpose of interviewing those who, owing to their official position, or for any other reason, could be relied upon to impart information at first hand. In short, recourse has been had to books only where no living authority was available. By such means, many apocryphal stories have been avoided or explained away.

In a work of this nature, ingenious theories and plausible explanations should find no place. Still less should generally accepted statements be complacently set down without inquiry. Of curious and out-of-the-way information there is in these days assuredly no lack. One can rarely take up a periodical without meeting with something new and strange of archæological interest. But, for the very reason that it is found where it is, it lays itself open to qualification. In another place the self-same subject may be presented in a totally different light. This is because ordinarily accessible information, such as is every day drawn upon by pressmen and magazine writers, is to a great extent conflicting and unreliable. Antiquaries are never so much at variance as when they are striving to make a very simple matter appear abstruse. Even grave historians will often be found romancing instead of adhering to sober fact. Take, as a solitary example, the ceremony of Kissing the Pope's Foot; or, as the vulgar will have it, the Pope's Toe. According to Matthew of Westminster this originated in an expedient of one of the Popes during the eighth century. Previous to his time, we are informed, it had always been the custom for the faithful to kiss the Pope's right hand; but on one occasion a woman clutched the hand of his Holiness with such fervour, that, foreseeing the danger to which he might be exposed, he deliberately cut it off, and was thereafter obliged to offer his foot. This story is as preposterous as it is unauthenticated. The most diligent search through the lives of the Popes has failed to elicit any information of the kind. But one need not take the trouble to wade through the history of the Church in order to be able to give the lie direct to such an unfounded assertion. There is not a Roman Catholic in the land, but who knows that a maimed priest could not on any account be allowed to exercise his sacerdotal functions. Yet this ridiculous story is repeated in most of the so-called books of reference which nowadays adorn our library shelves. It matters not upon what respectable authority such statements are put forth; if they cannot bear the test of studious inquiry, they should be rejected *in toto*.

It only remains to express indebtedness to many learned and influential gentlemen whose valuable time and generous assistance have been so largely laid under contribution for this work; notably, to M. S. S. Dipnall, Esq., late Secretary of Christ's Hospital, for some authentic particulars concerning the Blue-coat boys' costume; and to Louis B. Abrahams, Esq., B.A., author of "A Manual of Jewish History," for much of the material drawn upon in the Jewish section of this work.

L. W.

LONDON, 1894.

CONTENTS

REGAL AND ECCLESIASTICAL.

NAVAL AND MILITARY.

Courtship and Marriage.

Death and Burial.

Amusements of the People.

PATRON SAINTS AND THEIR ATTRIBUTES.

FESTIVALS OF THE CHURCH.

REGAL AND ECCLESIASTICAL

REGAL AND ECCLESIASTICAL

1. **Heraldry** is in all respects a complicated science; only those who are officially connected with that sombre-looking building known as Heralds' College, in Queen Victoria Street, or who have made armorial bearings their special study, can be expected to boast of something more than a superficial acquaintance with a subject so vast. Nevertheless, a few broad principles may be here laid down with advantage. It was Charlemagne who introduced heraldic devices—which had their origin in the military standards and symbolical marks of distinction on the bucklers of barbarian nations—into the Western World (*see* 36). Up to the time of the Crusades, however, such devices were strictly confined to rulers and princes. During the Crusades, when each and every knight had his face, in common with the rest of his body, encased in armour, the necessity for some means whereby one knight could be distinguished from another early suggested itself. To engrave his name upon his shield would have been useless, for in those days very few people could read. On the other hand, everyone could distinguish an animal from a bird, and although several knights might make a choice of the same animal or bird, there were a multitude of ways by which confusion was to be avoided. Each knight, accordingly, chose his own device, with the exception of a lion, which from being the king of beasts, and therefore regarded as the emblem of sovereign power, was appro-

priated by royal personages. When, for example, Richard I. returned from the Holy Land, he bore a crowned lion on the crest of his helmet, and three golden lions on his shield. For greater distinction our kings at a later date wore their crowns on their helmets in the battle-field, and earls and dukes their coronets. At the battle of Agincourt, the Duke of Alençon hewed off with one stroke of his sword part of the crown worn by King Henry V. Again, after the death of Richard III. on Bosworth Field, his crown was picked up out of a hawthorn bush by a soldier, who brought it to Lord Stanley; in memory of which incident Henry VII. chose a hawthorn bush and a crown above it for his own cognizance. Ordinary knights displayed their chosen devices on their helmets and shields; and as it was considered a great honour to have been a Crusader, the same devices were borne by their descendants, both in peace and war. Such was the origin of armorial bearings, or **Coats of Arms** as they were called, from being embroidered on the rich coats worn over their armour in the field, and upon their ordinary garments at home. When they appeared with their vizors down at tournaments, a herald sounded his trumpet and announced the name, family, and rank, as revealed by the devices upon the shield and horse-furniture, of each. At a subsequent period these devices became so complicated, owing to the union and "impalement" of the armorial bearings of different families, that it was found necessary to register and place them under official control. In this way **Heralds' College** was called into existence. The chief representative of the college in Scotland received the name of the **Lyon King at Arms,** from the lion rampant on the escutcheon of the Scottish kings; that of the English provinces north of the river Trent **Norroy,** literally north king; and that of the corresponding district south, at first **Surroy,** but at a later date

Clarencieux, from the nomination of the Duke of Clarence to this office by his brother, Henry V. A very short period elapsed before the heralds overcame the difficulties presented by an over-blazoned shield, by means of an abridgment in the form of a crest and motto. The earliest **Mottoes** were invariably the battle-cry or parole in some memorable engagement; but as time wore on imagination was called into play to devise mottoes of an original character. The idea of **Supporters of the Family Arms** was derived from the pages or esquires who bore the banner of a knight in the field; and, generally speaking, these supporters were an imitation of the beasts represented in the arms themselves. What are known as **Emblems** in armorial bearings were originally the devices displayed on the livery or worn as badges on the arms of servants and retainers of the nobility. Even tradesmen who had the privilege of supplying goods or provisions to a nobleman were expected to wear his livery and display his badge in mediæval times. From this custom the assumption of the royal arms on his shop-front by a highly-favoured tradesman took its rise.

2. **The Royal Arms of Great Britain** are familiar to everyone, yet those who understand the signification of their component parts are few. The **Three Golden Lions** on a red field in the first quarter are described in heraldic parlance as "gules, three lions passant gardant in pale or," *i.e.*, *gules*, from the French *gueles*, the red colour of the throat, and the Latin *gula*, a reddened skin; *passant gardant*, walking with the face looking sidewise; *in pale*, impaled with the arms of Scotland in the second quarter; *or*, from the Latin *aurum*, gold. Rulers and princes always chose *gules* for their royal colour in ancient times, because it was looked upon as the symbol of valour.

Scarlet is still the royal livery of England (*see* 5, 30). William the Conqueror and his successors had only two lions for their royal arms; these were derived from Rollo, Duke of Normandy, who bore the first in respect of his own province, and the second of that of Maine, after it was added to Normandy. The third lion was assumed by Henry II. in right of his queen, Eleanor, daughter of the Duke of Aquitaine. The **Lion Rampant** in the second quarter was the ensign of the Scottish kings from the reign of William the Lion—who received his surname on its account—down to the union of the two kingdoms in the person of our James I.; just as the **Harp** in the third quarter was that of the early kings of Ireland, having originally been adopted in compliment to their native bards. Gallant little Wales has never been represented in the British royal arms, obviously because it has never had any arms of its own; all it can boast of is an emblem, that of the **Leek** (*see* 421). Of the other national emblems which have been accorded positions in association with the royal arms, the **Rose of England** is the least time-honoured. Perhaps, however, it is invested with a more interesting story than all the rest, since it has entered so largely into the party strife of our country. To go back to the beginning, the red rose was the badge of John of Gaunt, the first Duke of Lancaster, and the white rose that of his brother Edward of Langley, the first Duke of York. The story of the "Wars of the Roses" forms one of the most exciting chapters in English history. Not less than thirty sanguinary battles were fought during this protracted struggle, nor was it until the union of the roses was effected by the marriage of Henry VII. with Elizabeth of York that peace once more reigned in the land. Ever since that date the rose has maintained its position as our national emblem. The **Thistle of Scotland** commemorates an incident whereby the Scots were saved from being surprised in a night attack. During that early period of their history, when their coasts were liable to frequent incursions by the Danes, it chanced that, although those piratical marauders considered it cowardly to attack an enemy under cover of night, they, finding the probabilities of success all in their favour, resorted to this expedient on one memorable occasion. With bared feet and noiseless steps they stole upon the Scots unobserved, until suddenly one of them planted his foot upon a thistle, which caused him to howl with pain. The alarm being thus given, the Scots fell upon the attacking party with such success that they put them to the rout with great slaughter. The **Shamrock of Ireland** is intimately associated with the life of St. Patrick (*see* 422). It may be mentioned that the trefoil finds a place not only in the royal arms, but also in the crown of the British sovereign, because it is emblematical of the three kingdoms in one. The motto, DIEU ET MON DROIT ("God and my right"), was the parole of the day given by Richard I. to his army at the battle of Gisors, in which the French were signally defeated; while that inscribed on the band or garter surrounding the royal arms, HONI SOIT QUI MAL Y PENSE ("Evil be to him who evil thinks"), forms the motto of the Order of the Garter instituted by Edward III. The **Lion and Unicorn** as supporters (*see* 1) are those of the royal arms of England and Scotland respectively; the latter was introduced when James VI. of Scotland became also James I. of England in the year 1603.

3. **The Plume of Ostrich Feathers**, and the motto ICH DIEN, were found on the helmet of the blind King of Bohemia after he was slain at the battle of Crecy, while serving as a volunteer in the army of the King of France, August 26th, 1346. In commemoration of his signal

victory on this day, though the English forces were nominally commanded by his father, Edward III., Edward the Black Prince adopted the plume and motto for his crest, and as such they have been borne by the Prince of Wales ever since.

4. **The Fleur-de-Lis,** which was the royal insignia of France until the Revolution of 1789, was chosen by Louis VII. as his emblem when, in conjunction with Conrad II. of Germany, he formed the Second Crusade. It has been stated that the fleur-de-lis received its name from the river Lis, which separated France and Artois from Flanders. By the marriage of Philip Augustus to the daughter of the Count of Flanders in the year 1191, Artois was united to the French crown; but as the Second Crusade was undertaken in 1147, the flower had already been accepted as the national emblem when the union took place (*see* 41).

5. **Red is the Royal Colour of England.** It was originally the distinctive livery of all Christian princes, but since it happens that red is also the colour of the field of the armorial bearings of England, other European sovereigns have thought fit to take their royal colour from the field of their respective arms. The English royal colour is well to the fore at Court, and on all occasions of State ceremonial. The throne, the woolsack, the seats of the peers, and the decorations generally in the Upper House of Legislature, are red. The Lord Mayor of London and the judges, as representatives of the Sovereign in the criminal courts, wear robes of scarlet. The royal livery has from the first been red, faced with gold. When Henry VIII. established a body-guard of fifty men, he put them into scarlet uniforms with gold facings. The cavalry of Elizabeth's reign were ordered to wear scarlet cloaks, similar to nobles and courtiers. Red is still the

predominant colour in the British army. Huntsmen following the hounds also wear red coats, in accordance with the mandate of Henry II. enjoining all who engaged in fox-hunting to wear the royal livery, because it was a royal sport. Red, too, is the distinguishing Post Office colour; the wall and pillar-boxes, the royal mail carts, and the facings of the letter-carriers, are all red. Formerly the "twopenny postman," and the drivers of the mail-coaches wore red coats. When we reflect that the Post Office grew out of a system of royal couriers established by Richard III. for the rapid transmission of intelligence during the Scottish campaign of 1482-3, the adoption of the royal colour in the British postal service will be at once understood (*see* 2, 30).

6. An undoubted relic of feudal times in our own age is the custom of the **Royal Champion** throwing down his gauntlet as a challenge to any person who dares dispute the right to the crown of the new sovereign at a coronation. A mere formal ceremony in these days, it was a matter of necessity in those troublesome times when the title to the crown was so far from secure that every sovereign required a valiant knight, renowned for deeds of arms, to assert and vindicate his just claims to it. In the event of the challenge being taken up by another valiant knight on behalf of a rival claimant, it fell to the lot of these two knights to fight a duel to the death, on an open field or *champ*—hence the term, "champion." As is well known, the Dymocks have held their estates ever since the year 1377 on condition of their providing a Royal Champion to ride into Westminster Hall at every English coronation (*see* 73).

7. **The Orb and Sceptre,** as the symbols of sovereignty, are very ancient. The orb, surmounted by an eagle and placed in the hand of a Roman emperor, typified dominion

over all the known world, but after the accession of Constantine the Great the bird gave place to a cross. The sceptre was originally the spear upon which a king leaned for support, and at a later period a staff or wand of office. In a MS. of the Cottonian Library we find the king represented as presiding over his Witenagemote with a sword in his right hand and a long staff surmounted by a cross in his left.

8. We have it on the authority of honest old Stow that what was known as **Touching for the King's Evil** originated in the dream of a young woman sorely afflicted with a scrofulous disease, that she could be cured by the simple operation of having the part washed by the king. So great was her faith in this remedy that her relatives at last made application to Edward I. on her behalf, with the result that that monarch at once consented to perform the disagreeable duty. After ordering a basin of water to be brought, he carefully softened the tumours until the skin broke and their contents were discharged. Then the sign of the cross was made and the patient retired, fully assured of her cure, which was effected within a week. How the disease came to be called the "King's Evil" is not quite clear, because neither Edward I. nor any of his predecessors are known to have been attacked by it. Nevertheless, from the time of the young woman's dream until the middle of the eighteenth century, the popular belief that the mere touch of the reigning sovereign would effectually cure a scrofulous patient was very deep-rooted. Dr. Johnson was touched for the King's Evil by Queen Anne in the year 1712.

9. In a primitive state of society, when the population of the earth was small, each individual family was governed by its own head or chief, called a **Patriarch**, but subsequently, when a diversity of interests arose, and the necessity for

providing for their common safety became paramount, these patriarchs made a choice of one person—"the bravest and best," as Carlyle would have put it,—and invested him with the proper authority for discharging so important a trust. Such was the origin of the **Monarchical System of Government.** For let it be remembered that the earliest kings and rulers exercised jurisdiction over a particular city or tribe only. In Genesis mention is made of the kings of Sodom and Gomorrah, of Gerara and Salem, of Sennaar or Chaldea, and of the Elamites or Persians. How well this system of local government has stood the test of time is evidenced by the existence of practically the same kind of thing at the present day: the mayor corresponds to the king and the aldermen to the patriarchs.

10. The indolent despotism which has for so many centuries distinguished the rule of an **Eastern Monarch** was inaugurated by Ninius, the son of Ninus and Semiramis, who shut himself up with his wives in his palace at Nineveh, and entrusted the management of the State, as well as the preservation of the integrity of the Empire, to the vast armies he had levied, and to the military commanders he had bound over to him by oaths of allegiance. Ever since his time an Eastern potentate has generally considered his person as too sacred a thing to be gazed upon by the people.

11. The celebrated **Hanging Gardens of Babylon** were constructed by King Nebuchadnezzar for the gratification of his wife, who was a princess of Media, and who wished to see in the plains of Babylon something to remind her of the woods of her native land.

12. One reason why the **Bull** entered so conspicuously into the religious rites and sacrifices of the nations of

antiquity was because the Egyptians believed that Osiris, the greatest of all their gods, dwelt in their midst in the form of a pure white bull with a black forehead having a square of white in the centre. When such a one was found it was held sacred during life and worshipped after death. A pure white bull is still held sacred among the Hindoos, while the Druids always sacrificed two white bulls when the sacred mistletoe was cut, at their annual festival of the winter solstice, on the 21st of December (*see* 464).

13. Among **Prohibited Foods** on religious grounds, pigeons and pork are the most noticeable. The orthodox Russian never eats the former, on account of the sanctity conferred upon the dove in both the Old and the New Testaments; the Jew refuses the latter, because the swine, which wallows in filth, is an emblem of impurity. The ancient Egyptians never touched animal food, consequent upon their belief in the doctrine of the transmigration of souls (*see* 222).

14. It has been asserted over and over again that the **Mohammedans Regard All Women As Soulless Creatures,** little removed from the brute species; and that, not expecting to participate in the joys of heaven, Mohammedan women never frequent the mosques for prayer. This monstrous imputation is very ably refuted by George Sale in the preliminary discourse to his verbatim translation of the Koran. Let it suffice to state here that the wives of Mohammedans can and do visit the mosques for devotional purposes; but it must be at a time when the men are not there, because the Moslems are of opinion that the mingling of the sexes is antagonistic to the spirit of true devotion. With regard to those females who are perpetually confined in the harems, the majority of them are not Mohammedans

at all: as for the rest, they are free to perform their devotions in private.

15. One of the most rigid penances enjoined upon a religious community in any part of the world is the Mohammedan **Fast of Ramadân.** From the first appearance of the new moon of Ramadân, literally, "the hot month," until that of the next new moon, all Mohammedans are prohibited from eating, drinking, smoking, bathing, or the indulgence of sexual intercourse between daybreak and sunset throughout the whole thirty days. Those who, by reason of sickness, or being on a journey, are prevented from keeping the fast in its proper season, are commanded to fast a like number of days on the first opportunity ensuing. The usual explanation of this fast, as tendered to Christian travellers, is that Mohammed fasted one day in Ramadân, but as the theologians were at variance as to the exact day, they resolved to impose the fast during the whole month, in order to make sure of it. This is a myth. The truth of the whole matter is very clearly set forth in the second chapter of the Koran, as follows:—"The month of Ramadân shall ye fast, in which the Koran was sent from Heaven, a direction unto men, and declarations of direction, and the distinction between good and evil."

16. **The Christian Sabbath** differs from that of the Jews because it was on the *first* day of the week that our Lord manifested Himself to His apostles after His resurrection, and also sent down the Holy Spirit upon them in the form of fiery tongues. Moreover, the apostles determined, at the very outset of their divine mission, that the day set apart to the particular service of the Lord should *not* be the Sabbath day of the Jews. Hence the Christian Sabbath is "The Lord's Day," rather than "Sunday," which term is a

relic of paganism, denoting the day appointed by the pagan Saxons for the worship of the sun. The **Mohammedan Sabbath** is Friday, in accordance with the belief that on this day God completed the work of creation.

17. Whatever may be the feeling among Dissenters relative to the payment of **Tithes**, it must be admitted on all hands that that portion of the Mosaic constitution which provided for the support of the priesthood was most reasonable. Possessing no land of their own, the tribe of Levi distributed themselves as a special element among the twelve tribes, for whom they officiated as priests, scribes, expounders of the Law, and in a general sense charged themselves with the moral and intellectual well-being of an agricultural population. In return for such services the Israelites were commanded to contribute tenths, or **tithes**, of the entire produce of the land, towards the support of the Levites, who were subject to the High Priest, the lineal descendant of Aaron, alone. This arrangement, which obtained among the Jewish people throughout the whole of their Biblical history, was found to be so equitable and reasonable that Christian monarchs were easily persuaded to make a like provision for the support of the priesthood. In this country tithes were claimed under the description of "God's fee" by St. Augustine, Archbishop of Canterbury, but they were given voluntarily until Alfred the Great, encouraged by the pious example of Ethelwulf, his father, who gave by a royal charter the tenth part of his land for the glory of God and his own salvation, imposed them upon all in the course of his brief but useful reign.

18. Everything in the **Roman Catholic Church** has a meaning. The **Altar** signifies the table upon which our Lord partook of the Last Supper with His apostles, and also

Mount Calvary, upon which He shortly afterwards offered Himself as a living sacrifice for the redemption of mankind. In all ages of the world the word "altar" has had relation to sacrifice; and as the Roman Catholic Church alone offers up sacrifice, it does not obtain and cannot be claimed by any other religious communion. The rubric that the altar must always be of stone is founded upon the circumstance that the Sacrifice of the Mass was originally offered up on the tombs of the martyrs in the Roman catacombs (*see* 224). The **Corporal** and **Linen Cloths** which cover the altar are symbolical of the linen cloths wrapped around the sacred body of our Lord when He was laid in the sepulchre. The **Candles** lighted on the altar signify the light of faith revealed to the Gentiles. The **Crucifix** is ever present in the centre of the altar to remind the worshippers of the Passion and Death of the Redeemer; the **Chalice** represents the holy sepulchre; and the **Patten**, the stone which was rolled against the entrance to that abiding-place of the sacred body of Jesus Christ. Quite as much meaning is conveyed by the different **Vestments** worn by the priest at the altar. The **Amice**, which, after holding it for a moment over his forehead, he fastens around his neck, represents the piece of linen with which the Jews bandaged the eyes of our Lord before they struck Him with the palms of their hands, saying, "Prophesy unto us, thou Christ, Who is he that smote thee?" The **Alb**, or long white robe, is symbolical of the garment which Herod put about the body of our Lord when he sent Him back to Pilate. The **Maniple**, pinned on the left arm, the **Stole**, which hangs around his neck, and the **Girdle**, represent the cords with which our Lord was bound when He appeared before Caiaphas, the High Priest. The **Chasuble**, or outer vestment, denotes the purple garment put upon Him by the soldiers when they mockingly saluted Him as King of the Jews, and the **Cross** embroidered upon it, the ignominious instrument of His death, which He bore upon his sacred shoulders up the hill of Calvary. Even the **Colour of the Outer Vestment** is significant. RED is used for Feasts of the Holy Ghost (*see* 57), and of the Martyrs; PURPLE in times of penance and mourning (*see* 206, 373, 379); WHITE on Feasts of the Blessed Trinity, of our Lord, except during His Passion, of the Virgin, and of the Saints, unless they are Martyrs; BLACK on Good Friday, and in Masses for the Dead; and GREEN on all other occasions, *i.e.*, when there is no special feast.

19. **The Burning of Incense** in the Roman Catholic Church is an observance borrowed from the Jewish ritual, and having the same signification, viz., that the prayers of the faithful may ascend to heaven "as incense in Thy sight." In addition to numerous allusions to incense burning in the Old Testament, we read in Luke i., relative to the history of Zacharias, that, "According to the custom of the priest's office, his lot was to burn incense when he went into the temple of the Lord. And the whole multitude of the people were praying without at the time of incense. And there appeared unto him an angel of the Lord standing on the right side of the altar of incense." Incense was also burned in the temples of pagan Rome (*see* 298).

20. In the porch of every Roman Catholic Church will be found a stoup containing **Holy Water.** This is a custom derived from the Jewish ecclesiastical law. We read in the Old Testament that God commanded Moses to make a laver of brass, which was to stand outside the Tabernacle so that the priests might wash before ministering to the Lord. Again: "And the priest shall take holy water in an earthen vessel" (Numbers v.). During the first centuries of Chris-

tianity all persons entering the church first washed their hands in the holy-water stoup; now they merely sprinkle themselves with the water as an outward manifestation of their intention to approach the altar with purity and innocence of heart. This holy water is pure water blessed, and containing a little salt. Salt enters largely into the ceremonies of the Church, being regarded as emblematical of incorruptibility. It had also the same signification among the pagans (*see* 161).

21. The object of the universal employment of the **Latin Tongue in the Mass** is very clearly set forth by Dr. Bagshawe, the author of "The Catechism Illustrated," and other works, as follows: "The Catholic Church is not the Church of one nation, speaking one language. Her children are literally of all nations and tribes and tongues; the languages spoken by them must be numbered by hundreds. It would never do to translate the solemn Sacrifice into the language of every barbarous tribe that embraces Christianity; therefore the Church chooses one language. For instructions, for all prayers in which the people can join, each nation uses its own tongue; but in the Sacraments and the Sacrifice they all employ the one language of the Church. Again, the Church is not of one age, but 'she subsists in all ages.' The languages of men are perpetually changing, and the lapse of a very few hundred years makes them unintelligible. For instance, when St. Augustine came to convert England there was no such language as English, and no such language as French; yet the Mass which he brought to England was almost word for word what it is now. Indeed, we find recorded as an event in the life of Pope Gregory, who sent him to England, that he introduced six words into the Canon of the Mass, which we now find there. Had the Mass been in the language of

the country, how many times must it have been altered since then!" To add any words of our own to the foregoing would be an insult to the intelligence of the reader.

22. **The Nimbus** or "Glory," which in Christian Art surrounds the heads of beatified personages, had a pagan origin. The statues of the gods were always decorated with a circle of stars around the head, expressive of the essence of divine power; and when the Roman emperors assumed all the honours due to divinity, they not only caused themselves to be represented with an aureole in statuary and upon canvas, but they even appeared in public crowned with a circle of rays imitating the glory of the sun. During the first centuries of the Church, the nimbus was studiously avoided in Christian representations, and its subsequent employment was due to accident rather than design. Without a thought of falling into heathenish practices, the clergy from the sixth to the twelfth centuries uniformly attached a broad circular brass plate upon the heads of statues situated in the open air as a slight protection against rain and snow. Such a disc-like aureole will often be met with in Roman Catholic churches at the present day. This suggested a like addition to the heads of such statues as were accommodated under cover, for the sake of ornamentation; so that when at length saintly legends came to be represented upon canvas, the aureole around the head of a beatified personage was never wanting.

23. The object of placing the **Altar at the East End of Churches,** so that the worshippers shall have their faces towards the east, is generally stated to be as a reminder of Christ, "the Day Spring and the Resurrection." But we can trace this custom much further back than the

commencement of the Christian era. The Greeks and other nations of antiquity not only buried their dead with the feet towards the east, but, like the Romans who came after them, they habitually turned their faces eastwards while praying. The true explanation of this must be sought in sun worship, which is the instinctive religion of all primitive races. The Jews turn their faces in the direction of Jerusalem, and the Mohammedans in that of Mecca, as indicated by a framed card containing the word *Misrach*, or East, among the former, and by a niche in one of the walls among the latter during prayers.

24. It is a curious but undeniable fact that the **Papal Tiara** or triple crown was, in its original form, nothing more pretentious than the Roman cap of liberty (*see* 119). All the images of the popes who preceded the reign of the Emperor Constantine appear with the head uncovered; whereas Silvester, whose pontificate was contemporary with him, wears the cap identical with that of the manumitted slaves. Whether it was assumed at the Emperor's order or of his own accord does not transpire; but that it was intended to signify the liberation of the Church from heathenish oppression and the many privileges granted to her by Constantine, there is no room to doubt. This is the conclusion arrived at by all authors who have made the subject their special study. The earliest instance of the coronation of a pope was that of Nicholas I., in the year 858, who added a gold circlet to his cap as the symbol of civil power. The second circlet was added by Boniface VIII. in the following century, as is generally thought, to denote his spiritual power over sovereigns; and the third by Urban V. in the year 1632, as a mere ornament, without any special signification. It should be added that the Pope ordinarily wears a mitre, the tiara being reserved for state

occasions. At the same time, whenever he says Mass in public the tiara is always laid on the altar.

25. **The Episcopal Mitre**, says the French numismatist Pellerin, "is the head-covering worn by the sovereign pontiff of the Hebrews, and was afterwards used, under the name of *Cidaris*, by the Oriental kings and the pontiffs of paganism with some small difference." It was not transferred to the priesthood by the early Christian Church, but after the eleventh century we meet with it in representations of popes, bishops, abbots, etc. The strict meaning of the mitre and its parts is thus expressed by Pope Boniface III., "The two horns are the two Testaments; the strings, the spirit and the letter." The mitre is worn by all Roman Catholic prelates from the Pope downwards.

26. Strictly speaking, the designation **Crosier** is applicable only to the official staff of an archbishop, which has a cross at its upper end; that of a bishop terminates in an ornamental curve in allusion to his pastoral functions, and should therefore be styled a **Crook**. An archbishop is distinguished from a bishop by having the crosier borne before him, while he, like a bishop, carries the crook. Du Cange is perhaps a little too fanciful when, speaking of the crosier, he says, "One part was crooked to draw the meek, the other to punish the contumacious." The Pope does not carry a crosier because, as has been suggested, the curve implies limited jurisdiction.

27. We are informed by Dudley Fosbrooke, in his "Encyclopædia of Antiquities," that "when Peter first preached at Antioch they shaved his head like a foole." However this may have been, it is certain that the **Tonsure** was not the distinguishing mark of the priesthood during

the first centuries of the Church. At the same time, all Christians were expected to avoid vanity in dressing their hair, and to keep it short; and since cutting the hair close was anciently the universal expression of mourning and penance (*see* 208), the primitive hermits shaved the whole head as a sign of greater austerity. Imitating their example, many of the fathers and doctors of the Church shaved their heads to a greater or a lesser degree according as their own fancy directed; but it was not until the fourth century that the tonsure was generally imposed upon the priesthood, and even then a further two centuries elapsed before its form, as indicating the rank or order of different priests, was determined. It may not be known that the monks of the Carthusian order shave the whole head to this day.

28. **Signet Rings** were in ancient times recognized as instruments of authority and investiture, strictly reserved for the use of kings and other privileged persons. The delivery of a signet, therefore, carried with it the power of making use of the royal seal, and implied the creation of a superior office of state. The investiture of the dignitaries of the Roman Catholic Church has always been marked by the delivery of a signet. Pope Gregory IV. ordered it to be worn on the fourth finger of the left hand, but after his death the order was reversed, on the ground that such a symbol of papal authority should be displayed to the best advantage. As the thumb and first two fingers of the right hand are employed for giving the blessing, and in various other ways at the altar, the fourth finger was chosen as the most convenient. On Good Friday the ring is laid aside, because the Church is then in mourning.

29. It is a noteworthy fact that no pope has ever borne the name of Peter. The custom of a newly-elected **Pope**

assuming a New Name was introduced in the year 844 by Peter di Porca, because he thought it would be presumptuous on his part to style himself Peter the Second. He therefore adopted the style of Sergius the Second. With this example before them, all the succeeding popes took a new name in imitation of the Apostle, whose original name Simon was changed to Peter, signifying "a rock," by our Lord Himself.

30. It is commonly but erroneously asserted that **Cardinals wear Red Hats**, birettas, and habits as a perpetual reminder that they should be prepared to shed their blood for the Church. Red was, during the Middle Ages, the distinctive royal colour throughout Christendom, just as purple was that of the Roman emperors. Only sovereigns and princes were allowed to robe themselves and decorate their residences with material of this colour. Red is still the royal colour of England (*see* 5). In the audience chamber at the Vatican, the chair of state reserved for kings and princes who in former times sought an audience with the Pope in person is, like the papal throne and the walls of the Pope's private apartments, covered with crimson damask. As "the father of princes and kings, the ruler of the world on earth, the vicar of our Lord Jesus Christ," according to the formula recited at his coronation, the Pope takes rank with sovereigns, and his cardinals bear the style of "Princes of the Church." This is why the latter wear red hats, birettas, and habits. In olden times the Pope's legate took precedence even of royalty.

31. Everyone knows that the **Franciscan Friars** originally bore the name also of the **Grey Friars**, from the colour of their habit. But the habit of the Franciscans to-day is brown instead of grey. To explain the reason of

this change, it will be necessary to go back to the time when the order was instituted. There was never any rule laid down to determine the colour of the Franciscan habit, further than it should be of some common earth or mould colour, whereby this particular order of mendicant friars might be identified with the poorest of the poor. As a matter of fact, St. Francis d' Assisi had from the very inception of his scheme for founding a new order, been struck with the distinctive garb of the poor shepherds of Umbria. This consisted of a loose gown of undyed (grey) wool, girdled round the waist with a rope. Now as nothing could have been more becoming to a set of religious devotees who voluntarily embraced poverty, this primitive costume of the Umbrian shepherds was at once adopted by St. Francis and all his followers. The change from grey to brown came about in quite a natural manner. In pursuance of the pious intentions of their founder, the Franciscans never lost sight of the distinguishing garb of the poorest classes of the community in whose midst they dwelt. Towards the close of the fifteenth century the poorest classes of Italy and Spain commenced to wear garments made of dyed materials, in imitation of those better circumstanced than themselves. Instead of affecting gaudy colours, however, they contented themselves with one of a sombre kind, well in keeping with the coarse nature of the material itself. Brown came thus to be the general colour of the poorer classes, as it was in England during the eighteenth century. Noting this, the Franciscans substituted brown for their original grey habits, and brown it has ever since remained throughout Europe. In Chili, on the other hand, the Franciscan habit is at the present day blue, this being the colour generally adopted by the common people, in contradistinction, as it were, to the better classes who affect brown and grey. With regard to Europe, there is every probability of the

Franciscan habit being once more grey. Already the Tertians or members of the Third Order of St. Francis, established for those living in the world, wear, when assembled in the churches, a grey habit closely resembling that of the poor shepherds of Lombardy of the time of St. Francis.

32. The religious order of the **Servites** was founded in the year 1283 by seven Florentine merchants, who had long been accustomed by mutual agreement to meet in a little chapel of the Annunciation just outside the city walls every day to chant the *Ave* and evensong in honour of the Blessed Virgin. For this pious practice they became so well known that in coming and going people generally pointed them out as the "servants of the Virgin." At last they determined to forsake the world, and having sold their possessions, each took up his abode in a hut on Monte Senario, a solitary mountain situated about half-a-dozen miles from the city. Their habit was originally white, in token of the purity of the Virgin whose servants they avowed themselves; but on a certain day one of their number had a vision from the Blessed Virgin, who charged them to assume a black habit in remembrance of her maternal sorrows and the death of her Divine Son. Accordingly, they have ever since worn a black habit. In the beautiful Servites' church, in the Fulham Road, a tablet containing the names of the seven founders may be seen.

33. Everyone has heard of the **Little Sisters of the Poor,** those pious gentlewomen who every day beg the scraps of food left over from the tables of the wealthy and middle classes, for the support of the orphan children and aged folk with which they charge themselves. Their London home is Nazareth House, Hammersmith, but a stone's throw from the busy Broadway. It may not be

generally known, however, that the sisters touch no food themselves except that which is returned to them from the tables of the inmates of their institution. The foundress of this noble religious order (Mother Marie Augustine) was originally a cook in the household of an English family at Dinard, in France. For some time she had been in the habit of selling the scraps from the kitchen as perquisites, until it occurred to her that they might be put to a far better use in the interests of the poor. Thereupon she left her situation, and went every day from house to house to collect the broken bits for distribution to the poor. This pious undertaking developed not long afterwards into the formation of a distinct religious order. Mother Marie Augustine died in 1893.

34. A beautiful ceremony is that of a novice **Taking the Veil.** This is a figurative as well as a literal expression. She has already taken the white veil, and conformed to all the rules of her order, but the moment she assumes the black veil and takes the vows of chastity and obedience, all the beauties of God's fair earth outside the convent garden are excluded from her sight, and relatives and friends are as dead to her. A solemn Mass is said, at which all the inmates of the convent assist; she is arrayed in bridal robes and wreath and veil, and in that character takes her vows, while a plain gold ring is placed on the fourth finger of her left hand, as the spouse of the Church. Finally she is shorn of her tresses, and her bridal robes are exchanged for the sombre religious habit. Her espousal ring, however, she retains during life, and even in her coffin after death.

35. **Bell, Book, and Candle** were the three instruments employed in the carrying out of a sentence of

excommunication. By the ringing of the bell all persons present in the church were apprised of what was about to take place; the sentence was read out of the book, and the lighted candle was then extinguished to denote the spiritual darkness in which the excommunicated person would for the future abide.

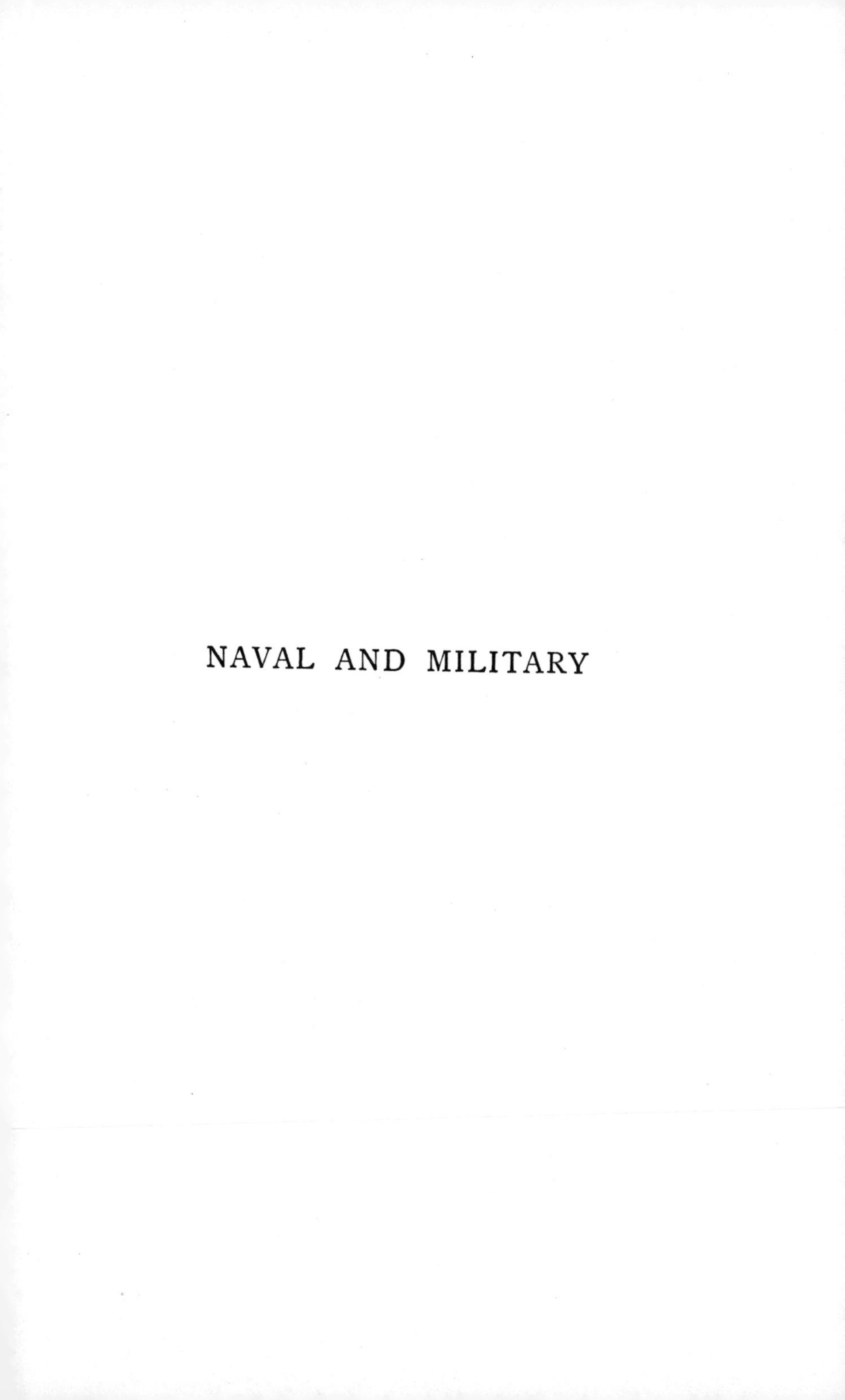

NAVAL AND MILITARY

NAVAL AND MILITARY

36. **Flags and Banners** originated in the **Ensigns** or **Standards** borne at the head of a barbarian host while marching into battle. When the Goths went to war, they sacrificed their horses to the gods and then cut off their heads, which they bore upon staves and spears as ensigns in the field. After their subversion of the Roman Empire, they bore the stuffed skin of a bear, in imitation of the Romans, who had their **Eagle**, the royal ensign of the ancient kings of Persia and Babylon, and of the Ptolemies of Egypt. Prior to the Cimbrian war the Romans had as ensigns in addition to the eagle, the wolf, the horse, the boar, and a multitude of other devices; but Marius retained only the eagle as the ensign of a legion, relegating all the rest to the cohorts. Thenceforward each cohort bore its own device emblazoned on the bucklers of its men (*see* 54). At the close of the war these bucklers were deposited in tents and magazines, but the cohort that had distinguished itself most in battle claimed the privilege of having its bucklers suspended for a time in the temples. The eagle is borne by the Emperors of Germany and Austria, and the Czar of Russia, who claim descent from the Cæsars. The **Two-headed Eagle** was first assumed by the Emperor Constantine, in token of his sovereignty over the Eastern and Western Empires; and next by Charlemagne, for the like reason. The second eagle in the imperial standard of Russia denotes the acquisition of that of Poland. The

ancient Phrygians chose for their ensign a sow, the Saxons a horse, the Flemings a bull, and the Mongols a **Dragon,** which is the device of the Emperor of China at the present time. The **Crescent,** the device of the ancient city of Byzantium, now Constantinople, was the symbol of sovereign power among the Greeks and Romans; to-day it is the ensign of the Turks. The **Red Flag** was the Roman symbol of war, and the accepted token of a call to arms. The **White Flag,** on the other hand, was the symbol of peace, and as such has from time immemorial been employed to proclaim a truce. In their civic processions the Romans invariably caused banners to be carried inscribed with the letters S.P.Q.R. These were the initials of the sentence, "*Senatus populus que Romanus*" ("The senate and the people of Rome"). In all representations of Roman life such banners are noticeable.

37. **The Royal Standard of Great Britain** is a flag emblazoned with the Royal Arms, and totally distinct from the "Union Jack," with which it is often confounded. The **Union Jack** is a combination of the military ensigns of St. George's Cross for England, St. Andrew's Cross for Scotland, and St. Patrick's Cross for Ireland. This combination was effected at the formal union of the three kingdoms in the year 1801. So much for the first part of the name. The origin of the second has always been a matter of dispute among antiquaries. By many it is thought to be a corruption of Jacobus or Jacques, *i.e.* James, in allusion to the union of England and Scotland under James I. Others, again, derive it from the *jacque*, or surtout of wadded leather strengthened by pieces of plate armour, and charged with the red cross of St. George, as anciently worn by all English soldiers. The latter is by far the more likely derivation. Let us just look into this for a moment. When our soldiers

were engaged in the field they wore the *jacque* both for protection and distinction. If, however, they had occasion to go on board ship, their *jacques* were placed close together along the bulwarks, exactly in the same way as the Romans and the Northmen disposed of their shields on board their galleys. Behind these *jacques*, then, they found protection from the arrows of their assailants, while the device upon them proclaimed their nationality. With the exception of the king's own ship of war, which had the royal arms embroidered upon a silken sail, no other indication of the nationality of a vessel was ever afforded. Now, although we are without any documentary evidence to prove to us in what particular manner these *jacques* came to give their name to the flag now flown from the bowsprit of a vessel, it is reasonable to assume that when in course of time the *jacques* no longer found a place along the bulwarks, a solitary *jacque* was displayed at the bowsprit, perhaps more for the sake of ornament than aught else; and this afterwards gave its name to the flag that superseded it. At all events, it is significant that the flag itself was called the "Jack," and the staff from which it was flown, the "Jack-staff," long before the union of the English and Scottish crowns called the designation "Union Jack" into being.

38. **The Tricolour of France,** as adopted by the National Assembly at the outbreak of the Revolution of 1789, is red and blue, the colours of the city of Paris, and white, the ancient colour of France, derived from the angel supporters in the royal arms. The selection of the last-named colour was due to M. de Lafayette, when it was pointed out that red and blue were already the colours of the House of Orleans. The flags of Italy, Belgium, and the Old North German Confederation were all three formed on the model of the French tricolour.

39. It is not true that the **Stars and Stripes** composing the American flag were taken from the arms of the Washington family, as seen on a brass in Brington Church, Northamptonshire, where the ancestors of George Washington lie buried. This similarity is merely an interesting coincidence. The flag of the American Union grew quite naturally out of the Union Jack, the same colours being retained from the first. In order to utilize the red field and the white saltire the field was cut up into thirteen stripes of alternate red and white, corresponding to the thirteen states or colonies, while the "constellation," or field of stars, was the outcome of a requirement for the remaining colour, the blue. Not before the year 1818 was the idea of adding a star for every new state formally adopted, although two new stars had been added to the original thirteen after the admission of Kentucky and Vermont to the Union on May 1st, 1795. The resolution of Congress establishing the Stars and Stripes as the national ensign was dated June 14th, 1777, but it was not officially promulgated until the 3rd of September following.

40. When we see a **Broom Tied to the Masthead,** we are given to understand that the vessel bearing it is for sale. This singular method of announcing a ship for sale is generally ascribed to the fact that Van Tromp, the celebrated Dutch admiral, displayed a broom at the masthead of his vessel to signify his intention of sweeping the English from their own seas. That he did display a broom in this manner is unquestionable, since, in retaliation, the English admiral tied a horsewhip to his own masthead, expressive of his determination to give the Dutchman a good thrashing. From this horsewhip the flying streamer or **Pennant** which now distinguishes all English ships of war has been derived. But the broom was a very old device at the time when Van Tromp made use of it. "The Friscans," writes John Evelyn,

"greatly infested the Danes, and those of Flanders, especially under William, the son of John, Count of Holland, and in the time of William the Good, Duke of Normandy. They were the first that bore the broome when, anno 1438, they had cleared the Levantine Seas, and subdued the Genoese." Here we have the origin of the broom at the masthead in the sense in which it was employed by Van Tromp; but the idea of an article sold being literally "swept away," is a little too far-fetched to satisfy us. Let us just see if the symbolism of the broom in connection with a ship for sale cannot be explained on more logical grounds. Looking around us, we find that at the periodical hiring of servants, which now takes place in country towns at Martinmas, but which formerly was intimately associated with what was called a **Mop Fair,** those servants who have not yet found a new master are distinguished from the rest by wearing twigs or small boughs in their hats. Now, the ancient Gauls always placed boughs on the heads of their slaves exposed for sale in open market, and from this custom other objects exhibited for sale came to have boughs fastened to them. Moreover, since these boughs invariably consisted of the broom-plant, the constant use of the term "broom" was easily mistaken in the course of time for the name of that article of domestic utility with which we are all familiar. As a matter of fact, the household broom received its name from its bristles being originally made of the broom plant. Hence the designation, "Mop Fair," by which was meant a fair exclusively held for hiring and selling, without any recreative adjuncts.

41. **The Fleur-de-Lis on the Mariner's Compass** was the cognizance of Charles d'Anjou, the reigning king of Sicily at the time when Flavio Gioja, the Neapolitan navigator, effected his improvements in the instrument first introduced to Europeans by Marco Polo some forty years

previously. It was in compliment to this king that Gioja adopted his cognizance as an ornamental indication of the direction due north (*see* 4).

42. For a very good reason there are always **Three Men stationed on a Lighthouse** off the British Isles. Formerly there were only two, but on a certain occasion one of the twain shut off from the world in a towering edifice constructed on the stormy rock-bound coast died, and, as frequently happens during the winter, since no boat could come near for some time, the survivor was obliged to keep the dead body of his comrade beside him until it had become putrid—a condition of affairs which almost drove him out of his mind. Had he disposed of the body by casting it into the sea, he would in all probability have been charged with murder, as he well knew. Happily, owing to the measures now adopted, such a terrible experience is not likely to again befall a British lighthouse-keeper.

43. That diverting marine saturnalia which, within living memory, always took place on **Crossing the Line,** when a vessel had "boys" on board who were passing from the north to the south latitudes, or *vice versâ*, for the first time, was nothing more than a burlesque of certain religious observances of the ancient mariners as they sailed out of the Mediterranean past the "Pillars of Hercules" into the broad Atlantic. In their time the exploration of that vast watery waste was supposed to be attended with peculiar dangers, which could only be averted by invocations to Neptune, the god of the sea, in much the same manner as they were accustomed to invoke him in their temples on the 3rd of December, the day set apart for a festival in honour of Neptune and Minerva. Consequently, in modern times, Neptune always came on board attended by his wife, to baptize those

"youngsters" who could not boast of having crossed the line before. On such occasions the fun ran fast and furious, though the victims doubtless held a different opinion. The introduction of steam navigation has been the chief factor in the abolition of this time-honoured revelry. In the old days, when a sailing vessel would be wind-bound under the equator, some diversion was needed to vary the monotony.

44. The nautical **Ahoy**, or, as it appears in old MSS., "aoi," was the battle-cry of the Norse and Danish vikings when they rushed their galleys upon the enemy.

45. When sailors on board ship indulge a tuneful "**Heave-oh!**" or "**Oh-yeigh-oh!**" to assist their labours at hauling in a cable, or while running round the capstan, they have no idea probably that this was the manner in which the slaves of the ancient world were inspirited to draw heavy burdens. Among the Egyptians, for example, we find from pieces of sculpture which have survived the ravages of Time, how huge blocks of several thousand tons' weight were drawn from the quarries to the places where some architectural work upon a grand scale was in progress, by hundreds of slaves yoked together in different rows by ropes to the sledge. On the top of the stone-block, or if it was a carved figure, seated on the knees, there was a kind of foreman or director, who, when a certain cadence of the song that he sang was reached, clapped his hands together as a signal for them to make a simultaneous forward movement. In the intervals of these exertions, a small body of men poured the contents of grease-jars upon the planks in front of the sledge, while others were in attendance to supply the labourers with water to drink. How true is the saying, itself as old as the time of Solomon, that "there is nothing new under the sun!"

46. Among the ancient Egyptians every soldier was compelled to wear a ring upon which a **Scarab**, or sacred beetle, was engraved. The object of this was to make him valorous in battle, the scarab being the symbol of regeneration or resurrection (*see* 432).

47. Some of our **Military Observances** have an interesting significance. When a **Salute is Fired** in honour of a person of distinction, it means that the peaceable nature of his visit is so well understood, that there is no need to keep the guns charged. Similarly, when the rank and file "**Present Arms,**" they virtually offer to deliver them into his hands, in recognition of his friendly disposition towards their commander; just as the **Lowering of Swords** by a mounted regiment expresses a willingness to stand unarmed before the distinguished person to whom honour is being paid. In active warfare, a superior officer on being taken prisoner **Surrenders his Sword** into the hands of an officer of corresponding rank on the enemy's side in token of submission, and that he places his life entirely at his mercy; but the sword is always as courteously returned to him.

48. **The Military Salute,** exactly as we now have it, has been in use in the British army from the very commencement of its history. Originally introduced at the tournaments of the Middle Ages, this raising of the hand to a horizontal position over the eyebrows expressed a compliment far more forcible than words. As soon as the "Queen of Beauty" had enthroned herself on the scene of the day's sports, all the knights who were about to take part in them filed past the *daïs* for her inspection, and as they did so, shielded their eyes from the blinding rays of her loveliness.

49. That interesting military display known as **The Trooping of the Colours,** was a device on the part of the Duke of Cumberland, when colonel of the First Foot Guards, to reform the uncertain gait of his officers on parade. In his time the hour of parade was six in the morning, and whenever he put in an appearance on the scene, he expressed himself highly scandalized at the unmistakable indications that his officers had not quite recovered from the effects of their previous night's potations. Accordingly, he invented a series of manœuvres, in the following out of which each officer would be required to walk slowly and separately in a straight line to a given spot, the least unsteadiness or irregularity being instantly detected. Though the necessity for such a test has long since ceased to exist, the parade has been retained as an annual ceremonial on the Queen's birthday.

50. The true origin of the nickname **Lobsters,** as applied to a British regiment, is given by Lord Clarendon in his "History of the Rebellion." In describing the stirring events of the Civil War during the year 1643, he says: "Sir William Waller received from London a fresh regiment of 500 horse, under the command of Sir Arthur Haslerig, which were so prodigiously armed that they were called by the King's party 'the regiment of lobsters,' because of their bright iron shells with which they were covered, being perfect cuirassiers, and were the first seen so armed on either side." The commonly accepted idea that our soldiers received this nickname on account of their red tunics is incorrect; the more so since a red-coat is popularly denominated **A Boiled Lobster,** in contradistinction to a policeman, who is **A Raw Lobster.**

51. The word **Lieutenant** was originally pronounced as

it would be if spelled "lewtenant," until by a printer's error the letter *v* was unwittingly dropped into the place of the *u* and suffered to remain. Thus in the "Colonial Records" relating to the State of New York, the word is spelled "lievtenant." It is the function of a lieutenant, conformably with the two words *lieu*, place, and *tenant*, holding, to supply the place of a superior officer in his absence.

52. Until recently, all the Hussar regiments of Europe wore the **Right Sleeve of the Upper Tunic Hanging loose** and useless down the back. This was in imitation of the custom of the original Hussars raised by Corvinus, King of Hungary, in the year 1445, for the national defence; the term **Hussar** being derived from "houtzar," which in the Magyar tongue means a twentieth, for Corvinus ordered all his people to furnish one man out of every twenty to the service of the State. The Magyars are justly regarded as the finest body of light horsemen in the world. Strong, hardy fellows, accustomed all their lives to the saddle in charge of large droves of cattle on the broad Hungarian plains, their sinews find active scope for development when, for the excitement's own sake, they employ themselves by capturing and taming wild horses. In this and their ordinary occupation they buckle their mantle under their right arm, so that the latter shall always be free and untrammelled. This, then, is why the right sleeve of the outer tunic of the original and all succeeding Hussar regiments never encased the arm. The oft-told story to the effect that a certain Hussar regiment was ordered out of camp to drive back a surprise party with such haste that the men had not time to get both arms into their coat sleeves, and that in commemoration of their success they allowed the right sleeve to hang loosely down the back ever afterwards, cannot be accepted seriously for one moment.

To say the least of it, it is most unlikely that all the men of the regiment, or even the greater part of them, would have been left-handed (*see* 54). It may be conveniently added that the **Scarlet Cloth Attachment to the Hussar Busby** is all that is left of the long narrow bag which the Magyars in battle allowed to fall over their left shoulder as a protection against sword slashes.

53. **The Broad Arrow** which appears on all Government stores, and which is used also to indicate points whence measurements in connection with the Ordnance Survey have been taken, was the badge or heraldic device of Henry Viscount Sydney, afterwards Earl of Romney, at the time when he held the position of Master-General of the Ordnance Department. It was he himself who originally caused it to be employed as the distinguishing mark for military stores.

54. In time of war it is the custom for military men and officers of state in Turkey to assign the left hand as the **Place of Honour** instead of the right. This is because the sword-arm is supposed to be always available for defence at such times. In this connection it may be asked, **How came Mankind to be right-handed?** The answer is very simple. When once it was discovered that the region of the heart was the most vulnerable part of the body, every man engaged in battle directed his blows upon the left breast of his adversary, who was naturally his *vis-à-vis*. Thus, arrows were shot from the right shoulder, and javelins were hurled with the right hand, while maces, battle-axes, and swords were dexterously wielded in opposition to the bucklers, whose primary object was to shield the heart from attack (*see* 73).

LEGAL AND PARLIAMENTARY

LEGAL AND PARLIAMENTARY

55. **The Law Terms** are an essentially Christian institution. Among the Romans the dispensation of justice took place daily, except during the Saturnalia, throughout the year; but after the establishment of Christianity this was prohibited by canonical authority, so that the festivals of the Church might be duly observed. Advent and Christmas gave rise to the winter vacation; Lent and Easter the spring; Pentecost the next; and haytime and harvest the long vacation between Midsummer and Michaelmas (*see* 56). Each term received its denomination from the festival immediately preceding its commencement; thus we have Hilary, Easter, Holy Trinity, and Michaelmas Terms. On one of the days in each term the courts do not sit at all, viz., Candlemas Day, Ascension Day, Midsummer Day, and All Saints' Day. The excuse for these holidays was in Catholic times purely religious; but after the Reformation they were turned to account as Reunion, or "Grand Days," at the Inns of Court. At the Universities these days are styled "Gaudy Days."

56. **The Long Vacation** in the English Law Courts has remained unaltered since the reign of William the Conqueror. The practical foresight of the Normans carefully adapted the suspension of litigation of all kinds to the season of the vintage, so that witnesses might not be drawn away from their wine-making employment; and the same

period was fixed in this country after the Norman Conquest (*see* 57).

57. An ancient custom lately revived in Catholic legal circles in London is the **Messe Rouge**, or Mass of the Holy Ghost, at the reassembling of the Law Courts after the Long Vacation. This Mass is attended by all the Roman Catholic judges and barristers, in the church of St. Anselm and Cecilia, otherwise the Sardinian Chapel in Lincoln's Inn Fields. As in France, where it has never been suffered to die out, it is called the "Messe Rouge," from the colour of the vestments worn by the officiating priests. The object of the Mass is to invoke the Divine blessing upon the work about to be undertaken; and it is especially offered up in honour of the Holy Ghost, so that the Spirit may give them wisdom. Masses of the Holy Ghost are all distinguished by the wearing of red vestments, in allusion to the fiery tongues which descended upon the heads of the Apostles on Whit Sunday.

58. The origin of the **Lawyer's Wig and Gown** is traceable to that period of our history when the study and practice of the law were strictly confined to the clergy. The gown is a relic of the cassock, the bands of those still worn by Catholic priests abroad, and the wig of the coif, or close hood, which when the restriction was removed in the time of the Plantagenets, was adopted by the lay lawyers as a compromise between the clerical tonsure and the capuchin, or hood with a long tail, generally worn by males. At first the coif was made of fine linen, but subsequently the material was changed to silk. The coif is still the distinguishing mark of a sergeant-at-law, though it has dwindled down to an insignificant black patch on the top of his legal wig. The attachment of this patch to his wig by the Lord Chan-

cellor forms part of the ceremonial of the creation of a sergeant-at-law at the present day.

59. The legal terms **John Doe and Richard Roe**, which previous to the year 1852 appeared in every process of ejectment in place of the names of the real parties, came into existence during the reign of Edward III., in consequence of that provision of Magna Charta which calls for the production of witnesses at every criminal trial. The fictitious names of "John Doe, plaintiff, and Richard Roe, defendant," were therefore inserted because they originally appeared as those of alleged witnesses. By the Act which abolished them on October 24th, 1852, it was ordered that every writ of ejectment should contain the actual names of the persons in possession of the property claimed, as well as a description of the property "with reasonable certainty."

60. **The Lawyer's Fee of Six-and-Eightpence** was fixed at the time when money was reckoned by pounds, marks, and nobles, instead of pounds, shillings, and pence. A mark was a silver coin, value thirteen and fourpence, but a noble, though worth only six-and-eightpence, or the third of a pound, was composed of the noble metal, gold.

61. **Barristers' Bags** are of two kinds, red and blue; but the former only may be taken into court; the latter must be left in the robing-room. Here we have another instance of the representative character of red as a royal colour. As a rule only a "silk," or Queen's counsel may carry a red bag (*see* 5).

62. **Punctuation** is a thing unknown in legal documents, because a "point" may have the effect of giving a sentence a totally different meaning from that intended.

63. An **I O U** should not be dated, because by dating it, it becomes barred by the Statute of Limitations after six years.

64. It was George the Third who first called the warriors of the law **The Devil's Own.** When the Temple Company of Militia was paraded before the king he asked the commander what his men were in private life. "They are all lawyers," was the reply. "All lawyers!" cried his majesty. "Then," he added, "we'll call them 'The Devil's Own.'" And "The Devil's Own" they have since remained.

65. The notion that the two **Sheriffs of the City of London** are also conjointly Sheriff of the County of Middlesex is very widespread, but this is a great mistake. It probably originated in the circumstance that a charter of King John, relative to both the City of London and the County of Middlesex, contains the word "Sheriffs," while another of Henry I., which relates to the County of Middlesex only, mentions but one Sheriff.

66. **The Judge's Scarlet Robes** are worn only in the Criminal Courts, where he represents the Sovereign (*see* 5, 30). In the Nisi Prius Courts he appears in his judicial undress, or violet gown, because he sits there merely to adjust the law between civilians.

67. **Gloves** are not worn on the Bench because, like priests, to whom the wearing of gloves is also prohibited, they are to perform their duties "with clean hands."

68. **White Gloves** are presented by the Sheriffs to the Judges in the Criminal Courts at what is called **A Maiden Assize,** by which is meant an Assize where there are no

capital charges; because they are the emblems of innocence. The original signification of the term was an Assize at which no criminal received sentence of death. The same custom obtains in a Magistrate's Court when there are no prisoners to try (*see* 210).

69. **Refusing to plead** was formerly punished in a very cruel and barbarous manner. The prisoner who obstinately "stood mute" when placed upon his trial was pressed to death. This was because, theoretically, as long as he refused to plead the civil authority had no power to act at all; and practically, because it is one of the fundamental principles of English Law that every person charged with any crime whatsoever, shall plead in his own defence. Instances are not wanting where a prisoner charged with high treason has preferred death in this manner to pleading, so as to preserve his estates to his children.

70. The State Robes of the English Judges, from the Lord Chancellor downwards, are lined with **Ermine,** because the animal whose fur it is has always been regarded as the emblem of purity.

71. The seat reserved for the Lord Chancellor in the House of Lords is a large sack of wool covered with red cloth, and officially denominated **The Woolsack.** This is supposed to constantly remind him of the great importance of the woollen manufacture of England.

72. **The Speaker of the House of Commons** is the first commoner in the land. Though he takes no part in the debates, it is a mistake to imagine that his voice is never heard. As the representative of the Sovereign in the Lower House of Legislature he presides over the debates,

puts the question, maintains order, and gives a casting vote when the numbers on both sides are equal; while it is through him alone that the Commons have access to the throne. When two or more members rise to address the House, the rule is for the one who is first observed by the Speaker to be allowed precedence. The necessity for such a rule was first experienced on November 26th, 1640, when several members rose and began to speak at the same time. At last the House decided for Mr. White to speak, and ever afterwards no member attempted to address the House except at the invitation of the Speaker. Hence the expression "**To Catch the Speaker's Eye.**"

73. **The Mace,** which is of Oriental origin, was anciently a spiked metal club hung at the saddle-bow of a mounted warrior prior to the introduction of swords. Afterwards, when the sword formed the personal armament of every horseman engaged in battle, the use of the mace was restricted to kings, princes, and a few privileged nobles. Finally, the king resigned that weapon into the hands of the valiant knight whom he appointed to be his Champion (*see* 6), and as the Champion always preceded him on State occasions, the mace that he bore came to be regarded as the insignia of royalty. When the time arrived that the royal champion was no longer needed except at coronations, the mace assumed an ornamental form. The spikes disappeared, the article itself was composed of massive silver-gilt, and its head was adorned with a crown symbolical of royal dignity. This is why the mace is borne before the Lord Chancellor and the Speaker, representatives of the Sovereign in the House of Lords and the House of Commons respectively. Likewise the mace lying on the table in front of these high legal functionaries signifies that matters of State are being discussed. In the absence of the

Speaker, that is to say, when the House of Commons goes into committee, the mace is put away under the table. As the representative of the Sovereign in the City, the Lord Mayor has his mace-bearer also. So, too, has the Pope.

74. **The Episcopalian Bench** in the House of Lords had its origin long before the Reformation. It is quite true that in the year 1540 Henry VIII. gave the privilege to all those bishops who acknowledged his supremacy as head of the Church to rank as barons; but we know also that the dissolution of the monasteries deprived twenty-six abbots and two priors of their seats in the Upper House, thus reducing the peerage by one third. As a matter of fact, the abbots and priors of ancient times were placed on the same footing in relation to the Crown as the nobility, by right of the lands that they possessed. Being landowners, they had to render military service, and could be summoned to Parliament.

75. **The Ladies' Gallery** in the House of Commons does not appear to be a very enviable place to occupy from the male point of view on the opposite side of the House. Why the fair sex should be imprisoned in a cage-like apartment is a mystery to most people; but the explanation is this:—On one occasion, before a separate gallery for lady visitors was provided, one of the daughters of Eve marked her appreciation of an eloquent member's speech by throwing him a bouquet as he sat down. This was considered such an unparliamentary proceeding that the total exclusion of lady visitors was contemplated. Eventually it was decided to prevent a repetition of the occurrence by imprisoning the fair ones behind a "grille." Although the matter has been much agitated of late, it is extremely unlikely that this detested obstruction will ever be removed.

76. **The Light on the Clock Tower** of the Houses of Parliament as a signal that the Commons are sitting is an old idea revived; it had its counterpart in the flag always displayed on the roof of a theatre in Shakespeare's day while the play was in progress. The Westminster light is not an electric light at all, as so many people fondly imagine, but old-fashioned gas. As long as the Speaker occupies the chair, it sends its rays across the metropolis; but the moment there is an affirmative response to the Speaker's question, "that the House do now adjourn," it vanishes. This excellent arrangement is due to the fact that a wire runs from the apparatus at the top of the tower to the Speaker's chair, behind which a man is stationed during the debates so as to be ready at any moment to switch off the light.

77. **The City Representatives**, on the assembling of every new parliament, wear scarlet gowns, and sit close to the right hand of the Speaker. This distinction emphasizes the importance of the Lord Mayor of London, who, as the representative of the Sovereign within the City, wears a scarlet robe of State (*see* 5, 73, 458).

78. **To Move the Previous Question** is a parliamentary subterfuge to ignore a question which one side of the House does not like to vote against, but which at the same time it has no desire to pass. As soon as the Speaker rises to put the original question to the vote, some member anticipates him by moving "that this question be *now* put," and if it is negatived there the matter ends, without any voting at all.

79. To move that a **Bill be Read this Day Six Months**

is the Parliamentary method of burking it, because the House will not be sitting in six months' time.

80. A privy councillor is entitled to be addressed as **The Right Honourable**, even though he be a commoner. This is because he constitutes one of "The Lords of Her Majesty's Privy Council." The Lord Mayor of London is styled "The Right Honourable" in virtue of his rank as an earl.

81. **The Ministerial Whitebait Dinner** at Greenwich was instituted by Sir Robert Preston, a Scotch baronet and merchant prince, who some time represented Dover in Parliament. This baronet had what he called a "fishing cottage" at Dagenham Reach, in Essex, to which he was accustomed to repair in the spring with his particular friend, "Old George Rose," Secretary of the Treasury, in order to escape from the cares of his mercantile and parliamentary duties. One day, while these two worthies were enjoying themselves at this place, Mr. Rose threw out a hint that their mutual friend Mr. Pitt would much delight in the comfort of such a snug retreat. The premier was at once invited, and received with the utmost cordiality at the "fishing cottage." On taking his leave he readily accepted an invitation for the following year, Sir Robert engaging to remind him of it at the proper time. For several years in succession Mr. Pitt, always accompanied by Mr. Rose, enjoyed the hospitality of Sir Robert Preston at Dagenham Reach; but as the distance was great, and railways had not then come into existence, the genial host at length discerned that his coming and going could not fail to be somewhat inconvenient to the First Minister of the Crown. He therefore proposed that they should in future dine together at some place nearer London. Greenwich was mentioned

as a convenient *salle à manger*, and this was agreed to. At their first meeting, however, the party was changed from a trio to a quartet, Mr. Pitt having requested that he might be allowed to introduce Lord Camden. It was not long before a fourth guest — Mr. Long, subsequently Lord Farnborough—was added to the little party. These were still the guests of Sir Robert Preston; but one by one other notables were invited, and at last Lord Camden proposed that as they were dining at a tavern, Sir Robert should be relieved of the expense. It was therefore agreed that each diner should bear his individual share of the cost, and on this plan the meetings were annually held until the death of Mr. Pitt. Sir Robert Preston was in the following year called upon to invite the several guests, the list of whom already included most of the cabinet ministers. It was then that the time of meeting was transferred to the end of the session. When Sir Robert died, the "fish dinner," as it was called, survived, and Lord Farnborough undertook to summon the guests from the list furnished to him by the private secretary of the late baronet, who had been in the habit of sending out the invitations privately. "No doubt eating and drinking," writes the author of a long and interesting letter on this subject in the "Times" for 1861, and of which the foregoing is an abstract, "are good for digestion, and a good digestion makes men calm and clear-headed, and calmness and a clear head promote logical reasoning, and logical reasoning aids the counsels of the nation, and *reipublicæ consilio* the nation goes on to glory. So I suppose in one way or another the 'Ministerial Whitebait Dinner' conduces to the grandeur and prosperity of our beloved country." It may conveniently be added that **Whitebait** owes its name to its silvery whiteness, and the circumstance that it was at one time employed exclusively for baiting crab and lobster pots.

82. The custom of **Wearing the Hat in Parliament** is alluded to in an old work entitled, "Rules of Proceeding, etc., of the House of Commons." It is there stated that when a member speaks he must stand up in his place with his head uncovered, and address his remarks to the Speaker and not to a particular member. This presumes the existence of the custom of wearing the hat when not actually engaged in debate. There are reasons why a member should always have his hat close at hand, though he may not care to keep it on his head. As often as he hears his name mentioned in the speech of another member he is expected to raise his hat deferentially, as an acknowledgment, and if at the moment he should happen to have it in his hand, or lying in his lap, he must instantly pop it on his head so as to be able to raise it with due respect. Sometimes, in consequence of a slight irregularity, a point of order arises, and if, at such a time, a member wishes to address the Chair, he must speak without rising from his seat, and with his hat on. Again, at a particular stage in private business, when the royal assent has to be intimated by a privy councillor, this is done by raising his hat. The process of securing seats in the House, at the opening of the session, or of a new parliament by placing hats on them is familiar to every newspaper reader. On such an occasion a member generally comes down to the House an hour or two before the sitting with an extra hat, and sometimes an armful of hats, which he places on behalf of dilatory friends who might otherwise find on arriving all the best seats occupied.

83. When a Member of Parliament wishes to resign his seat, he applies for the Stewardship of **The Chiltern Hundreds.** Technically, he cannot resign, but the acceptance of an office under the Crown debars him from further representing his constituency. The Chiltern Hundreds are

a range of chalk hills that separate Bedfordshire and Hertfordshire, and, traversing the middle of Buckinghamshire, extend as far as Henley in Oxfordshire. They comprise the Hundreds of Burnham, Desborough, and Stoke. Being at one time much infested with robbers, an officer of the Crown was appointed to protect them; but the office is now a sinecure, with a nominal pay. It is granted as a matter of course to a Member of Parliament who resigns his seat, and must be held by him until some other member who wishes to retire applies for it.

CIVIC AND SOCIAL

CIVIC AND SOCIAL

84. **Old London Bridge was built upon Woolpacks**, as was said, for the following reason. The bridge was commenced by one Peter, a priest of St. Mary Cole-church, which, previous to the Great Fire, stood on the north side of the Poultry. When the works were stopped for want of funds, Henry II. generously came to the rescue by imposing a tax upon his subjects' wool. This gave rise to the vulgar saying that Peter of the Poultry had reared the arches of his bridge upon woolpacks.

85. The so-called **Griffin on the Temple Bar Memorial** is not a griffin at all, but a dragon, which forms one of the supporters of the arms of the City of London, viz., the Cross of St. George, containing in the first quarter the sword of St. Paul (*see* 290). It will be noticed that the monster supports the City arms with one of its fore-paws. Possibly, had more space been available, both supporters would have been requisitioned. Let it be mentioned incidentally that the City's crest is a dragon's wing expanded to the sinister, and ensigned with St. George's Cross.

86. **The Dragon on the Spire of Bow Church,** Cheapside, has not hitherto been accounted for. Nevertheless, since we know that the church was dedicated to the Virgin, it is, or should be, by no means difficult to comprehend its signification. In all examples of Christian Art, the

Serpent which, as God foretold to the Mother of Mankind, would one day be crushed by a woman, appears in the form of a dragon (*see* 384).

87. **A Grasshopper** was formerly the usual grocer's shop-sign, in imitation of the family crest of Sir Thomas Gresham, which adorned his shop-front at the time when he resided in Lombard Street. The grasshopper on the Royal Exchange is believed to be one that was saved from the Great Fire of London, and also that of 1838, in which the second Exchange was consumed.

88. The subject of **Tavern Signs** has been so fully discussed in our "Names and their Meaning," that there is no need to revert to it here. Let it suffice to state that both shop and tavern signs were a necessity in the days when very few people could read, and when, consequently, it would have been useless for a tradesman to paint his name over his shop-front. Yet, while tavern signs had a purely heraldic significance, shop signs always had an intimate relation to the trades they advertised.

89. **The Pawnbroker's Three Brass Balls** were the arms of the Medicis of Florence, whose agent was the first to lend money on pledges in this country. As a distinguishing shop-sign, he employed the family arms, but subsequently, when the Jews of Lombardy flocked over to England and set up in the same kind of business, the sign was extensively copied. Roscoe, in his "Life of Lorenzo de Medici," published in 1796, attributes the origin of the family arms to an exploit of Averardo de Medici, one of the commanders of Charlemagne, who slew a famous giant named Mugello, and bore off his club, that had three iron balls sunk into it, as a trophy. Others, again, contend that the three brass balls

were simply gilded pills of large size. That the Medicis were Florentine physicians is well known; indeed, it is sufficiently established by their family name. It should be added, however, that the balls were originally blue; the brass balls did not make their appearance until some seventy years ago. Of course, there is such a thing as a blue pill, and the practice of our Continental neighbours nowadays is to gild their pills. The public money-lending establishments of France and Italy are styled *Monts de Piété*, from their sign, which consists of three mounds of earth, suggested by the three balls, surmounted by a *pieta*, a figure of Christ (*see* 282).

90. **The Barber's Pole** is a relic of the time when, under the style of barber-surgeons, the barbers of this country were also surgeons. It was customary then for the pole to be tightly grasped by a patient during the process of blood-letting, in order to make his veins swell, and the blood to flow freely. As the pole very soon became bloodstained it was painted a bright red, and, when not in use, hung outside the shop-door as a sign, swathed spirally with a narrow white linen band, in allusion to the bandage used for tying up the bleeding arm. In course of time it occurred to some sharp-witted member of the fraternity to have a dummy pole, painted with red and white stripes, permanently on view outside, and to keep the real one inside. From this time forward the barber's pole became a fixture. The gilt knob at the end of the pole is supposed to represent the brass dish or basin, with a notch-like cavity on one side of it to fit the throat, and which was employed to catch the lather when a customer was being shaved. The basin itself was generally suspended from the knob at the pole-end. To bring this basin to the ground by pelting at it from a distance was considered fine sport by the holiday-making school-boys on Shrove Tuesday a generation or two back (*see* 426).

91. The origin of the **Black Doll,** which not so very long ago was the recognized sign of a marine-store dealer, is not without interest. In the days when Indian and Chinese curiosity shops were common in all parts of London, such establishments always called attention to the character of their wares by means of a black doll or *joss*—a species of Chinese idol—exhibited outside. But there came a time when these shops dwindled down to an insignificant few; whereupon the dealers in cast-off clothing, who shipped large quantities of goods to Africa and other uncivilized lands, acquired the black dolls as an advertisement for their places of business, taking care to dress them up as gaily as they could in order to attract notice from a distance. By-and-by, these exporters of clothing degenerated into mere rag-and-bottle merchants, though the black doll, bereft of its finery, continued to be suspended over the door. It would, we fear, require an expenditure of much time and shoe-leather to discover such a sign in the byways of London in the present year of grace.

92. **The Chemist's Coloured Globes** are modern substitutes for the retorts and jars containing their various drugs and mixtures, of the apothecaries and alchemists of a bygone day. **The Doctor's Red Lamp** had a similar origin. After the Barber-Surgeons' Company (*see* 90) was dissolved, in the year 1745, the practice of surgery was placed in the hands of properly qualified surgeons, who set up a red globe—painfully suggestive of bleeding—outside their houses as a sign. As for the apothecaries, their invariable shop-sign was a **Wooden Phœnix,** owing to the association of the famous bird with alchemy. After the great Swiss alchemist Paracelsus wrote about it in the sixteenth century, the alchemists one and all employed it as the symbol of their vocation. The **Pestle and Mortar**

is still occasionally met with as a chemist's shop-sign. The pestle was originally the shankbone of a sheep.

93. **The Highlander at the Tobacconist's Shop Door** is still to be met with in the course of a day's walk, but the snuff-box from which he is supposed to be helping himself, does not always meet one's gaze. Why a Highlander should have been selected for this monotonous sentry duty can only be explained by the circumstance that our Scottish neighbours are notoriously fond of a pinch of snuff, and that a great deal of this article is nowadays made across the Border. Another tobacconists' sign, now fast disappearing, is the **Little Caribb,** with coloured feathers around his head and loins. This originally did duty for both tobacco and snuff, which are a West Indian production.

94. **The Draper's Farthing Change** was originated by a small linendraper in the Borough, who divined that an article ticketed "one and elevenpence three farthings" would be a more tempting bait for custom than another at two shillings, obviously because the farthing was knocked off. But his customers were not aware that he was by no means a loser by the transaction. At first he remitted the farthing per article or per yard only upon such goods as represented a large margin of profit, and the increased business was a clear gain to him. By-and-by, when the system became firmly established, he not only succeeded in having this supposed rebatement more than allowed for by the wholesale houses, but he had no compunction about actually marking *up* many a cheaper article to the popular "eleven three." Possibly the same thing is done now. The substitution of a packet of pins for the farthing change is the latter-day development of an exceedingly smart stroke of business.

95. **The Lion's Head on Public Drinking Fountains** has come down to us through the Greeks and Romans from the ancient Egyptians, who adopted it to symbolize the rising of the Nile, which takes place annually when the sun is in *Leo*.

96. The two words "**Ancient Lights**" signify that the owner of a building has had access to the light of day from a particular window for twenty years or more; therefore his claim to such light is made absolute by Act of Parliament (2 and 3 Will. IV., c. 71, s. 3), and no other building must be put up within a certain distance from the said window to which public attention is directed.

97. **Clubs**—in the modern sense of the term—came into existence in London soon after the Battle of Waterloo. The long-protracted war over, large numbers of naval and military officers were glad to retire on half-pay, but as they found the cost of living in London too great for their slender purses, they hit upon the plan of dining together at a central resort, each contributing his share of the expense. By this means a great saving was effected, and so satisfactory were the arrangements, that in a very short time they mustered sufficient members to establish what was styled "The United Service Club" in premises of their own. The United Service is, consequently, the parent of all the other London clubs.

98. The reason why **a Gentleman Escorting a Lady** should take the outside edge of the pavement is not so clear nowadays as it was in bygone times, when street brawls were matters of almost hourly occurrence, and the vigilance of the so-called preservers of law and order left much to be desired. By taking the side nearest the passers-by, a man

could, in those days, more easily protect his female companion from rough usage.

99. The expressions "**Near Side**" and "**Off Side,**" so commonly made use of by omnibus drivers and others, have no reference to the street pavements, as is generally supposed. The country waggoner, who walks by the side of his horse instead of riding on the shafts, invariably takes the left-hand side of the animal, so as to have the whip hand always ready. The "near side" of the horse is consequently close to his right hand, and the "off side" the farthest away from him. Opportunity may be taken here to state that the exclamation "**Wo!**" so well understood by horses, is a corruption of "Ho!" which was the signal for the cessation of the conflict at the tournaments of the Middle Ages.

100. Twenty years ago, or thereabouts, all the ladies of England who wished to be in the fashion affected what was styled "**The Alexandra Limp.**" This was because the Princess of Wales had sustained some injury to her knee and was walking lame. In this we see how history repeats itself. Alexander the Great had a wry neck, wherefore all his courtiers and generals considered it the correct thing to go about with their heads on one side. Another fashionable folly of a bygone day, "**The Grecian Bend,**" was originally intended as a mockery of the affected walk of the "Grecians" at our public schools, to show their manifest superiority over their neighbours; but the fashion once set, it was everywhere followed in all seriousness.

101. **A Lady's Curtsey** is a relic of those barbarous days when woman was expected to bend the knee on being ushered into the presence of men of rank and power, as an

acknowledgment of her inferiority. Says John Aubrey, writing in 1678: "Till this time, the Court itself was unmannered and unpolished. King James's Court was so far from being civil to woman, that the ladies, nay, the Queen herself, could hardly pass by the King's apartment without receiving some affront."

102. The custom of **Shaking Hands** originated in the ancient and universal practice of adversaries grasping the weapon hand during a truce as a precaution against treachery. But it will be asked, How came it that the chance meeting of *friends* was signalized by a shaking of hands? To this it may be answered that, just as the warrior clutched the weapon hand of his enemy to prevent mischief, so he freely extended his own weapon hand to a friend as a sign that he had no thought of standing on the defensive. It needs no great stretch of imagination to understand that the hand *shake* was but the natural outcome of a hearty and vigorous grasp. At one time strict etiquette demanded that a person should **Unglove the Hand** before offering it to another in friendly greeting. This was a relic of the days of chivalry, when a knight removed his gauntlet in token of perfect confidence in the peaceful intentions of his neighbour. Gloves are never worn in the presence of royalty.

103. **Uncovering the Head,** as a mark of respect on entering another's house or a place of worship, is a custom handed down to us from the days of chivalry, when a knight doffed his helmet to show that he relied upon the protection of his host as long as he remained under his roof, on the one hand, and that he was not afraid of being attacked in the House of God on the other. Owing to the peaceable nature of their vocation in life, women have always been exempted from uncovering their heads in the like circum-

stances. **Raising the Hat in the Street** had a similar origin. A mediæval knight always stood bareheaded in the presence of a lady. The Oriental custom of showing respect by **Removing the Slippers** originated among the Jews, in obedience to God's command to Moses from the burning bush, "Put off thy shoes from off thy feet, for the place whereon thou standest is holy ground." Our Jewish neighbours do not remove their hats in the synagogues; neither do they remove their shoes, because since the destruction of the Temple at Jerusalem, the Supreme Being is not supposed to abide in their ordinary places of worship. The primitive idea of uncovering the head in Christian churches was the Catholic belief in the Real Presence on the altar. No reasonable excuse can be assigned for the Quaker custom of keeping their heads covered in meeting-houses, further than that it is a relic of the war which George Fox, the founder of the sect, waged against ceremonies and conventionality. As David Hume tells us, speaking of Fox and his disciples, "Even the ordinary rites of civility were shunned as the nourishment of carnal vanity and self-conceit."

104. **The Quaint Dress of the Christ's Hospital Boys** is thought by some persons to be a modification of the ordinary habit of the Franciscan, or Grey Friars (*see* 31), whose monastery Edward VI. converted into the present educational establishment; and by others as simply that of the London apprentices of the Tudor period. It is, however, possible to arrive at the real truth of the matter. With regard to the blue colour of the gown, that certainly was common to all serving-men and apprentices from early times down to the sixteenth century. Pliny, the historian, tells us that the people of ancient Gaul clothed their slaves in blue as a mark of servitude. In the reigns of Mary and

Elizabeth the London apprentices were ordered always to wear blue cloaks in summer and blue gowns in winter. The privileged Scottish mendicants, known as "the King's bedesmen," still receive a new blue gown once a year, though no additions to their number have been made since 1833. When first admitted, the Christ's Hospital scholars were provided with a garb of russet cotton, very similar to the ancient Franciscan habit; but ere long this was exchanged for the blue gown and yellow stockings by which they have ever since been distinguished. The first time they appeared abroad in their blue gowns was when they accompanied the governor to hear the annual Easter sermons in the church-yard of St. Mary Spittle, where, subsequently, *i.e.*, in 1594, a gallery near the pulpit was specially constructed for their accommodation. Between the old monastic habit and the ordinary dress of the London apprentices, the new Christ's Hospital costume was a judicious compromise. The blue colour of the gown bespoke the charitable foundation, while its form retained something of the monkish character. The leathern girdle corresponded to the hempen cord, and the combined vest and petticoat, technically called the "yellow," to the sleeveless tunic or undergarment of the monastery. The stockings were yellow, in keeping with the petticoat; those of the town boys were white. As for the head-covering, a small cap of black worsted was supplied to them, but it was more usually carried in the hand than worn on the head. This singular custom must have been derived from the London apprentices, who, while stationed all day long outside their masters' shops crying, "What d'ye lack?" had no more thought of covering their heads than has the butcher's man or the draper's assistant at the present day. It should be recollected however, that although these juvenile traders might be exposed to the cold, the over-hanging stories of the houses of the age in which they lived effectually sheltered them from the wind and rain. To return to the Blue-coat boys. "In my time," writes our friend Mr. M. S. S. Dipnall, an old "Blue," and late Chief Clerk, *i.e.*, Secretary, to the Christ's Hospital Foundation, "the cap supplied to us was a black 'muffin' cap, which hardly covered the crown of the head, and was rarely worn in the streets; the custom or requisition having been to don it when about to pass the gate on a leave-day, or with an afternoon 'ticket,' and a minute after to doff it, and to consign it to the coat-pocket, or carry it in the hand. The cap was also donned on Sundays when going to church; and I have some impression that it was worn too when on Sundays we walked up and down the grounds by way of exercise before and after church." Here follows the most interesting part of Mr. Dipnall's communication. "For some time previous to 1829 there had been a considerable prevalence of ringworm in the school, and several years later the same complaint was troublesome. The boys' hair was cut about once a fortnight so as to render their heads of easier inspection; and this continued to be the case for many years. Much attention was paid also to cleanliness, especially of the head. A gradual disuse of the woollen cap ensued, and some thirty or forty years ago the issue of these caps was dropped. And, not much later, the 'yellow' was also disused, a vest and breeches being substituted for it." It only remains to be added that the pair of white bands are very similar to those still worn by barristers, and which were derived from the priests' bands at the time when the practice of the law was entirely in the hands of the clergy (*see* 58).

105. The fearfully and wonderfully made **Fardingale**, or hoop skirt of the Elizabethan period, was a device on the part of the ladies of the Court to ridicule the large trunk hose worn by the courtiers. Had the fair dames been satisfied

when the men confessed themselves completely outwitted in absurdity, no harm would have been done. But the wide **Hoop Skirts** thus worn for a brief space as an experiment became the rage. Before the close of the reign they had attained such alarming proportions that doors had to be widened, pews made double their former size, and carriages built on an extra large scale purposely to accommodate their wearers. These fashionable monstrosities never wholly disappeared until our own day; their size, indeed, was subject to fluctuations, but between the Elizabethan fardingale and the Victorian **Crinoline** there was no perceptible difference. For the love of our wives and sisters may we never see the like again!

106. **Fans** originated among the Chinese. Centuries ago, while a royal princess was taking part in the Feast of Lanterns, her face covered with a mask, as was usual in the case of distinguished personages, she found the heat so overpowering that, in order to cool her brow and conceal her features at the same time, she passed the mask quickly to and fro in front of her face. This action being observed suggested the fan.

107. **Patches** were at first employed by ladies of fashion simply to set off a dimple or other special beauty of the face; but it was not long before they grew into such excess that representations of a coach and four, a sun, moon, and stars without number appeared on a lady's face all at once.

108. **Powdering the Hair** was first adopted by the ladies of the English Court after the fops and gallants had taken up the fashion of wearing wigs or perukes during the Restoration period.

109. **Dressing the Hair with Ribbons** had its origin in the example of the Duchesse de Fontagne, the mistress of Louis XIV. This lady, while hunting one day in the year 1680, had her hat blown off, so in order to keep her hair out of her face, she tied it back with one of her ribbon garters. Shortly afterwards hairdressing with ribbons became fashionable, and has remained so, to a greater or a lesser extent, up to the present time.

110. **False Hair** was first regularly worn in England by Queen Elizabeth, who had upwards of fifty wigs of different kinds for her private use. After her death a few ladies adopted the French fashion of wearing wigs, but it was not until the Restoration that wigs, or more correctly speaking, **Periwigs**, came to be extensively worn by the sterner sex. These were introduced from the court of Louis XIV., where a natural head of hair was not considered sufficiently luxuriant for the artificial tastes of the times. The term "wig" is short for "periwig," which is a corruption of the French *perruque*. **Wigs** were originally adopted not as a remedy for baldness, but in the interests of personal cleanliness. The laws of ancient Egypt compelled all males to shave the head and beard. This explains why turbans were not worn by the Egyptians, the bushy artificial hair being regarded as a sufficient protection against the heat of the sun. The Romans, on the contrary, wore wigs because they were naturally bald.

111. The popular **Antipathy to Red Hair** arose from the tradition that Judas, the betrayer of Christ, had red hair. Hence the expression current in many languages, "Judas coloured hair." Cain, the first murderer, is also believed to have been a red-haired man. In England and the north of France the popular aversion was strengthened

in no small degree by the repeated incursions of the Danes, who were all red-haired, and heartily detested. By the Danes themselves red hair was and is still looked upon as a sign of strength.

112. As soon as the terrors of the French Revolution had subsided, fops and gallants took to wearing their hair cut very short, and called it **A la Guillotine** in memory of their relatives who had suffered death by that instrument.

113. The vulgar notion that the **Chinaman's Pigtail** is cultivated solely for the purpose of being pulled up into Heaven by it is altogether absurd. This *queue*, or pigtail from the hair of the crown, while the rest of the head is close shaven, was forced upon the Chinese by the Manchû, or Tartar conquerors of the Empire, in the year 1627, as an act of degradation. Inscriptions on old tablets in Japanese temples frequently refer to this humiliating requirement as one of the reasons why the people of Japan originally fled from China. However, John Chinaman has long since become reconciled to his pigtail; indeed, he would be loth to part with it on any consideration.

114. Like the **Small Feet of Chinese Ladies**, the cultivation of inordinately **Long Finger-Nails** by both sexes in the country of the Celestials is a recognized mark of distinction between the upper and middle classes, and those who are compelled to perform manual labour. The higher the social rank of the individual, the longer are the finger-nails. To preserve them from injury ladies enclose them in elaborate casings of gold and silver set off with precious stones; whereas the middle classes have recourse to pieces of bamboo cane extending beyond the tips of the

fingers. Bandaging the feet of female infants has been the fashion ever since the sixth century, but it obtains only in families that are more or less well-to-do.

115. It is a mistake to imagine that the **Turks compel their Wives to conceal their Faces** from the public gaze from motives of jealousy. Travellers in the East have assured us that it is rather owing to the homage which the Turks pay to female beauty, and to natural reverence for the modesty of women, that they impose such conditions; firmly believing that no man can look upon a beautiful face with a perfectly pure mind, and with perfect physical indifference. For a woman to have her face uncovered out of doors in the East is regarded as a sure indication of profligacy. Nor are the women so closely veiled but that they can see everything that passes around them. "If," as Lady Hamilton observes, "jealousy dictated such a disguise, it could not more effectually have defeated its own purpose; for the spirit of intrigue could surely suggest a more happy expedient to elude vigilance and to deceive without alarming suspicion." No man allows his wife greater freedom, or more disposes of his wealth so as to make her life enjoyable, than the Turk.

116. **Tattooing** may not inaptly be described as a primitive kind of heraldry. Just as the knights of chivalry needed some distinguishing mark by which they could be recognized when completely encased in armour, so the savages, who wear no clothing at all, must needs have recourse to some common device on their bodies when they make war upon a neighbouring tribe. By the particular style of ornamentation on their bodies only can friends be distinguished from foes. Among savages, therefore, tattooing serves the same purpose as the wearing of regimental

uniforms among civilized nations. In the exact proportion that clothing comes into use, so tattooing of necessity goes out.

117. The **Cocked Hat** became fashionable in the time of Louis XV. of France, but instead of being worn on the head, it was merely carried or *cocked* under the arm. From this circumstance the party badge or symbol which very soon found a place upon it received the name of a **Cockade.** Of course a hat of such dubious utility was practicable only in an age when the head was sufficiently protected against the elements by the peruke or court wig. It was during this period that the expression "knocked into a cocked hat," signifying to be completely doubled up, or flattened, first obtained currency. When George III. took to wearing the cocked hat on his military campaigns, it was abandoned by our fops and gallants in favour of the three-cornered hat. In a slightly altered form the cocked hat is still worn by our naval and military commanders.

118. **A White Hat** was formerly regarded as an infallible indication that its wearer was an uncompromising Radical, because Henry Hunt, the famous demagogue, was singularly partial to a white hat.

119. **A Red Cap** is the symbol of liberty, because when a slave was manumitted among the Romans, a small cap of red cloth was placed on his head, and his name was entered on the rolls of the City as a freedman (*see* 24).

120. **The Kilt** of the Scottish Highlanders is a relic of the dress of the ancient Gauls (the *Galli non braccati* alluded to by the Romans), to whom the wearing of breeches

was unknown. The word itself is the Gaelic and Irish *cealt.*

121. **Boots** were not worn by our countrymen until the popularity of the Hessian troops in English pay, in the time of the Georges, caused their foot-gear to be introduced among civilians on an extensive scale. Everyone betrayed a fancy for Hessian boots, to the great concern of the shoe and buckle makers. When the passion for Hessians had somewhat subsided, the short boot came into fashion, and remained until events on the field of Waterloo once more sent the people mad after military boots in honour of Wellington and Blucher. It is said that the town of Walsall, which at one time supplied the whole kingdom with shoe-buckles, was completely ruined by the introduction of boots.

122. **Stockings,** properly so called, came into existence when the wide Dutch trunk or petticoat breeches introduced during the Stuart period enabled the full hose or tights previously worn by both sexes to be dispensed with. In the time of Henry VIII., it is true, the tights were first divided just below the knee, the joining being concealed by a wide garter. This garter is seen in pictures of Queen Elizabeth's "Progresses." The hose then bore the names of upper hose and nether hose. After the Dutch trunks came in the upper hose was no longer worn. Ladies soon followed the example set by Elizabeth of wearing worsted stockings. Silk stockings were a rarity until the Restoration.

123. **Scarlet Neckcloths** are worn by all the porters and brakemen employed on the Great Northern Railway. This is because some years ago a collision was happily averted by a G. N. R. porter, who, with commendable

presence of mind, improvised a danger signal by covering a white light with the scarlet neckcloth which he happened to be wearing at the time. Ever since that event the directors of the Great Northern Railway have recognized the expediency of providing all their servants with scarlet neckcloths.

124. **The Agricultural Labourer's Smock** is not peculiar to this country. In all countries where peasants exist—and where do they not exist?—it will be found. Originally introduced into Europe by the Moors, it is nothing more than the evolution of man's primitive attire, viz., a sack, having in it a hole for the head and two holes for the arms. The Arabs of the present day wear a garment very similar to that of the agricultural labourers of the Western nations. In all probability the Roman *toga* owed its origin to the primitive garb of the East. Proceeding to the West we find but small difference between the Mexican *serape*, and the South American *poncho*, both, like the English smock, derived from Spain, and of Moorish origin.

125. The spirit of chivalry still lingers in the breasts of Englishmen. We, of all the nations of the world, give priority to the fair sex when we are addressing a public assembly. The stereotyped formula, "**Ladies and Gentlemen,**" however, has not yet attained its centenary. Previous to the year 1808 it was "Gentlemen and Ladies," answering to the French "Messieurs et Mesdames," and the German "Meine Herren und Damen."

126. The Scottish custom of **Licking Thumbs** on the completion of a bargain—of which the schoolboy ritual of attesting the truth is but a puerile imitation—conveys the

same meaning as the time-honoured practice of pressing the thumb upon the seal beside one's **Signature to a Document** as a mark of good faith. During the Middle Ages, when few witnesses could write their own names, it was incumbent upon all the contracting parties to impress their thumbs upon the wax while it was still warm, to remind them of the pains of hell-fire if they swore falsely, and then to make the sign of the cross beside it, as evidence that, being Christians, they pledged themselves by the symbol of their Faith. Even those who could subscribe their names (the rest had it filled in for them by the scholar or clerk) drew a rude cross on the document; but to save their thumbs from injury they wetted them with saliva before touching the molten wax. Hence the expression to "sign one's name." Hence also the original meaning of the illiterate witness's "× his mark."

127. Those who prefer **Tobacco Chewing** to smoking it in the ordinary way may have the consolation of knowing that their not very elegant habit is warranted by history. Plutarch says, "Chewing of mallows is very wholesome, and the stalk of asphodel very luscious." Whether this ancient biographer ever foresaw the possibility of ladies **Chewing Gum,** as they do in the United States, is more than we can say.

128. When the North American Indians **Bury the Hatchet,** while the calumet, or pipe of peace, is being passed round, the act poetically suggests that the implements of warfare must not even be visible during a peaceful conference. The acceptance of the calumet by a stranger on such an occasion is also intended to show that he harbours no suspicion of treachery. At a deliberation of war, the hatchet, painted a bright red, is always in evidence.

129. The origin of the **Baker's Dozen** must be sought in olden times, when, fearful of incurring the heavy penalties enforced for selling short weight, the London bakers threw in an extra loaf, which they called the "in bread," with each dozen loaves sold.

130. That we are reverting to some of the customs of our Anglo-Saxon forefathers is evidenced by our observance of the **Saturday Half-Holiday.** King Edgar ordered that there should be a general cessation of labour from Saturday midday until sunrise on Monday. A similar order was issued by William of Scotland in the year 1203; while that of Canute: "Let every Sunday be kept from Saturday's noon to Monday's dawn," has never been repealed. The like custom prevailed in the East as a means of gratifying Judaizing Christians. Josephus tells us that in his time there was scarcely a city in Greece that did not keep a portion of the seventh day holy. Not until after vespers on Saturday night did the Anglo-Saxons think of laying in their weekly store of provisions. This explains why the market-place of an English town invariably sprang up around the parish church.

131. To **Make the Grand Tour** was formerly incumbent upon the sons of every well-to-do English family on attaining their majority. This was but an ancient practice revived. The laws of Athens did not allow minors to enjoy the management of their estates until after they had spent a couple of years in travelling over the neighbouring countries.

132. The reason why there are so many **American Heiresses** in the European marriage market is because

wealthy parents in the United States invariably leave the bulk of their money to their daughters, and very little, comparatively, to their sons, who are expected to make their own way in the world by their natural gifts.

133. There is this much in common between the **Jews and Mohammedans**: while they do not hesitate to cheat and impose upon Christians, as the avowed enemies of their race, they are scrupulously straightforward in all their dealings amongst themselves. This singular trait in their commercial character is explained by a somewhat too literal interpretation of the religious law which regulates all their ordinary actions of life, and by which they are strictly forbidden to exercise usury, cheating, extortion, or over-reaching "among one another." Obviously their practice goes far to prove that those of a different race from themselves may be fleeced at pleasure.

134. The Germans and the Russians have a **Name Day** as well as a birthday. This is the feast of the saint whose name was chosen for them at their baptism, and who, throughout life, is looked upon as their patron.

135. **The Language of Flowers** was introduced into Europe by Lady Mary Wortley Montagu from Turkey, where it forms the amusement of the secluded fair ones in the harems.

136. The explanation why **Chinese and Japanese Pictures** appear to us so quaint, is because the people of the Far East have no idea of perspective; objects at a distance are depicted by them just as large as those in the foreground. A familiar example of this is the willow-pattern plate (*see* 144).

137. There is some analogy between a **Family Portrait Gallery** and the waxen busts of the deceased members of a Roman household (*see* 242). Even that unique arrangement was derived from the Egyptians, who had the painted coffins of their ancestors ranged in an erect position around the walls of the family vault, the features of the deceased being in every case very clearly shown, as may be seen from existing examples in the British Museum. In times of great distress an Egyptian was often compelled to borrow money on the security of the mummy of one of his ancestors —indeed no other kind of security was permitted by law— and if he could not redeem it he was publicly disgraced. Here, then, we discover an historical precedent for the occasional disposal of the family portraits by some impecunious nobleman at the present day.

138. **Grace at Meals** is not a modern observance; it existed amongst the Jews and the classical ancients. The latter also made an offering of the first fruits of the viands to the gods. This was commuted by the Anglo-Saxons into setting aside a portion of the meal for their guardian angel. Hence the saying, "Leave some for manners."

139. **Dressing for Dinner** is a custom handed down to us by the Romans, who put on a loose robe of light texture, and generally white, before sitting down to the most important meal of the day. Instances occur where it was kept in readiness for guests who came from a distance, and had had no opportunity of dressing before arrival.

140. In many parts of England what is called **Pudding Time** takes the place of "dinner time." This is because the pudding is always served before the meat, as was the custom formerly all over the country.

141. It will doubtless be news to many to learn that **Roast Lamb and Mint Sauce** was originally eaten by our forefathers in imitation of their Jewish neighbours, who ate bitter herbs with the Paschal lamb to remind them of the bitter oppression endured by the Israelites in the land of bondage, where, as we read, "the Egyptians made their lives bitter with hard bondage in mortar and in brick, and in all manner of service in the field" (*see* 397).

142. **Table Napkins** were articles of the utmost necessity in this country prior to the introduction of forks, which did not make their appearance even in polite society until the commencement of the seventeenth century. It was Thomas Coryate, that eccentric writer and wanderer, who traversed the greater part of the European Continent on foot, and afterwards hung up his old shoes in the parish church at Odcombe, Somersetshire, his native place, as relics of his extraordinary performance, who first brought the table-fork under the notice of Englishmen. "The Italians," he tells us in his "Crudities," "cannot by any means endure to have their flesh touched with fingers, seeing all men's fingers are not alike clean." We should think not indeed! And yet this social benefactor was abused on all sides because he "used a fork at feeding." In Hogarth's picture of the Guildhall Banquet, of "The Industrious Apprentice" Series, the absence of forks is plainly seen; all the guests eat with their fingers. Little wonder napkins were indispensable adjuncts to the dinner-table. The meal over, they also served the purpose of a towel when a general washing of hands took place.

143. The chief function of **Dish-covers** is obviously to keep the food hot during its passage from the kitchen to the dinner-table. But this was not at all the original idea of a

dish-cover. In the bad old times, when monarchs and nobles lived in daily fear of being poisoned by some unsuspected menial, dish-covers early suggested themselves as a necessary precaution ; and these were always padlocked in the kitchen, after the cook had been made to taste the food in the presence of a high official; thence the dish was carried up to the great man's table, where the steward of the household himself unlocked the cover and tasted the food before any of it was served. In this instance, verily, necessity was the mother of invention.

144. Thousands of English people to whom the **Willow-Pattern Plate** has been a familiar object all their lives are unacquainted with the meaning of the design. After all, it is the old, old story. In the mansion represented on the right dwelt a wealthy mandarin, with his only daughter, named Li-chi. This young lady fell in love with Chang, her father's secretary, whose residence, shown on the top left-hand corner, was on an island, seemingly at no great distance from the mainland. Now it chanced that one day the mandarin overheard the lovers interchanging vows of affection under the orange tree beside his house, and, pouncing down upon them, he then and there forbade their future meetings; whereupon they eloped, and for a time secreted themselves in the gardener's cottage beyond the bridge and the willow tree. The three figures on the bridge represent the mandarin and two of his servants on their way to the suspected refuge; but when they arrived there, the lovers had already escaped in a boat across the water to Chang's island home, whither, too, the mandarin followed, and would have carried out his determination to kill them, had not the gods promptly changed them into a pair of turtle-doves, as shown on the top of the picture. The name of the willow-pattern plate is given to the design because the

flight of the lovers took place during the season when the willow begins to shed its leaves.

145. **Toothpicks** are far from common in Italy. In *pensions* there may occasionally be met with small wooden picks, but quills never. The explanation is that one of the popes was poisoned by means of a medicated toothpick, purposely handed to him after dinner.

146. **To Toast a Person** is to drink his health. In the days of our grandfathers it was the time-honoured custom to put a piece of toast in the wine-cup before drinking, from a fanciful notion that it gave the liquor a better flavour. To pledge a person's health must, therefore, have been synonymous with "toasting" it from an early period. For the application of the term to the person himself we must turn to a presumably correct account of its origin in No. 24 of the "Tatler," as follows:—"It happened that on a public day a celebrated beauty of those times [Charles I.] was in the Cross Bath [at Bath], and one of the crowd of her admirers took a glass of the water in which the fair one stood, and drank her health to the company. There was in the place a gay young fellow, half fuddled, who offered to jump in, and swore, though he liked not the liquor, he would have the **toast.** He was opposed in his resolution, yet this whim gave foundation to the present honour which is done to the lady we mention in our liquor, who has ever since been called a toast."

147. The origin of the **Loving Cup,** or as it is called at the Universities, the **Grace Cup,** is attributed by Miss Strickland, in her "Lives of the Queens of Scotland," to Margaret Atheling, wife of Malcolm Kenmore, who, in order to induce the Scots to remain at table for grace, caused a cup filled with the choicest wine to be passed round to the dinner-

guests as soon as grace had been said. Without the Loving Cup no City banquet, or feast at the Inns of Court, would be complete. Grace being said, the Master and Wardens drink to the visitors, after which the cup is passed round the table. In his proper turn each guest rises and bows to his immediate neighbour, who, also rising, removes and holds the cover with his right hand while the other drinks. The meaning of this little ceremonial must be sought far back in Anglo-Saxon days, when Edward the Martyr was treacherously stabbed in the back by one of the servants of Elfrida, his mother-in-law, while drinking in the saddle, at the door of his house near Corfe Castle. To prevent the possibility of such lurking treachery for the future, a cover was provided for all manner of drinking-cups, the use whereof was this: By removing and holding the cover, the person offering the cup had his right, or dagger hand, sufficiently employed to assure the drinker, thus temporarily taken off his guard, of the honesty of his purpose. This was a wise precaution when no one else was standing by. At the banqueting-table, likewise, the assistance lent to the drinker by his immediate neighbour was regarded as a pledge of security while the former was unable to defend himself from attack by possible enemies around.

148. **The Stirrup Cup** may be traced to the *poculum boni genii* of the Romans, or the last cup quaffed at the festive board to a general "Good Night." The cold refinement of modern manners has almost banished this good old custom from the land, though our Scottish and Irish neighbours still offer the cordial stirrup cup to their departing guests.

149. Stinginess forms no part of the Spanish character. Without what is called **The Footbath** no Spaniard would think of serving or of accepting a drink. When a person

calls for a glass of wine or liqueur, it is customary for the waiter to fill it up until it overflows into the saucer. This is done to show an excess of liberality.

150. It was the custom not so very long ago to attribute every incredible story to **Miles's Boy.** People were also sent on fictitious errands, and, when they discovered how they had been hoaxed, the trick was laid at the door of "Miles's Boy." There is an old farce of this title, in which, though the youth does not appear in it himself, all the characters are put to no end of inconvenience by his pranks. We are indebted to Mr. Robins' "History of Paddington" for some definite information concerning the real existence of this notable young scapegrace. "At the beginning of this century," says Mr. Robins, "Mr. Miles, his pair-horse coach, and his redoubtable boy, were the only appointed agents of communication between Paddington and the City. The fare was two shillings and three shillings, the journey occupying more than three hours, and to beguile the time at resting-places, 'Miles's boy' (who presumably acted as a sort of guard to the coach) told tales and played on the fiddle."

151. The custom of saying **God Bless You!** on hearing a person sneeze is very old. The Greeks and Romans exclaimed "Long life to you!" on a similar occasion. The origin of this pious ejaculation is generally ascribed to a plague raging in Athens, in the course of which sneezing was regarded as a sign of convalescence. But to come to the Christian observance. When, five hundred and fifty-eight years after Christ, a universal epidemic broke out in Southern Europe, the reigning Pope recommended the faithful to exclaim, "God bless you!" whenever they heard a neighbour sneeze, as a kind of prayer that further evils might be averted. In this particular case a sneezing fit was fraught

with mischief, being the earliest symptom of the disease that threatened to lay a person low.

152. When mothers humour their children by offering to **Kiss the Place and Make it Better,** they little think they are only following up the practice of the sorcerers of old, who pretended to cure diseases by sucking the affected part.

153. The expressions **Sitting Round the Fire,** and **The Family Circle,** had a literal significance in the days of our forefathers, when the fireplace was built out in the centre of the room, much in the same manner as we still find it in Russia and Germany. Nowadays the family assembled on the domestic hearth is at best only a semi-circle.

154. That well-known expression **The Three R's,** was ushered into existence by Sir William Curtis, an illiterate alderman of the City of London, who, when called upon to propose a toast at a public dinner, electrified the entire company by giving, "The Three R's: Reading, 'Riting, and 'Rithmetic!"

155. **An Englishman's House is his Castle** because neither warrant-officer nor bailiff is empowered to force the door open if the master of the house refuses to admit him. In Scotland it is otherwise.

156. By the expression **The Fourth Estate** is meant journalists. It was first made use of by Edmund Burke, who said that in the Reporters' Gallery there was a fourth estate more powerful than any of the other three, viz., the Lords Temporal, the Lords Spiritual, and the Commons.

157. The expression, **A Nine Days' Wonder,** originated in the circumstance that kittens are born blind, and remain so for nine days.

158. **A Horseshoe** is considered a lucky find because it has seven nails in it. From the earliest ages, owing to the frequency with which it occurs in the Bible, seven has, all the world over, been regarded as a mystical number. An old horseshoe was formerly fastened upon the stable door to keep off witches, who were afraid of horses, and who had a reputation for riding through the air astride a broomstick.

159. **The Number Thirteen** is supposed to be unlucky because our Lord and His twelve apostles sat down together at the Last Supper. In some parts of the country the person who leaves the table first after thirteen have sat down to it, is believed to be the one to die first. This is because Judas, who was the first to quit the Supper Table, hanged himself shortly afterwards.

160. **The Friday Superstition** may be dismissed in a few words. In former times public executions always took place on a Friday, because this was the day of our Saviour's crucifixion between two thieves.

161. The widespread idea that **Spilling the Salt** is a bad omen, is of much older date than the time of Leonardo da Vinci, who, in his great picture of the Last Supper, has represented Judas overturning the salt-cellar while reaching over the table to dip his hand into the dish with our Lord. From the earliest times salt has entered into the sacred rites of the Jews, and, since the time of Jesus Christ, of the Roman Catholic church, owing to the universal belief in its

incorruptibility. At the present day the Arabs eat bread and salt together as a high mark of friendship, while to spill a man's salt wilfully, or to present him with bread without salt, is regarded as the surest evidence of hostility. Spilling the salt was regarded by the Greeks and Romans as a profanation of the table. Bread and salt, being necessaries of life, were formerly sworn by. Among the Russians, the bride and bridegroom sit down to bread and salt as a peace-offering (*see* 188).

162. **The Breaking of a Looking-glass** is everywhere regarded as an ill omen. It is a very old superstition, and doubtless found its origin in a mere association of ideas. The glass being broken, the reflected human image is destroyed; therefore sorrow in some form must be the portion of the wrongdoer.

163. **Walking under a Ladder** is supposed to be unlucky because the dead Saviour was taken down from the Cross by means of a ladder. This is sheer nonsense. Far more reasonable is the suggestion that the none too careful British workman may allow the tool he is using to slip from his grasp; the result being that although the passer-by may have the good fortune to escape actual personal injury by the mishap, his new silk hat will in all probability be ruined. It is not always a question of ill-luck that deters the average well-dressed citizen from passing under a ladder on which a bill-poster is at work.

164. **Looking Backward** is regarded as unlucky because Lot's wife paid the penalty of looking back upon the doomed city of Sodom by being changed into a pillar of salt.

165. **Making a Curtsey to the New Moon** on her first appearance is a relic of moon worship, the religion of primitive man, and one of the oldest forms of idolatry on the face of the globe.

166. **Tarring and Feathering** is not a new thing by any means. Roger de Hoveden, a chronicler of the time of Richard I., informs us that when that monarch set sail for the Holy Land he, among other laws designed for the regulation of his fleet, ordered, that "A robber who shall be convicted of theft, shall have his head cropped, after the manner of a champion, and boiling pitch shall be poured thereon, and then the feathers of a cushion shall be shaken out upon him, so that he may be known, and at the first land at which the ship shall touch he shall be set on shore." Whether the modern mode of tarring and feathering the entire body is an improvement upon the original is a question which can best be answered by the victim himself.

167. **The Ducking-stool**, or as it was often called, the **Cucking-stool**, was one of the oldest of popular punishments, being mentioned in Domesday Book. Its object was to cool the immoderate heat of shrews and scolds, who were fastened into it and then plunged into a pool of water. The number of dips was generally regulated by the degree of shrewishness in the victim. The term "Cucking-stool" was a corruption of *chucking* or *choking-stool.*

168. **The Brank**, or **Gossip's Bridle**, was an instrument of punishment formerly reserved for women whose tongues had engendered mischief. It was considered far more effectual than the cucking-stool (*see* 167), which allowed its occupant to wag her tongue between each dip. An interesting example of the Gossip's Bridle may still be

seen in the vestry of the parish church at Walton-on-Thames It bears this inscription : "Chester presents Walton with a bridle to curb women's tongues that talk too idle—1613." The presentation is believed to have been due to the fact that the person whose name is mentioned lost a valuable estate through the instrumentality of a gossiping woman.

169. **The Pillory** was originally devised for the punishment of mountebanks and quacks, who, because they harangued the people from banks and forms, were, as Rushworth says, "exalted in the same kind," but held close prisoners the while. It was subsequently used for cheats of all sorts, and, nearer our own time, for political offenders.

COURTSHIP AND MARRIAGE

COURTSHIP AND MARRIAGE

170. JOINING hands over a running streamlet was a favourite mode of **Plighting Troths** in former times. There is a pretty meaning in this. A modern poet has well expressed the sentiment in these words:

> "Like the waters at our feet, which never cease to flow,
> Constant love I crave from thee thro' life, for weal or woe."

171. One of the most popular love-tokens of a bygone day was the **Gimmal Ring,** a name derived from the Latin *gemellus,* joined, because the ring was composed of two separate bands fitting into each other with little teeth; thus allowing them to be divided at a betrothal, and put together again when the betrothed parties approached the hymeneal altar. Such a ring was devised to take the place of the **Broken Coin,** which among the Franks was the usual token of the conclusion of a bargain. When lovers plighted their troths in this way, the separated halves were always invested with mystic qualities in virtue of the vows of constancy exchanged over them. Sometimes the coin remained proof against breakage, and was merely bent; in which case a hole was bored through it, and one or the other of the parties wore it round the neck on a piece of ribbon, as a sort of talisman capable of warding off disease and evil spirits. In this we trace the origin of the popular idea that a coin with a hole in it is lucky. Many allusions to "Bowed Money" occur in the works of the old dramatists.

172. It would seem that a **Lock of Hair** naturally suggested itself to the minds of men and women as a love-token. But this was not the original meaning of the interchange of such a cherished treasure. In ancient times, whenever a person of distinction was taken prisoner in war, or held to ransom while on his travels, his relations were usually apprised of his captivity by the receipt of a lock of of his hair.

173. When lovers **Sit at the Feet of their Mistresses** they pay the same homage to beauty as was anciently paid to great people of both sexes. In Elizabeth's time this homage was considered the rightful heritage of all ladies who were being wooed; and to keep their lovers employed they gave them their wool to wind. Happy ladies!

174. **The Nuptial Kiss at the Altar** is all that remains to us of an ancient ceremony which always preceded the actual Marriage Service by a longer or shorter period, according to circumstances. This was the **Espousals**, or **Solemn Betrothal.** Generally speaking, the gift of a betrothal ring by the bridegroom-elect to the bride-elect was considered sufficiently binding; but in an age when it was the custom to invite the blessing of the Church upon all the more serious transactions of life, public espousals were, taking the population all round, matters of everyday occurrence. Besides, it often happened that a love-sick swain was not sufficiently endowed with this world's goods to give his future wife anything more substantial than an espousal kiss. When this was the case, he naturally wished all his acquaintance to bear witness to the fact that the young lady was solemnly engaged to him, and that he meant to carry out his intention of marrying her at the earliest opportunity. It was this espousal kiss, before witnesses, which marked the

difference between a sentimental compact, and one of a purely mundane character. The mere joining of hands following words of promise sufficed to ratify all ordinary bargains; but when the contractors joined lips as well as hands, they breathed into each other the breath of life, and their spiritual union was complete. Yet the kiss and joining of hands was only part of the espousal ceremony. Like the modern Jews, the betrothed pair went through a ceremonial which differed only from the actual Marriage Service in that their mutual promises therein were expressed in the future tense instead of in the present. In conclusion, they pledged each other in a cup of wine, as do the Jews and the Russians at the present day. This pledging each other in wine, it should be observed, is nothing more than a survival of the once universal custom of parties drinking together in ratification of a bargain.

175. **Marriage by Capture** was the universal practice in the early eras of civilization, as it still is among primitive races. Says Oldfield, speaking of the Maoris, "In Australia the men are in excess of the other sex, and consequently many men of every tribe are unprovided with the especial thing necessary to their comfortable existence—a wife, who is also a slave in the strictest sense of the word, being a beast of burden, a provider of food, and a ready object on which to vent those passions that the men dare not vent on each other. Hence, for those coveting such a luxury, arises the necessity of stealing the women of some other tribe; and in their expeditions to effect so laudable a design they will frequently undergo privations equal to those they incurred when in search of blood revenge." The disparity of numbers between the sexes here alluded to admits of a ready explanation; nor is it confined to savage nations. The cruel exposure of female infants by the Chinese—a

practice so justly reprobated by Christians—is but a form of the precautionary measures taken by all barbarian nations to prevent one portion of the population from becoming a burden upon the other. In a fighting community, the girl neither hunts nor engages in warfare; she does nothing but eat. Moreover, while unable to protect herself, she is at any time liable to be carried off by some neighbouring tribe, thus occasioning a constant watchfulness on the part of those to whom she belongs. Among the Arabs and Turks there is joy in the household on the birth of a son and heir, but the mother of a succession of daughters is generally despised, and often divorced. This much is certain: in a state of society but a trifle advanced from that of absolute barbarism, daughters are looked upon by their parents only as objects to be bartered for by their intending husbands as soon as they attain a marriageable age. Directly the pursuits of agriculture stimulated man to acquire, if only for the purpose of lightening his labour, such property as was represented by cattle, the original system of marriage was changed into what is called **Marriage by Purchase**. In many parts of the world wives are at the present day bartered for so many head of cattle. The presents which the young Indian of North America is expected to lay before his future squaw are only another form of purchase-money for her person. Among the Brahmins of India, up to the very moment when the father of the bride leads her to the bridegroom, saying, "I have no longer anything to do with you, and I give you up into the power of another," the latter is liable to be ousted from his position should any rival appear on the scene to offer a richer present to the father than his own. And amongst ourselves the presence of the bride's father at the marriage ceremony makes him a party to a transaction which in feudal times must have been thoroughly commercial in character. A few generations back the father did not put in an appearance until the ring had been placed on the bride's finger. This, to all intents and purposes, was to show that his consent had been wrung from him; that he countenanced the ceremony only to the same degree as a father would do whose daughter had been carried off by force. While the bride was attended to church by her maids and pages the father invariably loitered by the way.

176. **Wedding Presents** are a survival of feudal times, when tenants were bound to "render aid" at the knighting of their lord's eldest son, and at the marriage of his eldest daughter. When feudalism declined, the usual tribute on such occasions was commuted into a present, at the discretion of, and in accordance with the means of the individual, as a happy augury. Poor folk, who could afford nothing better, generally sent the bride the symbolical coronals mentioned in paragraph 188. During the reign of Elizabeth the most usual wedding present among the middle classes of society was "a pair of knives," *i.e.*, scissors, whose purpose is thus defined in Davison's "Poetical Rhapsody:"

> "Fortune doth give these paire of knives to you
> To cut the thread of love if it be untrue."

This explains why the gift of a penknife or a pair of scissors is regarded as an ill omen, because it cuts love in twain.

177. The origin of the **Wedding Ring** must be sought among the ancient Egyptians, who regarded the bracelet as the symbol of marriage, because, being round, it was endless. Egyptian wives wore no other ornaments than a pair of bracelets. Among the Assyrians, the Babylonians, and other nations of antiquity, the bracelet had the like signification. The Jewish women, we read, were so fond of these ornaments that they wore them on their ankles as well as

on their arms. Hence the allusion in Isaiah to "the jingling ornaments on the feet of the haughty daughters of Jerusalem." To this day married women in the East are addicted to wearing bracelets so massive as to greatly oppress the wearer. This, like the long finger-nails of the Chinese, is looked upon as indicative of high birth, inasmuch as they are thereby rendered incapable of personal exertion. On the overthrow of the Persian empire by the Greeks, they, being a highly imaginative people, and observing that most of the leaders of the vanquished host wore bracelets on their wrists as ornaments of distinction, invested their brides-elect with a miniature bracelet, to be worn on the medicated finger (*see* 178); and themselves bestowed bracelets upon their heroes and generals as rewards of valour. By this means the original symbolism of the bracelet was in part destroyed; but a deeper significance attached itself to the plain gold band upon the finger, which was supposed to have a direct communication with the heart. The Romans, who copied nearly everything from the Greeks, also rewarded their military heroes with bracelets as badges of honour. Like the Greeks, too, they bestowed a plain gold ring upon their brides-elect, in strict accordance with a time-honoured custom amongst themselves of delivering a ring as an earnest upon the conclusion of a bargain. In the course of the marriage ceremony, however, the betrothal ring was exchanged for the bridegroom's signet, the emblem of investiture and authority (*see* 28), to show that the newly-made wife was fully admitted into her husband's confidence, that he endowed her with equal rights with himself over his property. Though at first the marriage ring was a signet, it eventually gave place to a plain one of iron, called a *pronubum*, symbolical of the lasting character of the contract. It was not until after they had seen the wedding ring come into general use among the Roman conquerors of the East that the Jews adopted it in their own marriage rite. Wedding rings did not obtain in the Christian Marriage Service until the ninth century. The Anglo-Saxons established the custom of wearing plain gold rings, and these have been worn by married women ever since. There is no rubric on the subject; a ring is all the Church stipulates for. Consequently, we sometimes hear of a bride being married with the ring of the church-door key, in the absence of the more desirable article.

178. The custom of wearing the **Wedding Ring on the fourth Finger of the Left Hand** had unquestionably a pagan origin. Both the Greeks and the Romans called the fourth left-hand finger the **Medicated Finger,** and used it to stir up mixtures and potions, out of the belief that it contained a vein which communicated directly with the heart, and therefore nothing noxious could come in contact with it without giving instant warning to that vital organ. When the ring supplanted the bracelet as the symbol of matrimony (*see* 177), the deep sentimentality of the Greeks dictated that it should be worn on the medicated finger. The fallacy of the connection between that finger and the heart was in more modern times completely exploded, but after such long usage the so-called medicated finger still continued to be the annular. Some attempts were indeed made to improve matters by shifting the ring on to the corresponding finger of the right hand, as was, and is, the custom of bishops and cardinals (*see* 28); yet it was not long before the improvers reverted to the old order. To commence with, the left hand was found to be more suitable, because less used, as the depository of such ornaments than the right. With regard to the finger, our forefathers knew very well that the fourth finger was used much more sparingly than any of the others, so a ring placed

on that finger would be little liable to be bruised or damaged; for whereas the other fingers can be put out singly to their full length, the fourth, or ring finger, cannot be extended in this way except in company with the rest.

179. If any evidence were needed to lend weight to the generally-concurred opinion that **The Best Man** was originally one of the belligerents who assisted the bridegroom to carry off the bride by force (*see* 175), it would be found in the fact that in Sweden formerly marriages always took place under cover of night. This custom obtained from a very early period of Scandinavian history, for no warrior considered it dignified to woo a woman himself. He waited until she had been successfully wooed by another, then, when the marriage was about to take place, he sallied forth with his companions with the object of wresting the bride from the bridegroom. Knowing this, the latter took such measures as were calculated to frustrate the designs of the rival that threatened. Behind the high altar of the ancient church at Husaby, in Gothland, a collection of long lances, with sockets for torches, are preserved. They were formerly served out to the groomsmen as weapons of defence, as well as for illumination, when marriages were being solemnized by night. All these groomsmen were styled "Best Men," because they were the strongest and bravest obtainable for the purpose. The assailant also had his "Best Men," as valiant as himself. At the present time we have but one "Best Man," who is the particular friend of the bridegroom; the remainder of the male witnesses to the ceremony are simply "guests."

180. **The Bridesmaids** and **Groomsmen** had formerly many important duties to perform. For some time previous to the great event, the first bridesmaid placed her-

self at the disposal of the bride-elect. She attended her in all her shopping excursions, gave advice as to the choice of colours and materials, applied herself most diligently to all the necessary needlework, and with hand and brain lent assistance in every possible way. The making of the bridal wreath devolved upon her alone. To console the bride on the wedding eve, to superintend, if not to prepare with her own hands, the decoration of the festal banquet, to dress the bride, with the assistance of the other bridesmaids, on the eventful morning, and to hold her fan and scent-bottle for her in church—these were her especial duties. Then, when the day was spent, she and the others undressed and put the bride to bed. Corresponding services were rendered to the bridegroom by the groomsmen. The "Best Man" was always charged with the sole management of affairs, even to the paying of the customary fees. During the days of feudal England the "Best Man" was supposed to be prepared to shed his blood, if need be, for his friend the bridegroom (*see* 179).

181. It is still the custom in many parts of the country for the officiating **Clergyman to Kiss the Bride.** This is a relic of the benedictional pax, which in Catholic days always brought the marriage ceremony to a happy ending. After all the parties had regaled themselves with the light refreshment provided (*see* 187), the priest gave the pax, or kiss of peace, to the bridegroom, who communicated it to the bride, at the same time as an ecclesiastical assistant conveyed another holy kiss from the lips of the priest to the groomsmen, bridesmaids, and other persons present, kissing each of them in succession. The same ceremony, in a slightly altered form, takes place immediately after the Communion in the Catholic churches at solemn High Mass. Its origin is traced to St. James the Greater, who,

when one of the soldiers deputed to bind and drag him along to the place of execution, was so touched by his gentleness that he supplicated to be allowed to die in his company, kissed him and said, "Pax vobis!"

182. The object of **Publication of Banns** is, and has been from the first, to prevent marriages within the forbidden degrees of kindred; but it was not until midway in the thirteenth century that such announcements became canonically established. Long before, it had been the custom for all "good knights and true," who elected to take part in the tournaments, to hang up their shields in the nearest church for some time prior to the event, so that, in the event of any taint being discovered, they might be prohibited from entering the lists. There is good reason, therefore, to believe, that it was from this knightly custom that the publication of the banns of marriage on three consecutive Sundays in the parish church took its rise.

183. **Orange Blossoms** were first worn at weddings by the Saracens, who regarded these flowers as the emblems of fecundity. Like many another Oriental custom, it was introduced into Western Europe by the Crusaders.

184. **The Bride's Wreath** is a Christian substitute for the gilt coronet which was the especial adornment of a Jewish bride. The Jews have always regarded the promotion of marriage as a meritorious act, and by crowning a bride they paid her the highest possible honour. The Russians and the Calvinists of Holland and Switzerland still adhere to the ancient practice of crowning a bride during the nuptial ceremony.

185. **The Bride's Veil** has been derived from the

flammeum, or large yellow veil which completely enveloped the Greek and Roman brides during the celebration of the marriage rite. Such a one is still in use among the Jews and the Persians. In those parts of the world where marriage by capture still prevails a sheet, or other voluminous drapery, is thrown over the bride so that she may be the more readily borne away by her captors.

186. A great deal of speculation has been rife concerning the celebration in bygone days of **The Marriage Rite in the Church Porch.** But the truth is, that the porch was never regarded as an integral portion of the sacred edifice. Even the nave was, down to a comparatively modern period, utilized for secular purposes. We all know how Old St. Paul's was converted into a fashionable promenade, and worse, for tradesmen's stalls and carpenters' shops were actually set up in close proximity to the choir. Elsewhere there was more reasonable excuse for such an apparent desecration of a house dedicated to the service of God; because, in those days when parochial affairs were necessarily discussed in the vestry—hence the modern designation "vestry hall"—the public had no sheltered place of common resort except the church itself. In the nave of the church it was that the earliest plays were represented; in the same place the people assembled for social diversion on great occasions; there, too, it was, when the distance to the bride or bridegroom's house was great, and the roads to be travelled over were bad, that the marriage feast was not unfrequently spread. In many respects, therefore, the parish church fulfilled a two-fold purpose. It was at once a place of public worship and a place of public meeting. When all England was Catholic the lamp perpetually burning in front of the altar proclaimed that it was there, in the tabernacle, where God particularly dwelt. Though the

same roof extended over all, the nave was apportioned to the people, not merely on Sundays, but on all high holidays; and if this was true of the nave it was still more so of the porch. In no sense was it considered a portion of the church itself. All day long its doors stood invitingly open for gossips to assemble, children to play in wet weather, and tired wayfarers to find a shady retreat from the sweltering sun. In the larger centres of civilization commercial matters were freely discussed in the church porch, and money passed from hand to hand—it was in fact a primitive Royal Exchange. Infants were christened in the porch before, literally and metaphorically, they were admitted into the church; women, too, were "churched" there after childbirth. In this connection it may be stated that part of the ceremonial incidental to both christenings and churchings still takes place outside a Roman Catholic church proper. In the porch, again, the funeral service was read over the dead, and marriages were solemnized. Does not the poet Chaucer tell us how the wife of Bath was married to her five husbands in the church porch? The sole reason why the marriage rite was performed virtually outside the walls of the church, was because the clergy looked upon marriage as, first and foremost, in the light of a civil contract. Not for 1,500 years after the introduction of Christianity did the Church decree matrimony to be a Sacrament, although its benediction had always been invoked by way of ratifying the contract which owed its origin to the law of the land. When, therefore, marriage became a spiritual as well as a civil institution the actual rite was still performed in the porch as of old, and the solemn blessing of the spirituality took place at the altar rails in the church itself.

187. In these days the term **Wedding Breakfast** is a misnomer, for no one would think of going through such

a trying ordeal breakfastless. In pre-Reformation times, however, the bride and bridegroom, before leaving the church, were expected to hear Mass and receive the Holy Communion. The attendance of the witnesses was naturally enjoined also, but in their case the Communion was optional. At the conclusion of the Mass the officiating priest solemnly blessed some wine, cakes, and sweetmeats, which were then handed round to the company. This slight repast was, in every sense of the word, a breakfast, since in the Roman Catholic Church none can receive the Holy Communion who have not fasted from the previous midnight.

188. **The Wedding Cake** is the modern development of an ancient practice which had its origin in the Roman form of marriage called *Confarreatio*, or eating together. When the Roman bride gave her right hand to the bridegroom, she held in her left three wheat ears, symbolical of plenty; and at the conclusion of the ceremony all the contracting parties sat down together to partake of a cake made of flour, salt, and water (*see* 161). In the reign of the Emperor Tiberius this *Confarreatio* was suffered to fall into general disuse, though the wheat ears continued to play their original part in the marriage ceremonial as a happy augury of future plenty. All through the Middle Ages, and long afterwards, the symbolical wheat ears were never wanting in one form or another; *i.e.*, either carried by the bride or worn as a chaplet on her head. Eventually it became a custom with the marriageable girls of the neighbourhood to assemble outside the church porch with full measures of wheat, the contents of which they threw over the head and shoulders of the bride as soon as she reappeared after all was over. This idea was doubtless derived from their Jewish neighbours who, while the bridegroom walked three times round the bride, threw handfuls

of wheat over them, exclaiming, "Increase and multiply!" as their descendants still do to-day. Then ensued a scramble among the witnesses for the grains as they lay scattered on the ground; in compliment to the bride it was considered the proper thing to eat them on the spot. At last, however, there came a time when people lost their appetite for uncooked kernels, and the natural outcome of man's ingenuity was a kind of biscuit. Easy enough it would have been to distribute portions of the wedding biscuit; but popular sentiment demanded that it should be broken over the bride's head, and scrambled for in the good old-fashioned way. In the Scottish Highlands at the present day an oatmeal cake is broken over the bride's head by the best man and first bridesmaid as she enters the house on her return from church, and distributed to the company. By the time of Elizabeth these thin dry biscuits began to take the form of small rectangular cakes or buns, made of eggs, milk, sugar, currants, and spices. The number of such articles always brought together at a wedding was very considerable; for not only did every guest make his appearance with a packet, but all the neighbours were expected to send in their contributions before the bride returned home from church. The instant she crossed the threshold, those members of the household who had remained at home to prepare the feast, energetically threw the whole collection over her head. Those which by any chance alighted upon her head and shoulders were prized most of all; they were eaten at once by the married, but by the single they were religiously preserved in order to be placed under their pillows at night, so as to make them dream of their future partners for life. The remainder were divided into two equal portions; the one distributed to the poor who had followed the party home from church, the other placed in a huge pile in front of the happy couple on the festive board.

Towards the conclusion of the repast the newly-made husband and wife exchanged a kiss over the dish of cakes, and then proceeded to distribute them. The next step in the direction of the modern wedding cake was the coating of the little square cakes with almond paste or comfits. After this, it needed little to convert the pile into a single mass, covered with hardened white sugar and ornamented with tiny cupids and other devices suggestive of matrimonial bliss. This occurred during the Restoration period, when the art of preserving fruits was first cultivated, and, thanks to the ingenuity of the pastrycooks, dainties found their way into English households such as had never before been heard of. It only remains to be added that the cake continued to be broken over the bride's head, or rather tossed and suffered to break on the ground, long after its introduction in the modern form; but, in order that its appearance on the table might not be spoiled, good housewives generally provided two cakes—one for the table, the other for breaking and distribution. Nowadays the cake cut by the bride is considered all-sufficient.

189. Instances have not been wanting in this country in which a bride has gone through the marriage ceremony, attended by the usual witnesses, in her shift. This was known as a **Marriage in Chemise.** It was done with the object of absolving her husband from such debts as she had contracted before marriage. According to the strict letter of the law a man is not responsible for his wife's past debts, unless he has received property with her. Needless to state, this disrobing of the bride before the ceremony was a subterfuge both unnecessary and invalid from a legal standpoint.

190. In one part of the world only is **The Nuptial**

Knot literally as well as figuratively tied. This is in India, at the marriage of a Brahmin. No sooner has the father, in words as plainly as can be, **Given the Bride Away** (*see* 175), than the bridegroom places the *Tali*, or insignia of marriage, consisting of a piece of ribbon with a gold bead suspended upon it, round her neck, and ties the knot. It is this knot which actually secures her to him, and makes the marriage indissoluble, for the Brahmins do not recognize divorce.

191. **The Breaking of the Wine-cup**, after the bride and bridegroom have drained its contents, is common to both the Jews and the members of the Greek Church, with this difference, that among the former it is dashed against the wall or on the ground, whereas among the latter it is trodden under foot. There is also this difference of signification. The Russian bridegroom exclaims: "May they thus fall under our feet, and be trodden to pieces, who shall endeavour to sow dissension or discontent between us!" The Jew, on the other hand, shatters the vessel in memory of the destruction of the Temple. In some places ashes are put on his head for the like reason, and with the bride he wears a black cap, the ancient sign of mourning (*see* 203).

192. **As Marriage is a Serious Business**, some indication that the parties most immediately concerned are fully alive to this fact would be generally welcome. At every Roman wedding the bridegroom, on emerging from the temple with the bride, threw a handful of nuts among the bystanders. This was to show that he considered himself a boy no longer; that the sports and fancies of youth were now entirely abandoned; that he was standing on the threshold of a new existence, ready to assume all the re-

sponsibilities of a citizen. An analogous custom prevails at the present time in Java and in Japan, where a bride casts all her childish toys and trinkets into the fire, to evince her determination of becoming a woman. The object of the presents which the company then make her is to replace the treasures she has thus sacrificed.

193. The Scottish custom of **Lifting the Bride over the Doorstep** is a relic of barbarism. Most savage tribes carry their wives to their tents. Bruce, the traveller, found the same custom in Abyssinia as in Mexico: "The bridegroom takes his lady on his shoulders and carries her off to his house." The Canadian Indians always carry their wives on their bent backs to the tent prepared for their reception. In China the bride is carried into the house by a matron, and lifted over a pan of charcoal at the door. Whenever a bride is borne off by force, enveloped in a sheet, on horseback, in accordance with the primitive custom of marriage by capture, she is naturally carried into the house by the bridegroom (*see* 185).

194. **Ill-Assorted Marriages** were formerly resented in a very peculiar manner. Whenever such a ceremony was known to be taking place, the neighbours collected all the old tin pots, pans, and kettles they could find, and at times even invaded the church porch with their noisy manifestations of disapproval. All day long and far into the night some of them would be picketed outside the house of the far from happy couple, their inharmonious serenade being at length terminated by the heaping up of all the utensils in the doorway.

195. The meaning of **Rice Throwing at Weddings,** as an auspicious "send-off" to the happy couple, is not far

to seek. Inasmuch as rice is the most prolific of grains, it has always and everywhere been regarded as emblematical of God's command to Adam and Eve, and after the Deluge to Noah, to "increase and multiply, and replenish the earth." Among the Brahmins of India this rice throwing forms part of the marriage ceremony. Instead of rice, the Jews throw wheat, and the Russians oats or barley, upon the heads of the bridal couple, saying, "Increase and multiply" (*see* 188).

196. Of all the lingering customs of a bygone age that of **Throwing the Shoe** after a newly-married couple just off on their honeymoon will probably die the hardest. This is a relic of the Jewish mode of completing a transfer of land in ancient times, as illustrated in Ruth iv. 7. Here we find the shoe constituting a recognized symbol of possession. There is yet another virtue in an old shoe. As the shoes are always taken off indoors throughout the East, they serve as a ready means of inflicting correction on a child that disobeys its parents. When it is recollected that not only in the East, but in mediæval England, grown-up daughters were subject to be whipped up to the time of their marriage day, one can readily understand how the shoe came to be regarded also as a symbol of parental authority. In those Eastern countries where the Jews still abound the shoe plays no insignificant part in the marriage ceremonial. Directly the bride makes her appearance, her father presents a shoe to the bridegroom as a token that he yields his authority over her into the hands of her husband; who, thereupon, gently taps his newly-made wife on the nape of the neck to impress upon her that she must in future obey him. The self-same observance obtained among the Anglo-Saxons, with this addition, that the bridegroom caused the shoe to be placed on the pillow on his side of the bridal bed. If, as sometimes happened, the bride was inclined to be at all strong-minded, a

practical joker generally transferred the shoe to that lady's pillow, as a warning to the bridegroom of what he was to expect. Of course, the original significance of a custom which has travelled all the way from the East is subject to considerable modifications among different peoples in process of time, if, indeed, it is not wholly lost. The Highlanders, for example, always try to strike either the bride or the bridegroom with an old shoe for luck—a practice formerly in vogue throughout our own country, as the works of the old dramatists amply testify. In some parts of England, too, the flinging of the shoe is said to be a mode of chastising the bridegroom for taking away the bride; in other words, a survival of the barbaric custom of claiming a wife by capture; while elsewhere the shoe is intended merely as a reminder that the bride has left the house for good. Needless to state, all these customs have their common origin in the shoe anciently received by the bridegroom with the bride. In the New England States of North America, where many old English customs yet survive, the popular expression, "to live under the shoe," is tantamount to living under the ferule.

197. For the duration of the bridal tour, styled the **Honeymoon**, we are indebted to the Scandinavian races, who drank hydromel, or diluted honey, for thirty days after a wedding.

198. What is styled a **Wife's Pin Money** was originally devoted to the purchase of pins and nothing else. That was, of course, at a time when pins were neither plentiful nor cheap. Indeed, they did not resemble our modern pins at all. The pins of our great-grandmothers were, in fact, skewers, made of ivory, bone, steel, tortoiseshell, or silver, according to the quality of the purchaser.

199. **The Dunmow Flitch of Bacon Custom** really originated in a joke on the part of the monks of Dunmow Priory, in Essex, in the year 1244. These good easy men, who must have had plenty of time on their hands to enable them to reflect upon such things, could not conceive the possibility of a newly-married couple preserving their connubial bliss for any length of time; so, as a practical test, they offered a reward of a flitch of bacon to the man and wife of twelve months' standing who should come forward and maintain upon oath under cross-examination, while kneeling on sharp-pointed stones, that they had never had a quarrel, had never wished themselves single again, and if at liberty to make another choice, that they would make exactly the one they had made. It speaks very little for the perfect harmony which is supposed to dominate married life—at least by those young persons who have it in contemplation—when it is stated that exactly two hundred years elapsed before the flitch of bacon was even laid claim to! When, in common with all other religious establishments, Dunmow Priory was dissolved by the so-called Defender of the Faith, the land fell into the hands of a secular proprietor who either had the good sense to continue the old custom on his own account, or else he felt himself under some sort of solemn covenant to do so. At all events, the bacon was saved, and people had the same encouragement to strive to lead happy wedded lives as of yore. Thanks to the efforts of that distinguished novelist, William Harrison Ainsworth, the Dunmow Flitch of Bacon Custom has frequently been revived within the last half century.

DEATH AND BURIAL

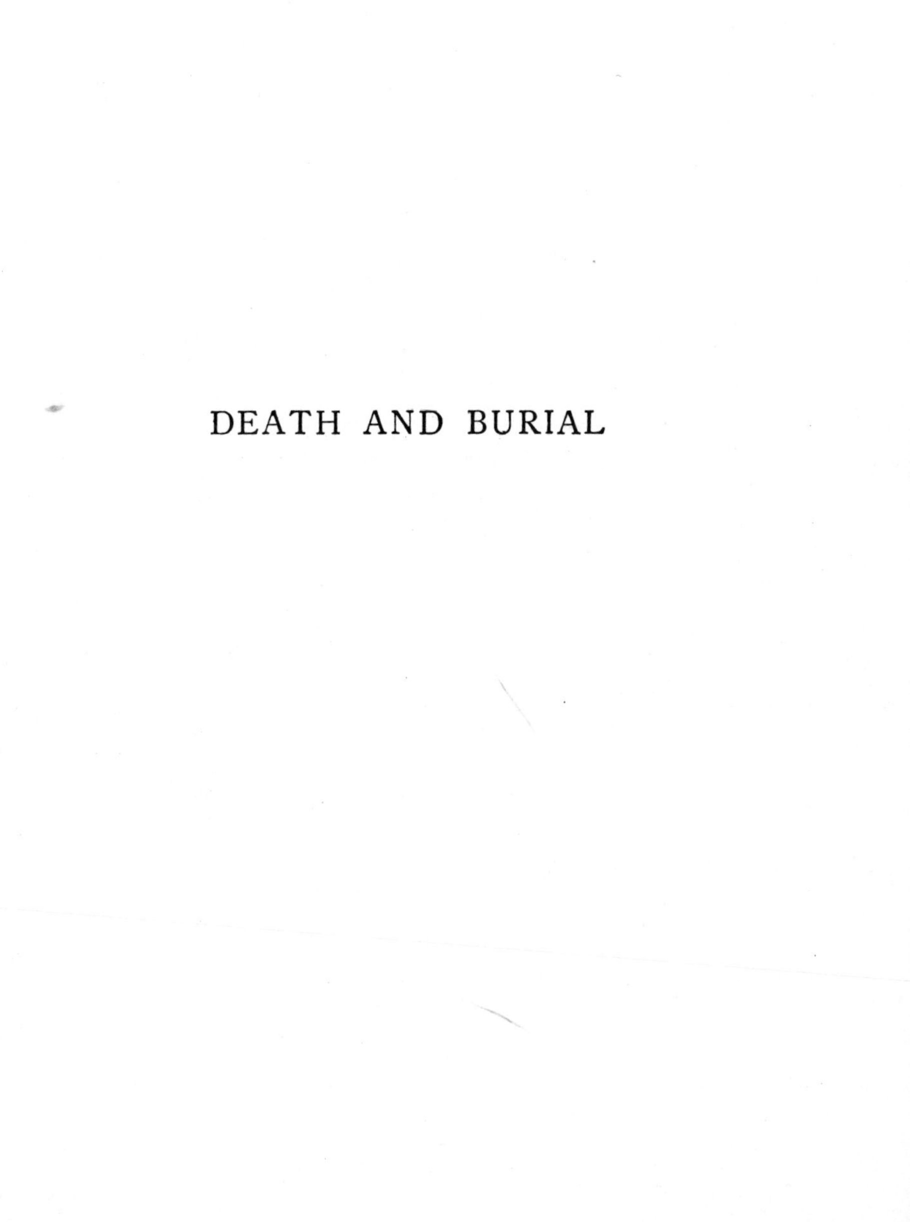

DEATH AND BURIAL

200. The cause of the **Death Rattle** is thus explained by Sir Henry Halford, the eminent physician :—"The lungs are the last to give up the performance of their functions and die. As death approaches they become gradually more and more oppressed; the air-cells are loaded with an increased quantity of the fluid which naturally lubricates their surfaces; the atmosphere can now no longer come into contact with the minute blood-vessels spread over the cells without first permeating this viscous fluid—hence the rattle; nor is the contact sufficiently perfect to change the black venous into the red arterial blood; an unprepared fluid consequently issues from the lungs into the heart, and is thence transmitted to every other organ of the body."

201. The custom of flying a **Flag Half-Mast High** as a mark of mourning and respect arose out of the old naval and military practice of lowering the flag in time of war as a sign of submission. The vanquished always lowered his flag, while the victor fluttered his own flag above it from the same staff. To lower a flag, therefore, is a token of respect to one's superior, and a signal of mourning and distress.

202. **Tolling the Church Bells** on the death of a distinguished person arose out of the **Passing Bell** formerly tolled in the parish church, the moment any member of the congregation passed away, to invite the prayers of all

the other parishioners for the repose of his soul, and also to drive away wicked spirits, who could not bear to hear the sound. Says Jurandus, "It is said that the wicked spirits that be in the region of the air fear much when they hear the bells ringing; and this is the cause why the bells be ringing when it thundereth: to the end that the foul fiend and wicked spirits should be abashed, and flee, and cease from moving of the tempest."

203. "Why does the judge in a criminal court assume the **Black Cap** when pronouncing sentence of death?" is a question frequently asked. This is because covering the head has from the earliest times been regarded as a sign of mourning. Numerous examples of this occur in the Scriptures, in the classics, and in modern literature. "The ancient English," says Dudley Fosbrooke, in his monumental work on archæology, "drew their hoods over their heads at funerals." We read also in Peck's "Dissertata Curiosa," of "the congregation, a very great one, sitting in the choir to hear the funeral sermon, all covered," at the burial of Bishop Cox in Ely Cathedral in the year 1581. Not only do the Jews keep their hats on their heads at funerals, but in some countries they still wear black caps at weddings, in token of mourning for the destruction of the Temple. Another reason is that the black cap forms part of the full dress of a judge, which is worn only on extraordinary occasions. When the new Lord Mayor is presented in the Court of Exchequer on the 9th of November, the judges receive him with their heads so covered.

204. **The Black Flag** hoisted upon prison walls as a signal that the last sentence of the law has been carried out, was first employed by Tamerlane, Khan of the Tartars, in the fourteenth century. Whenever a beleaguered city refused

to surrender after a certain period, he displayed a black flag, to proclaim that "the time for mercy is now past, and the city is given up to destruction."

205. **A Military Funeral** is always an impressive spectacle. When such a one takes place in time of peace, the ceremonial is exactly the same as it would be in camp or on the battle-field. A gun-carriage forms an improvised hearse, the drums are muffled out of respect for the dead comrade, and all arms are carried reversed to show that the company deputed to perform the sad office count upon the forbearance of the enemy for the time being, consequently they do not fear an attack (*see* 379). In the case of a cavalry officer being buried, his horse is led behind the body; this is a survival of ancient times, when an officer's charger was universally sacrificed at the grave-side and buried with its master. At the conclusion of the ceremony a salute is fired over the grave to intimate to the enemy that they are once more ready to act on the defensive.

206. **The Mourning Colours of Different Nations** are not devoid of meaning. BLACK is the accepted colour throughout Europe. It expresses the solemn midnight gloom, the total deprivation of light and joy on account of the loss sustained. In Shakespeare's time the stage was draped with black during the performance of a tragedy. This accounts for the opening line in his "Henry VI.," "Hung be the heavens with black;" the "heavens" answering to our "borders" and "flies." WHITE is the emblem of Hope, the Chinese colour of mourning. The ladies of Rome and Sparta dressed in white during the period of mourning. Prior to the year 1498, when Anne, queen of Charles VIII., of France, surrounded her coat of arms with black drapery and dressed herself in black on the

death of her husband, in opposition to the prevailing custom, widows in England, France, and Spain generally adopted white mourning. Mary, Queen of Scots, received the name of "the White Queen," because she mourned in white for the death of her husband, Lord Darnley. White coffins for children are still popular; while in some parts of the country white hat-bands in mourning for the unmarried are the rule rather than the exception. BLACK AND WHITE STRIPED express Sorrow and Hope. This is the mourning colour of the South Sea Islanders. The ancient Egyptians mourned in yellow, "the sere and yellow leaf." So do the Burmese, whose monastic habit is the same colour. In Brittany widows' caps are invariably yellow. PALE BROWN, the colour of withered leaves, is the Persian mourning colour. The inhabitants of Ethiopia affect GREYISH BROWN, the colour of the earth, to which the dead return. In Syria and Armenia SKY-BLUE is the colour of mourning, indicative of the assurance that the deceased has gone to heaven. PURPLE was formerly the mourning colour of all Christian princes. All the kings of France mourned in purple. Charles II. of England mourned in purple for his brother Henry, Duke of Gloucester, when he died in the year 1660. On Good Friday the cardinals, who bear the style of "Princes of the Church," wear purple habits because they are then in mourning for the death of Christ. So, also, on the death of the Pope, or of one of their number. This mourning colour of Christian princes in general, and of the princes of the Roman Catholic Church in particular, has been derived from the purple garment which the Roman soldiers put about our Lord, and mockingly saluted him as "King of the Jews" (*see* 18, 373, 379).

207. **Mourning Hat-bands** are a survival of the liripipe, or long tippet, depending from the hood worn by males

in this country during the Plantagenet period. When the hood was exchanged for the hat in the reign of Henry VIII. the tippet was retained in the form of the hat-band. Modern hat-bands, designed for ordinary wear, are so narrow as almost to pass unnoticed, but our mourning hat-bands are identical with those adopted during the Tudor period.

208. **Widows' Caps** are accounted for in this way: The Egyptians and Greeks shaved off their beards and cut off their hair in times of mourning. The Romans did not cultivate beards, but cutting off the hair as a sign of mourning was common to both sexes. To supply the want of a natural head-covering, the men wore wigs, and the women caps. This practice fell into disuse after the Romans abandoned Britain; nevertheless, widows studiously concealed their hair during the whole period of mourning.

209. **The Piece of Crape worn on the Sleeve**, which has latterly superseded the hat-band as a sign of mourning, is the recognized military badge of mourning, derived from the scarf tied by each "Sovereign Lady" round the left arm of her chosen knight, in the days of chivalry, to bind him to her faithful service. No good knight and true was ever known to part with his lady's kerchief except at the cost of his life.

210. **White Gloves** are presented to the undertaker's men at a funeral for the same reason that they were formerly given to the coachmen at a wedding, viz., because they are the emblem of innocence. At such a time the mourners, like the bride and bridegroom of a bygone day, wish to show that they are at peace with all the world; and as the undertaker's men are virtually strangers to them, they well represent the world at large. In former times a white glove

was usually suspended in the high street or in the market-place of a country town during the annual fair; this ensured to criminals and debtors immunity from arrest for the time being.

211. **Undertakers' Mutes** were originally Roman lictors dressed in black who marched in the funeral procession under the direction of the master of ceremonies. The object of stationing a couple of mutes at the house-door, from the moment when the undertaker was called in until the funeral, was to guard the body on behalf of their master until his responsibility in the matter had ceased with the interment. Latterly their presence seems to have been required only on the day of the funeral. They are rarely to be met with nowadays.

212. **The Pall-bearers** at the obsequies of the great are invariably well chosen. When the Duke of Wellington was buried in St. Paul's Cathedral, the pall was borne by the officers who had fought by his side in his many campaigns. This custom of appointing such pall-bearers as the deceased worthy might have desired to carry him to the grave has been derived from the Romans. Æmilius Paulus had for pall-bearers the chief men of Macedonia who happened to be in Rome at the time of his death; Julius Cæsar had magistrates; Augustus Cæsar had senators; while Caligula had tribunes and centurions.

213. **Throwing a Handful of Earth upon the Coffin,** after it has been lowered into the grave, was first ordered by a rubric of the Church in the year 1542. This is in allusion to the passage in Scripture, "For dust thou art, and unto dust thou shalt return." By a rubric of 1552 it was permitted to be done "by someone standing by."

Nevertheless, the priest who reads the Burial Service is still regarded as the proper person to perform this duty.

214. **Funeral Feasts** were instituted by the Romans, who made the public exposure of a corpse on the day of the funeral the occasion of a solemn festival. The object of such exposure was to satisfy the relatives and friends of the deceased that he had died in a perfectly natural manner. In this may be traced the origin of **Viewing the Body at an Inquest.** When all the persons so convoked had practically exculpated the heir from the least share in the death, an offering of wine, milk, and honey, mingled together in a small plate decorated with flowers, was made to the manes of the deceased. This singular rite arose out of the pagan belief that the dead were capable of drinking the health of their friends on earth. Subsequently the whole company sat down to a feast of baked meats. At the conclusion of the repast everything that remained was distributed among the former employees of the deceased.

215. The popular notion that **Burial at the Cross Roads,** where a cross was generally set up, was reserved in former times for executed malefactors and suicides, as the next best place to consecrated ground, is not quite correct. The true reason was this : the Teutonic nations always set up their altars at such places, and as criminals were sacrificed to the gods, the place of execution was there. Hence, after the introduction of Christianity, malefactors and suicides were buried at the cross roads during the night, in order to convey as strong an impression as possible of a heathen burial. Christian burials, on the other hand, were, and are, conducted in the broad light of day, in contradistinction to the pagan Romans, who laid their dead to rest by night; the word **Funeral** being derived from

the Latin *funeralis*, a torchlight procession, from *funis*, a torch.

216. The carved representation of a **Skull and Cross-bones** at the entrance to some of the old disused church-yards in the City, is indicative of the burial-place of the early victims of the Great Plague of London. When these consecrated burying-grounds were all filled up, recourse was had to enormous plague-pits outside the City.

217. **The Yew Tree** and the **Weeping Willow** are appropriate to churchyards; the former on account of its umbrageousness and gloomy aspect; the latter, because its drooping branches are typical of sorrow and desolation. The suggestion that yew trees were first planted in English churchyards so that a sufficient supply of bow-staves might be forthcoming for the encouragement of archery practice, is by no means well supported. To commence with, it would have required a full century's growth to meet the demands of a single year. Secondly, that the bow-staves of the Tudor period were obtained from abroad is shown by certain enactments of Henry VIII., whereby all ship-owners were compelled to import bow-staves in proportion to their ordinary cargo, such compulsory cargo being admitted duty free.

218. In these days the full significance of **Monumental Brasses and Sepulchral Effigies** is little "understanded of the people." The following hints may, therefore, be of some service. SAINTS AND MARTYRS always lie to the east of the high altar (*see* 23), and are elevated above the ground exactly in proportion to their acknowledged sanctity. HOLY MEN, not canonised, lie level with the ground, while FOUNDERS OF CHAPELS may be known by

their monuments built into the wall. Cross-legged Figures are Crusaders, or those who at any time during their lives made a vow to proceed to Palestine, there to fight the Infidel under the banner of the Cross; where the figure is in the act of sheathing his sword, it means that his vow has been fulfilled. Recumbent and Kneeling Figures are ordinary knights; those with a chalice in their hands are priests, or if with mitre, crosier or crook, and pontificals, prelates; whereas female figures wearing a mantle and a ring are nuns (*see* 34). When Husband and Wife lie close together on a table-tombstone, it is not difficult to tell if they lived during the age of chivalry or after. In the former event, the universal homage paid to woman demanded that she should occupy the place of honour, viz., at a man's right hand. Since the decline of chivalry she has everywhere been placed on his left-hand side. The presence of a lion at the feet of a monumental effigy of a man is symbolical of courage and magnanimity, exactly as a dog at the feet of a woman symbolizes affection and fidelity. Crusaders are often represented with a dog at their feet, indicating by this means that they followed the standard of the Cross as faithfully as a dog follows his master. The effigy of Edward the Black Prince in Canterbury Cathedral furnishes an example of this kind. Kneeling Boys on tombs remind us that formerly children were not allowed to sit down unless bidden, but were expected to kneel upon cushions when in the presence of their parents.

219. It is not unusual in old churchyards to meet with tombstone inscriptions commencing with the words, "Stop, Traveller!" Now, although it is true that, except in cases where a cross-cut from the public high-road leads directly through the God's acre, few "travellers" ever visit the earthly mansions of the dead, it should be remembered

that the Romans invariably buried their warriors by the side of some great military road, and placed a monument over their bodies, the inscription on which was headed *Siste, viator* (Stop, traveller). In their case, at least, the injunction was sufficiently appropriate.

220. **The Jewish Mode of Burial** is simplicity itself. There is not the slightest need to call in an undertaker, the whole of the arrangements being carried out by the officials of the synagogue at a fixed charge. From the moment of death until the interment the body is never left alone. Two days is the limit of time during which the dead are allowed to remain above ground. There is no adornment of the wooden coffin, nor are flowers permitted to be placed either inside or on the lid. Velvet and feathers are likewise prohibited. All expenses over and above those incurred in respect of the actual interment are discountenanced. The burial-grounds are euphemistically called "Houses of Life," though they are virtually mansions of the dead. Family vaults are unknown, because a corpse can on no account be suffered to repose on a shelf; it must be placed six feet beneath the surface of the earth. Neither is it permitted for one coffin to be placed above another. No prayers are said at the grave-side, except "May he [or she] go into his [or her] place in peace." The orations which on rare occasions are delivered at the interment of a distinguished person must be brief. Hats are not removed at any time. Females are never allowed to follow a corpse to the grave. Priests may not enter a burial-ground at all, except at the interment of a near relative, such as a father or mother. In Biblical times, those who had suffered defilement by coming in contact with a dead body were compelled to attend a purification service in the Temple; nowadays, all persons on leaving the cemetery must wash their hands. The only

food laid before the mourners on returning to the house consists of hard-boiled eggs and salt, the respective symbols of regeneration and incorruptibility. For seven days all mirrors are covered over, so that none shall see the reflection of his face or any sign of joy. During this period the members of the household sit on lower chairs than usual; they do not wear boots, and all manner of work is suspended. To meet the case of the poor in this respect a monetary allowance is made.

221. The Parsee mode of disposing of the dead is exposure on **The Towers of Silence.** Perfectly naked, the bodies deposited on these lofty structures become the prey of vultures perpetually hovering around. To make room for fresh arrivals, it is the business of an attendant to topple the newly-pecked bones to the foot of the tower with the aid of a pair of tongs. This final destruction of the body awaits all classes, from the highest to the lowest. According to the Zoroastrian religion neither fire, which is the common object of worship, nor the earth, which produces fruit, must be defiled by contact with a dead body.

222. The custom, universal among the ancient Egyptians, of **Embalming the Dead Body** is easily accounted for. It was one of the fundamental articles of their religion that after a period of three or four thousand years the soul would return to the body, therefore the latter had to be preserved from corruption. Meantime the soul was destined to occupy the bodies of a succession of inferior animals. This was why most of the lower animals were held sacred, and flesh meat was never eaten.

223. Modern researches have proved beyond a doubt that

the **Pyramids of Egypt**, both great and small, were constructed for no other purpose than to contain the embalmed bodies of notable personages. Knowing this, one need not be surprised to learn that the entire number of pyramids in Egypt—between sixty and seventy—are spread over that extensive necropolis near the city of Memphis in which the people were known to bury their dead. When first explored all the chambers in the interior of these pyramids contained sarcophagi. In one case the sarcophagus enclosed a coffin, the inscription upon which showed that it had at one time contained the mummy of a king. The chief reason why the aristocracy of Egypt affected this costly and enduring mode of sepulchre was the universal dread which the pillagers of the tombs anciently inspired among the people. Not even the tombs of the kings were safe from the visitations of these plunderers. The three largest and principal pyramids were certainly constructed by three kings of the fourth dynasty as places of sepulture for themselves. Labour was cheap in those days, and kings were tyrants. Cheops, the builder of the Great Pyramid, had no compunction about impressing a hundred thousand men during a period of twenty years—leaving out of count the ten years required to construct a causeway from the Nile bank to the actual site of the work —in the colossal undertaking upon which he had set his heart. On the outside of the pyramid, when completed, was set forth in Egyptian characters the enormous sums expended while the work was in progress for the radishes, onions, and garlic supplied to the labourers, but nothing is mentioned about wages. It is a sad reflection that the greatest monuments which now excite the wonder and admiration of our species were reared at the cost of an incalculable amount of human suffering in an age when a monarch's will was law, and a universal system of slavery prevailed.

224. There is no longer any room for doubt concerning the primary object of the **Roman Catacombs.** Neither disused sandpits, turned to good account by the early Christians for places of refuge and secret worship, nor *puticoli*, or pits, into which, as has been said, the Romans flung the bodies of their slaves, because they considered them unworthy of decent sepulture, were originally these subterranean galleries, which, after having been closed and forgotten for hundreds of years, may now once more be traversed. The *arenariæ*, or sandpits, which are common enough around Rome, exist in a different stratum altogether from the Catacombs. When persecution increased in severity, and the ordinary approaches to the hiding-places of the Christians became known to their persecutors, a secret entrance through some disused sandpit may in many cases have been constructed for greater convenience and security. But that the Catacombs themselves, with their storied galleries one above another, and countless ramifications extending for miles in different directions, could ever have been excavated without the knowledge of the authorities was impossible. The whole truth of the matter is this: the Catacombs were, from the first, the recognized burial-places of the early Christians. The pagan Romans had their family burial-places, too, but these, styled *columbaria*, from their resemblance to dovecotes, were simply depositories for the urns containing the ashes of the cremated body. The Christians, on the other hand, as Minucius Felix reminds us, "execrated funeral pyres, and condemned the sepultures of flame." This is easy to understand. Being for the most part a Greek-speaking community of converted Jews, the earliest followers of the new religion desired to bury their dead, as had always been the Jewish custom, and because the Son of God had Himself been laid in a rocky tomb. Although advocates of cremation themselves, the Romans placed no

restrictions upon those who held an opposite view. Those who wished to bury their dead, either out of preference for such a mode of sepulture, or because they could not afford to pay the usual charges for cremation and the exclusive right to a *columbarium*, had full liberty to do so. This liberty was extended also to the Christians; indeed, it was the only Christian office that they were allowed to perform undisturbed. Fortunately for the Christians the Romans paid the utmost respect to all places set apart for the burial of the dead, such places enjoying the special protection of the municipal authorities. The formation of the Catacombs had very humble beginnings. First of all a small plot of ground was secured and consecrated. The next step was to run an underground gallery around the enclosed area, and construct stairways in connection therewith. On both sides of the gallery, *loculi*, or cavities for the accommodation of the dead, were then cut. As soon as the first series of galleries was fully tenanted, a second series was commenced on a lower level; and, in due course, a third, on a still lower level. Frequently as many as five such stories of galleries are to be met with. If it chanced that a person of distinction in a wealthy family desired a private vault, such a one, called a *cubiculum*, was excavated out of the earth lying between two main corridors. In these small rectangular chambers the martyrs were usually buried, their tombs serving as altars upon which Mass was celebrated. Thus, when the persecutions at length broke out, this subterranean city became at once a secure asylum for the living, and a safe burial-place for the dead. For three centuries it was the palace of the Popes, and the home of the Spouse of Christ.

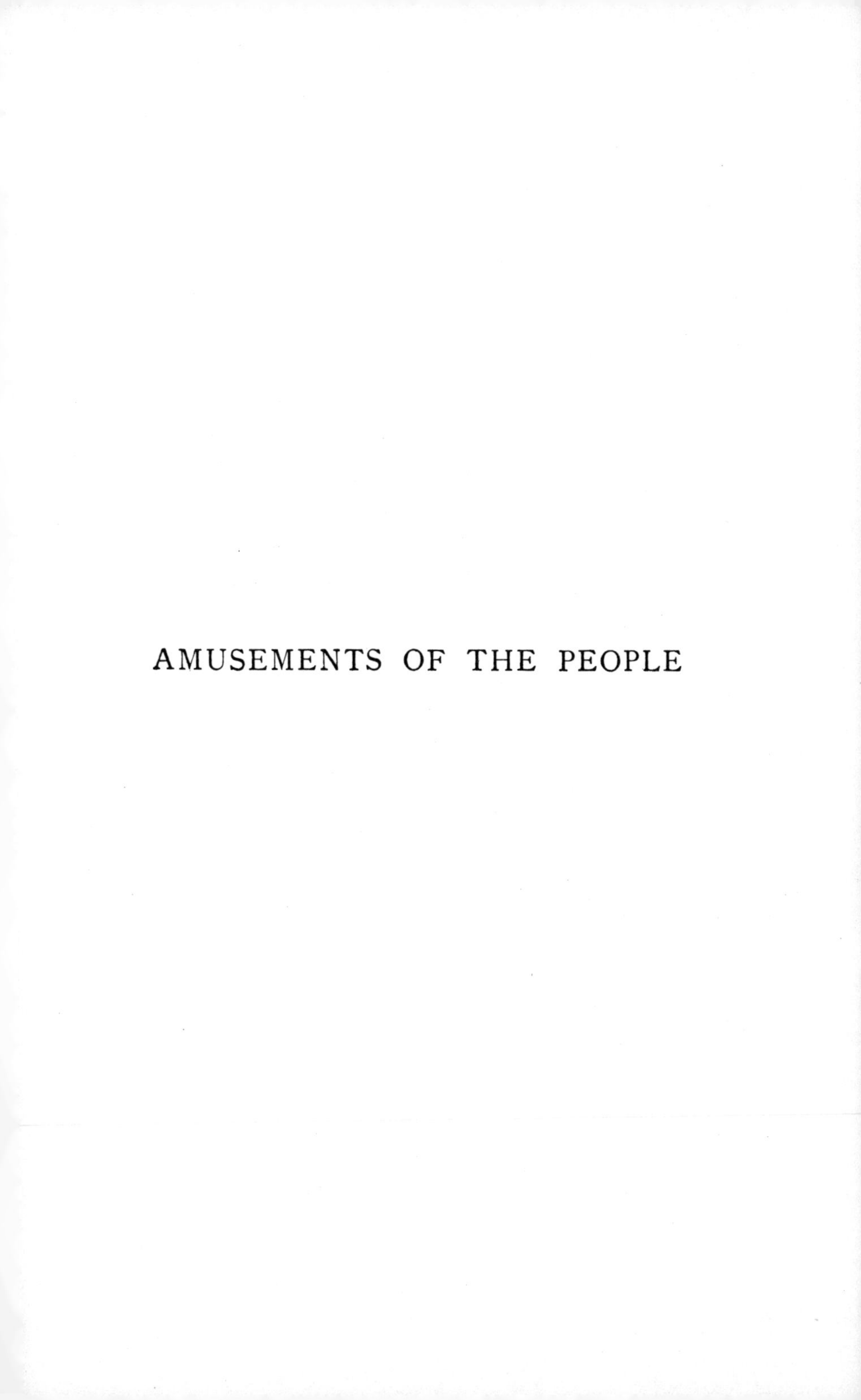

AMUSEMENTS OF THE PEOPLE

AMUSEMENTS OF THE PEOPLE

225. ALTHOUGH Thespis, mounted on his cart, was unquestionably the father of the Greek drama, the **Origin of Dramatic Representations** of every kind must be sought in an idolatrous form of public worship. When Danaus, a son of Belus, having quarrelled with his brother, Ægyptus, with whom he shared the throne of Egypt, set sail with a numerous retinue in quest of a new settlement, he in due time landed near the city of Argos, of which he presently became king. Here he instituted festivals in honour of Bacchus, a god synonymous, as is generally believed, with the Egyptian Osiris. These festivals soon became popular all over Greece, but, owing to the low state of literature at the time, the songs were very mean, and the festivals were conducted in a most licentious manner. In after years, however, when literature had made some advancement among the various tribes, and these licentious revels had, in a great measure, filled the minds of the Athenians with disgust, a praiseworthy attempt was made to honour the god in a more befitting manner; they gave him the appellation of Dithyrambus, and the odes sung at the celebration of his festival, Dithyrambs. But the Athenians did not stop here. True to their character as patrons of learning, they offered a prize for the best Dithyramb, delivered *extempore* in a wild, enthusiastic manner. The prize was a *tragos*, or goat, and he who gained it had the privilege of sacrificing it to the god. From this circumstance every theatrical representation in which the

life of a person was supposed to be taken came to be denominated a **Tragedy**, or song of the goat. Some years later a second prize, consisting of a cask of wine, was offered for the best comic song delivered *extempore* in praise of the same god, each competitor having his face besmeared with the lees of wine. As these comic performers were not tolerated in the city, but were compelled to abide in and around the villages near Athens, the comic ode thus strangely called into existence received the name, first of a village song, and then vintage song; until at last the Greek term *Komus* was applied to every festal procession and dramatic representation not purely tragic, and in which singing bore a part. Hence the modern word **Comedy**. The drama remained in this rude state until Thespis, a native of Icaria, appeared on the scene. Taking his subjects from history, he introduced a singer who addressed himself to the chorus in a monotonous strain, and they in return addressed themselves to him. By-and-by it occurred to Thespis to make an actor recite the brave deeds of some hero, between the singing, and so relieve both the chorus and the singer. This introduction proved so satisfactory to the Athenians that many among them materially assisted the foundation of a regular drama by applying themselves to the composition of tragedies and comedies. But the great reformer of the ancient drama was Æschylus. He introduced dialogue, and diminished the length of the chorus singing, which had no longer any reference to Bacchus, but partook of the subject of the play. The portable stage he abolished, having a regular theatre built, replete with scenery; he also introduced a chief character or hero of the play, whom he raised above all the others by means of the *cothurnus*, or buskin, and dressed the whole of the performers in elaborate costumes; so that little remained to be done by Sophocles, a later reformer and writer of tragedies, except to add a third speaking character, and to dress each performer in a habit suited to the character he played.

226. **Pantomime** had its origin among the Romans. One day, while Livius Andronicus, a favourite actor and poet, was reciting his own pieces in the theatre, he was encored so many times that he became quite hoarse, and was unable to finish his performance. Seeing which, the audience compelled another actor to recite the words, and entreated Andronicus to supply the action. In this novel form of entertainment the poet acquitted himself so well that his admirers insisted upon a repetition of it on the following day, and pantomime, or the art of mute gesture, at once became popular. An early step in the development of this new art was the selection of a singer who possessed a voice closely resembling that of the pantomimist. The singer was generally stationed out of sight of the audience. When several singers accompanied the actions of the pantomimist, a man wearing iron shoes beat time for them with his feet. Pantomime was brought to the highest state of perfection under the Empire by two incomparable exponents of the art. These were Pylades of Cilicia, and Bathyllus of Alexandria. The former represented tender, graceful, and pathetic characters; while the latter excelled in comedy. The subjects of the *pantomimus*, or pantomime, in which they appeared were taken from the myths of gods and heroes; and as no other actors were considered sufficiently talented to lend them support, the representations of all the different characters, both male and female, by turns devolved upon them alone. From first to last they were never off the stage for an instant. Scenic and mechanical accessories were wanting altogether, but a choir, accompanied by flute-players, sang the text of the play all through. A later stage in the development of the Roman pantomime was the introduction

of a number of dancers of both sexes, whose gestures conveyed a distinct dramatic idea. This species of performance was clearly the *ballet d'action*, which employs the talents of so many Continental pantomimists of the present day.

227. The elements of the **Italian Comedy**, which was the parent of that portion of our English pantomime denominated the **Harlequinade**, were drawn from the oral drama of the Romans rather than from the *pantomimus*. Contemporary with the *pantomimus* there existed two other highly popular forms of theatrical representation in the days of the Empire—the *Atellana* and the *Mimus*. Both were a species of improvised burlesque, though differing widely in many respects. The *Atellana* received its title from the Oscian city of Atella, where it first came into notice. As originally performed by young citizens, in typical masks, it was simply a caricature of the persons and a parody of the private lives of the trading classes; but in proportion as it became popular it developed into a regular comedy, and at length found a place in the theatre as a comic relief to the serious drama. The four chief characters in the *Atellana* were identical with those afterwards revived in the Italian comedy, and styled "the Four Masks," viz., Harlequin, Pantaloon, Brighella or Clown, and the Doctor. Like the *Atellana*, the *Mimus* was pressed into service as an interlude or postlude to the regular drama. The dialogue was always witty, occasionally not only coarse, but highly indecent. Its principal character was Archimimus, dressed in the particoloured costume of a harlequin, with the addition of a short cloak. To him all the other characters were subordinate; he was, in short, the catechiser of them all. Armed with a short staff or wand—which survives to-day in **Harlequin's Wooden Bat**—he conducted a conversation with his companions upon current events, and the witty retorts

he elicited in answer to his various questions were well calculated to raise a laugh on the part of the audience. This was the origin of the **Topical Allusions** in our modern pantomimes. In the Italian comedy the fun was kept alive all through by Harlequin; but after the death of John Rich, the original Harlequin on the English stage, this character degenerated into a mere dancing lover, whose business it was to protect Columbine and play off tricks upon his boorish rival, the Clown, and the father of his beauteous sweetheart, Pantaloon; and when Joe Grimaldi appeared upon the scene his genius invested the part of Clown with an importance before undreamt of. It is a fact very little known that Rich made Harlequin speechless not only to afford himself scope for his marvellous pantomimic abilities, but because he was such a "bad study" that he never could learn a speech of any kind by heart.

228. **The Dress of the Pantomime Clown** was a blending of the costumes of the French Pierrot and the old English court jester introduced by Grimaldi himself; the floured face and white garments of the former being used as a groundwork for the variegated spots and patches of vermilion paint. The closely-shaven head was from time immemorial a characteristic of all fools, while the tail of a hare took the place of the cock's comb generally worn by the jesters of a bygone age. The **Pantaloon's Dress** is, according to Goldoni, the historian and reformer of the Italian comedy, that of a Venetian merchant of the time of the Republic. "The red waistcoat, and breeches cut like drawers," says he, "and red stockings and slippers, represent exactly the dress of the ancient inhabitants of the Adriatic lagoons, and the beard, which was a great ornament in those distant days, has been carried to a grotesque extreme in these latter days." **Harlequin's Black Mask**, which, as may

have been noticed, he pulls over his forehead when the Clown and Policeman attempt to lay hold of him, is a relic of the magic cap which in fairy legends afforded its wearer the power of becoming invisible at any moment by simply turning it round. His parti-coloured dress and wooden bat have already been accounted for (*see* 227). With regard to the latter, it should be added that it performs certain magical changes because the Fairy Queen is supposed to resign her magic wand to Harlequin directly he is introduced in the transformation scene (*see* 230).

229. **The Pantomime Opening** now demands our careful attention. In the days of Rich and Grimaldi this was by no means the chief attraction of the evening's entertainment, being merely intended to lead up to and introduce the Harlequinade, or Pantomime properly so-called. But, after the death of Grimaldi, when good clowns were hard to find, managers had to rely principally upon an elaborate scenic display, and the Harlequinade sank into insignificance. It is a remarkable fact that the Pantomime "Opening" found its origin neither in the opera nor in the drama, but in the puppet-shows. During the Restoration period these puppet-shows became the rage of London; so much so that the regular actors petitioned the king for the removal of a puppet-show in Cecil Street, Strand, on the plea that it interfered with the prosperity of Drury Lane Theatre. Nor was it the drama alone that had cause to fear competition from the puppet-showman; his success affected even the opera. From an account of a dispute between Powell, the proprietor of a celebrated puppet-show in Covent Garden, and the managers of the Italian Opera (*temp.* 1711), we learn that "the Opera at the Haymarket, and that under the Piazza of Covent Garden are at present the two leading diversions of the town; Powell professing in his advertisements to set up

'Whittington and his Cat' against 'Rinaldo' and 'Armida.'" We are told by Strutt that the subjects of the puppet-show plays were always taken from popular stories of knights and giants, therefore the foundation of our modern pantomimes upon well-worn nursery legends and fairy tales is no new thing. Perhaps this was the secret of the success of the puppet-shows. They contained all the essentials of the opera, which was closely imitated, even to the mechanical effects and the apotheosis in the final scene. If the musical portions of the puppet-show performance were far below the level of those of the opera, these shortcomings were atoned for by the interest of the story, which could be understood by young and old alike. Children were delighted with the puppet-shows, and so were their parents, who had long been surfeited with mythology and ancient history at the opera. Barring the quality of the music, the only material differences between the two forms of dramatic representation were the subject of the story, and the substitution of fairies and demons in the puppet-shows for the "goddesses" and "furies" of the opera. The self-same arrangement was introduced in the pantomimes. The "Demon Scene," with its red fire and trap business, invariably discovered on the rising of the curtain upon a pantomime of the old-fashioned order, is now a thing of the past; but the fairies, the fairy ballet, and the transformation scene remain (*see* 230).

230. It is to the masques that we must look for the origin of the **Transformation Scene**, and, indeed, of every other kind of spectacle that now captivates the eyes of the beholder on the boards of a theatre. These **Masques**—so called from the masks originally worn by the male performers—were the private theatricals of the nobility, and of royalty at the court. "But while the public theatre continued long in this contracted state," writes Isaac D'Israeli,

in his "Curiosities of Literature," speaking of the drama during the reign of James I., "without scenes, without dresses, without an orchestra, the court displayed scenical and dramatical exhibitions with such costly magnificence, such inventive fancy, and such miraculous art, that one may doubt if the combined genius of Ben Jonson, Inigo Jones, or Lawes, or Ferobosco, at an era most favourable to the arts of imagination, has been equalled by the modern spectacle of the opera." It was directly from these masques that the scenic embellishments of the theatre and the English opera itself took their rise (*see* 231). The organization of a court masque involved preparations on a most extensive scale, and employed the talents of some of the foremost men of the time. We read how Lord Bacon, Selden, and Whitlock sat in committee for days together in order to work out the details of the last grand masque set before Charles I. Not only did they invent the devices, but they formed the processions and arranged the dances. When the eventful day arrived, they took upon themselves all the responsibilities of the stage management; while Lawes, Inigo Jones, and Ben Jonson, who had lavished their entire resources upon their respective departments of the production, took care to work the machinery themselves as a safeguard against hitch or accident. It is gratifying to learn that the success of this masque was so great that the enthusiasm of those who were privileged to witness it knew no bounds. Now this, similar to every other masque, had, for its "last scene of all," an apotheosis gradually led up to by a series of picturesque mechanical changes to the strains of melodious music, and amid a perfect blaze of illumination, similar in all respects to the modern transformation scene.

231. Considering the part played by music in the early Greek drama, **The Opera** can scarcely be regarded as an in-

vention of modern times. All musical authorities are agreed that the opera had its origin in the tragedies of the ancient Greeks, of which the dialogue and chorus parts were rendered in a kind of rhythmic monotone or chant (*see* 225). To trace the gradual development of music until it culminated in the opera would be an onerous task; but it may safely be assumed that for this form of theatrical representation we are indebted to the Italians, who are, as a nation, ardent lovers of music, and whose soft language lends itself so admirably to musical setting. The first musical piece of which we have any record was "Pomponiano," a tragedy, partly sung and partly recited, which was produced at Rome in the year 1480. Eighty years afterwards Alfonso delle Viola set a drama to music; while a so-called opera was performed for the entertainment of Henry III., of France, on his return from Poland, at Venice, in 1574. Most people imagine that the opera was introduced to our countrymen by the Italians, but this is a mistake. The opera in England is an institution of native growth. Curiously enough, it came about in consequence of the interdiction of all theatrical representations and public amusements during the Commonwealth. Effectually though the Puritan *régime* crushed every attempt to re-establish the drama in the public theatres, it never succeeded in suppressing the masques in the private mansions of the wealthy (*see* 230). Profiting by the loophole thus presented for the re-introduction of the drama under a musical disguise, Sir William D'Avenant produced at Rutland House, Charterhouse Yard, on May 23rd, 1656, what was styled "An Entertainment of Declamation and Musick after the Manner of the Ancients." This was the first attempt at a musical piece in this country, and it proved highly successful. The following year the same astute manager produced what purported to be an opera, though described as "The

Siege of Rhodes; a Representation by the Art of Perspective in Scenes, and the Story Sung in Recitative Musick." It is undeniable that this was the first opera ever heard of in England. Encouraged by its success, Sir William D'Avenant had the plays of "Macbeth" and "The Tempest" converted into operas; but before these were ready for production he died, and it devolved upon his son, Sir Charles D'Avenant, to bring them out at the Lincoln's Inn Fields Theatre, under royal and distinguished patronage. From this time forward the opera and the drama flourished in the open light of day side by side.

232. **The English Concert** came into existence under the following circumstances. During the early part of the year 1672 John Banister, "the king's first violin," and conductor of the court band of Charles II., incurred the mortal displeasure of his majesty by observing that the court band should, in all fairness to native talent, be composed exclusively of Englishmen instead of foreigners. For this indiscretion he was promptly cashiered. Whereupon he at once converted his house "over against the George Tavern," in Whitefriars, into a "Musick School," and determined, in the course of the ensuing winter, to give a series of concerts at which the public might derive pleasure from hearing good music, similar to that which the king and court had every day at their command at Whitehall. A gallery erected for the instrumentalists in the largest room of his house was, with singular modesty, shut in with curtains, while the ground floor was filled with small tables and chairs in ale-house fashion. A shilling was charged for admission, returnable in refreshments. According to advertisements in the "London Gazette" the concerts were held daily at four o'clock in the afternoon. This was six years anterior to the establishment of those select musical

assemblies by Thomas Britton, the "Musical Small-Coal Man" in Clerkenwell, which so many excellent people believe to have given rise to the English concert. That Banister's enterprise must have been attended with considerable success is evidenced by the fact that his advertisements are traceable in the "Gazette" until the close of 1678, or within a year of his death.

233. The first London **Music-Hall** was the Canterbury, in the Westminster Bridge Road, opened in 1848. Under another name, however, the music-hall can boast of an antiquity as venerable as the opera and the stage of the Restoration. When the Civil War scattered the players it did not spare the musicians, who were compelled to seek their livelihood as best they could. A few of the more favoured ones visited the houses of the gentry, the rest resorted to taverns, where they invited the public to hear them play. The taverns at which such entertainments, both vocal and instrumental, were given, took the name of "Musick Houses," to distinguish them from taverns of an ordinary kind. They were established in all the most populous parts of the town, and adapted for the reception of all kinds of visitors. Pepys speaks of the Dolphin Tavern in St. Paul's Churchyard as having "an excellent company of fiddlers;" and in another place he tells us how, at the Globe Tavern at Greenwich, he heard the music led by a woman "with a rod in her hand keeping time." At the Castle Tavern in Paternoster Row second-rate singers from the operas were regularly engaged, in addition to the best instrumentalists in town. We hear also of famous music houses at Wapping and in Moorfields, which were kept open day and night, and had bands of fiddlers and dancers for the entertainment of visitors. The Moorfields establishment is described as built in the form of an amphitheatre,

the dances taking place on a circular platform in the centre. The Wapping Music House was elaborately decorated and had numerous apartments, both above and below ground, all calculated to give greater zest and variety to the pleasures of the hour. Sadler's Wells Theatre was originally a "Musick House" where tumbling, tight-rope dancing, and other performances of the "variety" order took place. And what in after years became the Grecian and Britannia theatres were at first "saloons" devoted to instrumental music, singing, dancing, and variety entertainments. Nor must we omit to mention the far-famed Evans's Supper Rooms, in "the Joyous Neighbourhood of Covent Garden," which were at the height of their popularity a quarter of a century ago. To trace the origin of the variety show it will be necessary to go back to feudal times, when every castle throughout the land had its own music-hall in miniature. "At evening in the castle hall, when the lord and his retainers sat at ease over their measures of wine or ale, the minstrels sang their ballads, acrobats tumbled and wrestled, dancers twirled and pirouetted, jugglers threw balls and swallowed swords, and trained beasts were put through their paces." Truly a lineage so ancient as this cannot be laid claim to by the British drama itself.

234. Oddly enough the prototype of the **Court Fools and Jesters** of a bygone day was a woman. We read in Greek mythology that when Ceres went in search of her daughter, Proserpine, she was accompanied by Iambe, one of the merry maids of the Queen of Eleusis, who enlivened her with her witty sayings. As this Iambe kept a sort of commonplace book filled with short satirical verses written in a novel measure, it is from her that the designation "Iambic Verse" has been derived. The professional humorists whose business it was to make princes and nobles

"laugh and grow fat" were early introduced into Northern Europe from Italy. They were of two distinct kinds. The first, a jester, dressed in a parti-coloured costume, was the constant attendant upon his royal or noble master; whereas the second was a half-witted fellow, attired in fantastic garments, whose place was in the scullery, to afford sport for the retainers and menials. The latter undoubtedly suggested the fools of Shakespeare's plays, and survives to-day in our **Circus Clowns.** The French Pierrot and the English pantomime clown had a different origin altogether (*see* 227, 228).

235. The perennial **Christy Minstrel Entertainment** was originally a very different thing from that with which we are all familiar at the present day. Instead of, as they often are, operatic artists and low comedians in disguise, the companions of the world-famous Ned Christy were accomplished imitators of the darkies of the sunny South; rendering their plantation songs and dances exactly as they had been handed down from generation to generation. Their funny sayings and droll antics were also drawn from life. Recourse was therefore had to the burnt cork only to make the impersonation the more perfect. No mawkish sentimental ballads entered into their programme. Their costume was that commonly met with on the cotton plantations. It was, in fact, Ned Christy's darling idea to transplant the negro life of the South to the North. For a time his experiment was tried upon a very small section of the public, albeit it proved successful from the first. Arriving in the spring of 1842 at a lake-side hotel in Buffalo City, he made a proposal to the hostess of that establishment to give a series of darkey impersonations there for the entertainment of the visitors. It mattered not to him that he was single-handed. With the assistance of the son of

the hostess (who, under the assumed name of Charles Christy, afterwards introduced the minstrel entertainment into England), and a young man named Vaughan, Ned Christy gave his nigger show once or twice every day, to the intense delight of the guests at that lake-side resort. The instruments played upon by these three imitation niggers were a banjo, violin, tambourine, triangle, and bones. By the month of June these concerts had attracted so much attention that the proprietor of the Buffalo Theatre was induced to allow the black-visaged trio to occupy his boards for four nights in succession. This daring innovation proved an immense success. An extending tour followed, until at last Ned Christy, with an augmented troupe, pitched his tent at the Mechanics' Hall, 472, Broadway, New York City, where he remained for several months, giving two performances daily. Such was the origin of the Christy Minstrel entertainment. Although the gentlemanly performers at St. James's Hall and elsewhere have nowadays little or nothing in common, either in regard to their songs or manner of speech, with the darkies of the sunny South, it is not likely that they will ever abandon the use of burnt cork. This is because there are times and seasons when, in the absence of a more remunerative engagement on the operatic stage or in the concert-room, vocalists of high standing will often condescend to appear with the minstrels under an assumed name, and proof against recognition behind their sable disguise. To this fact the excellent vocalization of the burnt-cork entertainers at St. James's Hall is in a large measure attributable.

236. Playing the audience out with "**God Save the Queen**" at the close of an entertainment had its counterpart in the London theatres of Shakespeare's day. As soon as the epilogue was spoken, all the performers came on the

stage, and, kneeling down, prayed for their noble patrons, whose "servants" they were. "Her majesty's servants" always prayed for the queen. The first public performance of the National Anthem is reported in the "Daily Advertiser" for Monday, September 30th, 1745, as follows:—"On Saturday night last the audience at the Theatre Royal, Drury Lane, were agreeably surprised by the gentlemen belonging to that house performing the anthem, 'God save our noble King.' The universal applause it met with—being encored with repeated huzzas—sufficiently denoted in how just abhorrence they held the arbitrary schemes of our enemies, and detest the despotic attempts of Papal power." The enthusiasm displayed by the patriotic auditors on this memorable occasion doubtless accounts for the idea that a modern audience should stand up while the National Anthem is being played, to show their loyalty. Though the actors no longer appear on the stage at the conclusion of the night's performance, the chorus still sing "God save the Queen" before the orchestra strikes up the overture on the opening night of the opera season.

237. The fact that **Women rarely applaud** at the theatre or in the concert-room is no evidence that they do not appreciate a fine performance. To tell the truth, their hands are not well adapted for any great demonstration of their feelings; moreover, they have their gloves to consider. As for shouting "Encore!" or indulging in any other vocal manifestations of approval, such a proceeding would be regarded as highly indecorous. On the other hand, laughter and tears are easily induced, and these may be looked upon as legitimate outlets for their feelings.

238. Equestrian artists, acrobats, and other "variety" performers invariably make their obeisance to, and acknow-

ledge the plaudits of the audience by **Kissing and Extending the Hand**; or, in the case of females, both hands, in addition to bending the knee. This was the Roman mode of saluting the statues of the gods, the emperor, and other exalted personages. Charioteers in the circus likewise saluted the populace with the whip-hand as they flew round the arena; but actors in the theatre kissed both hands and bent the knee.

239. The reason why the **Tuning up of Musical Instruments** always takes place in the orchestra itself is, because the temperature of the ante-room being different from that of the theatre or concert-room, if the instruments were tuned up in the former place they would instantly get out of tune again in the latter.

240. **The Construction of a Modern Theatre** differs in no essential respect from that of the Elizabethan playhouses, which did not require to be built at all, being ready to hand in the London inn-yards. The galleries ranging one above the other round the yard served for the more select portions of the auditorium, and are evident in the tiers of a modern theatre; while our pit, or floor of the house, was derived from the inn-yard itself, where were congregated the City 'prentices, tradesmen, sailors, and the rougher element of playgoers—the "groundlings," as they are styled by Shakespeare.

241. **Panoramas** were the invention of Robert Barker, an Irish portrait painter residing in Edinburgh towards the close of the last century. It was within the narrow confines of a prison cell that the idea of the panorama first arose in his mind. By all accounts, life in a Scottish Debtors' Prison was very different from that in the Fleet,

whose inmates, of whatever station, were compelled to herd together. In his Edinburgh prison-house, at all events, Robert Barker had a cell to himself. This cell was so feebly lighted by means of a small air-hole in one of the corners, that the only way in which he could read the letters that came to him was by holding them up at arm's length against that part of the wall which was opposite to the air-hole. By so doing the words not only became perfectly distinct, but the effect produced was very striking. It then occurred to him that if a picture were placed in a similar position it would produce a still more wonderful effect. Having plenty of time on his hands, he devised first of all the illuminated panorama in a darkened room, and subsequently the circular panorama, which after his liberation he patented on June 19th, 1787. "Out of evil cometh good." If he had not been imprisoned for debt in Edinburgh he would never have amassed a considerable fortune by his Panorama in Leicester Square.

242. **The Waxwork Exhibition** had its origin in a custom of the Romans, who caused a waxen bust of a distinguished citizen to be borne in front of the bier at his funeral, and afterwards assigned it to a particular niche in the vestibule of the house (*see* 137). The vulgar notion that wax models of illustrious personages were first produced and exhibited by the far-famed Madame Tussaud is altogether wrong. Around the walls of Islip's chapel in Westminster Abbey there may yet be seen, preserved in glass cases, the waxen effigies of royal and other exalted personages which, from their faded and dilapidated appearance, have merited the description of "The Ragged Regiment." These comprise Queen Elizabeth, Charles II., William III. and Mary, Queen Anne, John Sheffield, Duke of Buckingham, with his Duchess and child, the Duchess of Rich-

mond, William Pitt, Earl of Chatham, and Lord Nelson; and, like the busts of the Romans, they originally played an important part in the obsequies of the persons represented. Arrived at the tomb, the counterfeit presentment of the deceased worthy was left there as a temporary monument until such time as it could be replaced by a more enduring one of stone. These figures are clearly of French workmanship, and very faithful portraits they are too. Modelling the human figure in wax was a favourite pursuit during the Middle Ages, and the revival of art in the fifteenth century gave it a new impetus, more particularly in Italy and Germany. One of the masterpieces of the Florentine ceroplastor, Orsini, is now preserved in the museum at Lille. Other examples by the same hand were dedicated as votive offerings to the shrines of saints by the friends of Lorenzo di Medici, in thanksgiving for his escape from death at the hands of the conspirators of the Pazzi in the year 1478. The earliest printed account of a group of wax figures exhibited to the public for payment occurs in "The Enterprising Correspondent" for 1738, which gives a detailed description of "The Nativity in the Stable at Bethlehem," then on view in the Maze at Amsterdam. Now this *subject* was not at all new, for the visitors must have met with the very same thing in the churches every year at Christmas time. Indeed, there can be no question that the travelling waxwork show originated in the "Crib," which proves such an attraction in all Roman Catholic churches during the Christmas season; for it is a fact that until the period of the French Revolution none but Biblical subjects were chosen. Such groups as "The Death of Abel," "The Judgment of Solomon," and "Daniel in the Lions' Den," are still as popular as ever at country fairs. Madame Tussaud was not the foundress of the first permanent exhibition of life-size wax models of celebrated personages, either in Paris or elsewhere. The credit of founding a cosmopolitan portrait gallery, such as has now for many years constituted one of the sights of London, belongs to her uncle, J. C. Curtius, who shortly before the outbreak of the Revolution of 1789 had two distinct exhibitions in the French capital—one in the Palais Royal, containing the counterfeit presentments in wax of celebrities of all kinds; and another on the Boulevard du Temple, exclusively set apart for those of murderers and other sensational notorieties. The latter collection was undeniably the original "Chamber of Horrors." It was from M. Curtius that his niece, Mdlle. Marie Gresholtz, afterwards Madame Tussaud, learned the art of modelling in wax.

243. **Fairs** originated among the ancient Egyptians. At the periodical overflow of the Nile, when the lower levels of the Nile valley were converted into a watery waste, it was the custom for the entire population to crowd in barges to the various festivals held in the principal towns or in the neighbourhood of the great temples. At these places the scene was one of unusual bustle and activity; produce and manufactures of every kind found a ready market, while the priests made a rich harvest by practising astrology, computing genealogies, consulting oracles, and in divers similar ways turning popular superstition to their own profit. This periodical flocking to the great festivals, and the marts and amusements carried on there, obtains at the present day among the Hindoos and other Asiatic races. The Greeks and Romans had their fairs also, when labour and law pleadings were for the nonce suspended. In the early days of the Church these assemblages always took place on the festival of the patron saint of the town in which they were held, or else on the anniversary of the day upon which the parish church was dedicated to him. Tradesmen were then

allowed to display their wares for sale in the churchyard, and all who came could, if they were so minded, quench their thirst with excellent ale brewed by the clergy themselves, the proceeds being given to the poor (*see* 445). Instead of fairs, however, these annual merry-makings were styled **Wakes**, because the faithful were supposed to spend the vigil in watching and offering up prayers to the local patron saint. Descending to more modern times, we find the religious element altogether wanting, and the term "Fair" substituted for the old-fashioned "Wake." Country fairs were little short of a necessity in the days when the population was small, and facilities for reaching the larger commercial centres were few. At the present time those which still remain have long since outlived their usefulness. It is easy to understand that the shows, swings, booths, etc., were merely the incidental adjuncts to the commercial fair (*see* 333).

244. It is interesting to learn how and when the **Rival Blues** in the Oxford and Cambridge boat-race first became settled. When on June 10th, 1829, the first inter-University contest took place, the Oxford crew adopted the colours of one of their colleges, Christ Church, then head of the river, and which had four of its men rowing in the boat. Those colours were dark blue. The members of the Cambridge crew were drawn from two colleges only, and as they could not agree about the colours, they wore their respective college colours, over which each man had a pink sash, in compliment to their captain, whose colours were pink. The second University boat-race was not rowed until 1836. It was on this occasion that the colours were determined. Oxford had their dark blue, but the Cambridge boat displayed no colour in her bows. Just before the start many suggestions were made, and no agreement could be arrived

at until a famous oarsman rushed into an adjacent haberdasher's shop, asked for a coloured handkerchief or a piece of Eton light-blue ribbon, got it, and affixed it. The light blue then became the Cambridge colour; while the Oxford blue was in the following year deepened, to make the distinction the more marked. For the foregoing account of the origin of the colours we are indebted to one of the three survivors of the first crews, the Very Rev. Charles Merivale, Dean of Ely.

245. It is not simply for amusement that the Eastern shepherds beguile the time by **Playing on the Pipes.** According to a very general belief in the East, music renders sheep docile, and makes them fatten readily.

246. **Playing Cards** were invented about the year 1390, for the amusement of Charles VI., of France, who had relapsed into a very melancholy state of mind; who the inventor was is not recorded. The French playing cards are the same now as they were five centuries ago. And, since the court cards bear different names upon them, this helps us not a little to determine their meaning. The four KINGS are David, Alexander, Cæsar, and Charlemagne, representing the four celebrated monarchies of the Jews, Macedonians, Romans, and Franks under Charlemagne. The QUEENS are Argine, Esther, Judith, and Pallas, typifying noble birth, piety, fortitude, and wisdom, the four qualifications supposed to reside in the person of every queen. A key to these names is furnished us by the circumstance that Argine is an anagram for Regina, meaning queen by descent. The KNAVES are the servants or pages of the knights, represented by what we call the "spades." Knave is an old English term for servant; witness the allusion in an old translation of the Scriptures, where St. Paul is styled the *Knave* of

Jesus Christ. To come now to the suits, or colours, as they are called in France. These suits were intended by the inventor to represent the four orders or classes of men in the king's dominions. The HEARTS, or Cæsars, are the *gens de chœur*, choir-men and ecclesiastics. The Spaniards, who undoubtedly derived their playing cards from the French, have instead of hearts *copas*, or chalices, which mean the same thing. The SPADES are an imperfect representation of the ends or points of the pikes anciently carried by the nobility, forming the prime military section of the people. The Spaniards make use of *espades*, or swords, in lieu of the pike ends; which being so, perhaps accounts for our misapplication of the figure. The DIAMONDS denote the order of citizens, merchants, and tradesmen. The French term for this figure, *carreaux*, square stone tiles or the like, is translated by the Dutch *Stienen*, literally stones, but applied in the sense of diamonds or precious stones. The Spaniards substitute a coin for this figure. Lastly, *Treste*, the trefoil or common clover, signifies the husbandmen or peasants. The English term CLUBS has been derived from the Spaniards, who employ staves or clubs.

247. The invention of **Chess** is ascribed to a Chinese general who was put to the necessity of devising some means of reconciling his soldiers to pass the winter in uncomfortable quarters in the country of Shensi; the cold and dreary aspect of which were likely to have occasioned a mutiny amongst them. That was nearly two thousand years ago. The story goes that when the emperor learned how well the troops had employed themselves, he sent for the inventor, and desired him to teach him the game. So delighted was he with it that he offered the general whatever remuneration he cared to name as the reward of his discovery. When the latter replied that he would be satisfied with a grain of corn

for the first square of the chess-board, two grains for the second, four for the third, and so on, reckoned by a simple process of doubling until the sixty-fourth square was reached, the emperor expressed his astonishment at such a modest request; but he very soon found that the sum total would represent an altogether fabulous amount. According to this computation the total number of grains would be 18,446,743,573,783,086,315, and if placed side by side they would reach 3,883,401,821 times round the world. This then must have been the origin of the story of the horse-shoe nails. By the Chinese the game is styled *Chong-he*, signifying a royal game. The European term "Chess" is most probably a corruption of Shensi, the name of the country where it was first played.

248. **The Game of Dominoes** was invented by a couple of French monks, who amused themselves with square flat stones marked with spots. When the game was up the winner declared his victory by reciting the first line of the Vesper Service, "Dixit Dominus Domino Meo." The game eventually became the recreation of the whole convent, and the Vesper line being abbreviated into "Domino," suggested a title for the game itself.

249. **The Game of Marbles**, so popular in its due season among boys, was originally an imitation of another popular game among boys of a larger growth—Bowls. The bowls of the ancients were of marble, hence the name of the diminutive bowls that came after them.

250. **The Game of Quoits**, which is similar to that of the *discus* of the ancients, grew out of the rural pastime of throwing an old horse-shoe to a required spot as a trial of skill. In some parts of the country a quoit still goes by the name of "the shoe."

251. **Cock-fighting**, as a form of sport, was introduced by Themistocles. Having one day chanced to see a couple of cocks fight, he instituted periodical contests between such birds, from a notion that they would encourage bravery among the people that witnessed them. These cock-fights became exceedingly popular among the Greeks and Romans. The birds were regularly fed, and after the contest the victor was, like a hero, crowned with palm. But this was not all. So addicted to the sport did the people become, that as often as a favourite gamecock died he was accorded a solemn funeral and a monument suitably inscribed.

PATRON SAINTS AND THEIR ATTRIBUTES

PATRON SAINTS AND THEIR ATTRIBUTES

252. **St. Genevieve** (January 3rd) is the patroness of Paris, because she was chiefly instrumental in banishing paganism from that city. Notwithstanding the singular piety of her life, says the Golden Legend, she was beset by demons. Often during her vigils the tapers would be extinguished, and as quickly re-kindled by her prayers and faith. "For God never permitted her to remain in the dark when she prayed for light." Hence she is represented in Christian Art with a lighted taper in her hand, and a demon trying to blow it out from behind her shoulder with a pair of bellows. (Died 507.)

253. **St. Julian Hospitator** (January 9th) is represented in Christian Art with a stag by his side, because it was while pursuing a stag to the death that he formed the resolution to forsake worldly pleasures and devote the remainder of his life to good works. After journeying into a distant country, he established a hospital on the bank of a great river, in crossing which many travellers were drowned. There he took upon himself the duty of ferrying all comers across in person, and such as were sick or infirm he tended in the adjacent hospital. On this account he is regarded as the patron of travellers, boatmen, and ferrymen. (Died 313.)

254. **St. Anthony** (January 17th) is the patron and protector of animals, on account of his intense regard for the brute creation during his lifetime. He is inseparably associated in Christian Art with a pig; not because he was ever a swineherd, nor, as Fuller observes, since by living in a cave, and feeding upon roots, he and the hogs had something in common; but rather for the reason that the hog is typical of the demon of gluttony and sensuality, which St. Anthony is supposed to have vanquished by the exercise of piety and the Divine assistance. As the founder of monachism, he wears a monk's habit and cowl. The crutch upon which he leans is given to him out of respect for his age; while the bell suspended from the crutch, or carried in his hand, indicates his power to exorcise evil spirits (*see* 202), because he withstood so many demons and temptations. (Died 356.)

255. **St. Sebastian** (January 20th) was bound to a stake and made a target for arrows, which stuck so thickly in his body that it resembled a pin-cushion full of pins. For this reason both archers and pin-makers claim him as their patron. He is also the patron of soldiers, because he was a centurion, or leader of a hundred Roman soldiers. By Italian and especially Roman women, he is held in great veneration on account of his youth, courage, and beauty of person, combined with the attractiveness of his story, into which a woman's charity enters so conspicuously. Above all, he is regarded as the saviour against pestilence and plague. In the year 680 a terrible scourge ravaged the city of Rome for three months, at the end of which time it was revealed to a holy monk that if an altar were set up in honour of St. Sebastian the martyr, the pestilence would be stayed. This was done, and, accordingly, by the saint's intercession, the dread visitant speedily took its departure.

All along the east coast of Italy, from Venice to Bari, St. Sebastian is specially invoked when pestilence threatens. In Christian Art he is represented bound to a tree or stake, with a multitude of arrows piercing his naked body. (Martyred 268.)

256. **St. Agnes** (January 21st), the patroness of maidenhood, is specially invoked by Roman women for the gifts of meekness and chastity. In Christian Art she is represented with a lamb by her side, because, according to the legend, when the Christians visited her shrine on a certain occasion they were rewarded with a vision of the saint, accompanied by a lamb whiter than driven snow. (Martyred 304.)

257. **St. Vincent** (January 22nd), Deacon of Saragossa, is represented in Christian Art in a deacon's dress, and with a crow, having a pitchfork in its mouth, by his side. We are told that his flesh was lacerated by iron forks, and that, after his body was cast up by the sea on the promontory now designated Cape St. Vincent, it was protected from wild beasts that came there to devour it by crows or ravens. (Martyred 304.)

258. **St. Ignatius**, Bishop of Antioch (February 1st), was devoured by lions in the amphitheatre. In Christian Art, therefore, he appears in the dress of a Greek bishop, and with a lion, or two lions, by his side. (Martyred 107.)

259. **St. Blaise**, Bishop of Sebaste (February 3rd), is the patron of wool-combers, because his flesh was torn off by iron wool-carding combs. His attribute in Christian Art is, therefore, an iron comb. Finally he was beheaded A.D. 316 (*see* 419).

260. **St. Agatha** (February 5th) is invoked by sufferers from diseases of the breast, because her breast was ordered to be torn by two slaves with iron shears. She is protectress, also, against fire, from the particular mode of her martyrdom, her body being exposed to the flames, although, to increase the torture, she was not permitted to be burned to death, but taken back to her dungeon, there to die in agony. The legend tells us how, a year after her martyrdom, when Mount Etna was in eruption, the affrighted inhabitants of Catania, in the district, took refuge at her shrine, and finding there her veil, they stuck it on a lance and marched towards the mountain, invoking her intercession, with a result that the fire was at once put out. The veil of St. Agatha, we learn from the same source, was drawn tightly round her lacerated bosom when, by God's command, St. Peter came into her dungeon to heal it with precious ointments. Hence she is usually represented wearing a long veil. The shears are always in evidence, either in her hand or lying beside her. Sometimes she has a dish or salver containing a female breast. (Martyred 251.)

261. **St. Dorothea of Cappadocia** (February 6th) is represented in Christian Art with roses in her lap or in her hand; or, as sometimes occurs, with an angel standing by offering her three roses and three apples. According to the legend, her profession of faith to the pagans was this: "I serve the Son of God, Christ, mine espoused! His dwelling is Paradise; by His side are joys eternal; and in His garden grow celestial fruits and roses that never fade!" While on her way to execution she was scoffingly asked by a young lawyer to send him some of the roses she had spoken of on joining her bridegroom. Whereupon she answered, "Thy request, O Theophilus, is granted!" Immediately after her martyrdom an angel appeared to him with a basket of celes-

tial fruit and flowers, saying, "Dorothea sends thee these!" and then vanished. (Martyred 303.)

262. **St. Apollonia of Alexandria** (February 9th) was flung into a fiery furnace, which consumed her; but as a preliminary she had all her beautiful teeth pulled out one by one. Hence she is regarded as the protectress against toothache. In Christian Art she appears with a pair of pincers, either in her hand or lying beside her. (Martyred 250).

263. **St. Matthias** (February 24th), the Apostle chosen by lot to take the place of Judas, is represented in Christian Art with a battle-axe, the instrument with which he was beheaded by the Jews.

264. **St. David** (March 1st), patron saint of Wales, was the son of a prince of Cardiganshire, of the royal line of Cunedda Whedig. On the spot where he received his education, now St. David's, he founded a convent with a most rigorous rule; and when, after the synod at Brevy in 519, Dubricius, of Dyvrig, Archbishop of Caerleon, resigned the See to him, he removed the archiepiscopal seat to the same place. He died in 554, and was buried in the Cathedral, where a simple monument marks his tomb.

265. **St. Thomas Aquinas** (March 7th) is represented in Christian Art with a large open book or books on his knees and a sun on his breast, because he was a distinguished theologian and luminary of the Church. Sometimes a human eye appears within the sun, in allusion to his far-seeing wisdom, inasmuch as he composed the Office of the Sacrament, which is still in use. The Sacramental cup is generally in evidence. As a Dominican, he wears the habit of his order. (Died 1274).

266. **St. Longinus** (March 15th) is the patron of Mantua, where his relics are preserved. He is believed to have been the centurion who pierced the side of the crucified Christ with a lance, and after witnessing the Divine manifestations around him, exclaimed, "Truly this man was the Son of God!" In Christian Art he wears the dress of a Roman soldier, and has a lance or spear in his hand. (Beheaded 45).

267. **St. Gregory the Great** (March 12th), the greatest of all the Popes, is represented in Christian Art in his pontifical robes, and with an infant angel holding the tiara. According to the legend, his mother had a vision of St. Anthony, who promised her that her infant son should one day wear the papal tiara. (Died 604).

268. **St. Patrick** (March 17th) is the patron of Ireland, the people of which country he converted to Christianity. His exorcism of the venomous reptiles has a similar significance as the dragon stories of the East, symbolising the conquest of good over evil, the triumph of Christianity over paganism. In Christian Art he is always represented with a serpent at his feet. (Died 464.)

269. **St. Benedict** (March 21st), the founder of the Benedictine order of monks, has several attributes in Christian Art. The broken pitcher, or glass, or wine-cup is in allusion to the attempt of some perverted monks to poison him in a cup of wine; but which, when the saint made the sign of the Cross upon it, instantly fell from the hand of the traitor, to be shattered on the ground. The loaf of bread, with a serpent creeping from it, similarly expresses the attempt of the monk Florentius to poison him with a loaf of bread, under the instigation of the Evil One. The asperge

for sprinkling holy water is given him because he so often resisted the attacks of the demon; and the thorn bush, because, when the demon tempted him by conjuring up a vision of a very beautiful woman, St. Benedict cast himself into a thicket of briars and nettles. The roses said to have been propagated from these briars are shown in the monastery garden of Subiaco in Italy. (Died 543.)

270. **St. Ambrose** (April 4th) is the patron of Milan, because he was consecrated bishop of that city eight days after his conversion. His peculiar attributes in Christian Art are a knotted scourge with three thongs, symbolical of the penance he inflicted upon the Emperor Theodosius for his ruthless massacre of 7,000 unoffending human beings; and a beehive, owing to the legend that when he was a child a swarm of bees settled upon his mouth without inflicting the slightest injury. Strangely enough the same story is told of Plato and Archilochus. (Died 397.)

271. **St. George** (April 23rd) is the patron of Christian chivalry, owing to the signal assistance which he rendered to Godfrey of Boulogne in the first crusade. He is the patron saint of England, because Richard Cœur-de-Lion, while in Palestine, placed himself and his army under his special protection. For the like reason he is the patron of soldiers and armourers. He is represented in Christian Art young, or in the prime of life, and beardless. He wears either the dress of a Roman soldier or a complete suit of armour. His shield bears the Latin cross, which, until the union of the three kingdoms, formed the national standard of England. When mounted he holds in one hand a white banner with a red cross upon it. His lance is generally broken, from the account in the legend that "his lance

being broken, he slew the dragon with his sword." The slain monster lies at his feet. (Died 303.)

272. **St. Mark** (April 25th) is the patron of Venice, because about the year 815 some Venetian merchants obtained possession of his relics and buried them on the spot where the church dedicated to him now stands. As the historian of the Resurrection, his familiar attribute in Christian Art is a lion, conformably to the Oriental fable that the lion's whelp is born dead, but after three days its sire breathes upon it and so gives it life. He holds a pen in his right hand and the Gospel in his left. (Died 68.)

273. **St. Peter Martyr** (April 28th) was a Dominican monk murdered by hired assassins of two noblemen of the Venetian States whom he had handed over to the secular authorities, and who, in consequence, had been imprisoned. He is represented in Christian Art with an axe buried in his head and blood trickling down his face, and a sword piercing his heart. This was the manner in which the assassins accomplished their fell work. (Martyred 1252.)

274. **St. James the Less** (May 1st) is said to have resembled the Saviour so closely that, to quote the words of the Golden Legend, "the holy Virgin herself, had she been capable of error, might have mistaken one for the other." This was the reason why Judas saluted his Master with a kiss. Though commonly described as "the Lord's brother," St. James minor was really the son of a sister of the Virgin. He is represented in Christian Art with a fuller's club, the instrument with which Simeon the fuller dashed out his brains. (Martyred 63.)

275. **St. Philip** (May 1st) has for his attribute in Chris-

tian Art a pilgrim's staff with a cross upon it. This is because he carried the Gospel into Scythia, and was eventually crucified (the Greeks say head downwards), and then stoned, A.D. 90.

276. **St. Florian** (May 4th), one of the eight titulary saints of Austria, is exceedingly popular all over Germany. As the protector against conflagrations his effigy will often be met with on pumps, as well as at street corners, or in open spaces, to mark the spot where a destructive fire was once arrested. This is because, among other miracles attributed to him, he on one occasion put out a fire with a bucketful of water. He was a Roman soldier, and in that character usually figures in Christian Art. (Martyred *c.* 300.)

277. **St. Victor of Milan** (May 8th) is the great military saint of North Italy. He was a Roman soldier, beheaded by the Emperor Maximus, after enduring many torments. One of his attributes in Christian Art is an oven, because he was thrust into a hot oven. More frequently however, we see him on a white charger leading his troops to victory. (Martyred 303.)

278. **St. Pancras** (May 12th) is the patron of children, because he was martyred by Diocletian at the age of fourteen. He is generally represented in Christian Art trampling upon a Saracen, in allusion to his hatred of infidelity; and bearing in his hand a stone or a sword, the implements of his martyrdom. (Martyred 304.)

279. **St. John Nepomuck** (May 16th) is the patron of silence and protector against slander, because rather than reveal the confession of the Empress at the command of the Emperor Charles IV., of Germany, he allowed himself to be

cast into the river Moldau from the bridge at Prague, on the precise spot where in modern times a statue has been set up in his honour. Hence he is regarded also in Bohemia and Austria as the patron of bridges and running water. In German pictures he is often represented with a padlock on his mouth, in token of silence. (Martyred 1383.)

280. **St. Yves of Bretagne** (May 19th) is the patron of lawyers, because he was learned in canon and civil law. By the Bretons he is invoked as "the poor man's advocate," on account of the good use that he made of his knowledge in the interests of the oppressed during his lifetime. In Christian Art he is represented as a Doctor of Laws holding a paper in his hand. (Died 1303.)

281. **St. Dunstan** (May 19th) is the patron of goldsmiths, because when Abbot of Glastonbury he worked at the forge as an amateur artificer of church plate. His attribute in Christian Art is a pair of pincers, for, according to the legend, the devil paid him a visit one day in the form of a beautiful woman; but finding he could not tempt him in that character, he appeared *in propriâ personâ*, whereupon the saint tweaked his nose with the red-hot pincers so unmercifully that the howls of the Evil One were heard by all the neighbours. This incident suggested the sign of the celebrated Devil Tavern in Fleet Street, hard by St. Dunstan's Church. (Died 988.)

282. **St. Bernardino of Sienna** (May 20th) might well be described as the patron of those who are compelled from time to time to have recourse to the pawnbroker. He was the founder of those very serviceable institutions which in France and Italy are styled *Monts de Piété*. Conscious

of the miseries endured by the poor of his own country, owing to the exactions of the Jewish usurers, he everywhere advocated the establishment of public loan societies, where money might be lent on small pledges disinterestedly and beneficially. For this reason St. Bernardino is represented in Christian Art with a *Mont de Piété* in his hand, consisting of a little green hill of three mounds, surmounted either by a cross, or a standard having on it the figure of the dead Saviour. Such a figure in Italy bears the name of a *pietà*, in France, a *piété;* this on the three mounds is symbolical of a Christian money-lending establishment. Another attribute of St. Bernardino is a square tablet having the letters I.H.S. upon it within a circle of rays. One day a man who had earned a good livelihood by carving dice and chessmen, came to him complaining that since gambling had gone out of fashion he could no longer subsist by his art. Whereupon the saint told him that if he could carve ivory tablets with the name of Jesus upon them, he would no doubt find many purchasers amongst the faithful followers of Christ. The man did so, and soon became wealthy by this new occupation. (Died 1444.)

283. **St. Elmo** (June 3rd) is held in peculiar veneration in Sicily and Spain. The celebrated Neapolitan monastery of this name is placed under his special protection. His attribute in Christian Art is a wheel or skein upon which silk is generally wound, because, so says the legend, seeing that he withstood all ordinary tortures, his entrails were wound round such a wheel. (Martyred 296.)

284. **St. Boniface** (June 5th), the patron and apostle of Germany, was a Saxon monk of the Benedictine Abbey at Nutsall, near Winchester. His life was sacrificed while preaching the Gospel to the pagans in Friesland. In Christian

Art he usually appears with a copy of the Gospels transfixed by a sword. (Martyred 755.)

285. **St. Barnabas** (June 11th), the schoolfellow of St. Paul, is represented in Christian Art as a man of majestic presence, with a copy of St. Matthew's Gospel in his hand. This was the substance of his preaching in Asia Minor, Italy, and Greece; and whenever he encountered any who were sick, he healed them by placing the book on their bosom. (Died *c.* 38.)

286. **St. Vitus** (June 15th) is the patron of dancers, and particularly of those afflicted with the nervous disorder known as the St. Vitus Dance, because, as the legend tells us, when his father looked in upon him through the keyhole of the dungeon into which he had been cast for openly professing himself a Christian, he beheld him dancing with seven beautiful angels. One of his attributes is a cock, from his habit of early rising; hence he is often invoked by persons who are addicted to oversleeping themselves in the morning. Another of his attributes is a cauldron of boiling oil, the instrument of his martyrdom. Sometimes, too, he has a lion beside him, in allusion to his exposure to lions in the amphitheatre; or a wolf, which is said to have kept faithful watch over his remains. In all cases he is represented as a very beautiful youth. (Martyred 303.)

287. **St. Alban** (June 22nd) was the first English martyr. His attributes in Christian Art are a sword and a fountain, because, when he reached the summit of the hill where he was to be beheaded, he prayed for water to quench his thirst, and immediately a spring appeared at his

feet. His burial-place was afterwards revealed to King Offa, who erected a sumptuous shrine over his remains at what is now St. Albans, in Hertfordshire. (Beheaded 305.)

288. **St. Martha** (June 29th) is the patroness of good housewives. She is represented in homely garments, with a ladle or skimmer in her hand, and a bunch of keys hanging from her girdle. Occasionally we see her with an asperge and holy water, and a dragon at her feet. This is because, according to the legend, she delivered the neighbourhood of Aix, in Provence, of a dragon that lay concealed on the banks of the Rhône. (Died 84.)

289. **St. Peter** (June 29th) is the patron of fishermen, because he was himself a fisherman. His attributes are the keys, in allusion to his custody of the portals of Heaven, and a book or scroll. When our Lord said to him, "And I will give unto thee the keys of the kingdom of Heaven" (Matthew xvi. 18), He employed a set form of words well understood by the Apostle. A key was anciently the recognized symbol of authority, and the presentation of a key the usual mode of investiture with supreme authority. Thus we read in Isaiah xxii., 22, "And the key of the house of David will I lay upon his shoulder: so he shall open, and none shall shut; and he shall shut, and none shall open." The cross keys constitute the arms of the Archbishop of York, and also, when one is of gold and the other of silver, the Papal insignia. The church of St. Peter-upon-Cornhill has a gilt key for a vane. The usual weather-cock on church steeples was adopted at an early period of Church history as an emblem of clerical vigilance, in commemoration of the cock that crowed thrice after St. Peter denied the Saviour during His Passion. St. Peter was

crucified with his head downwards, A.D. 65, because he did not consider himself worthy to die in the same manner and posture as his Divine Master.

290. **St. Paul** (June 29th) is the patron of the City of London, the church rebuilt upon the site of an ancient temple of Diana having been dedicated to the Apostle by Sebert, King of the East Saxons, about the same time as that monarch founded the Benedictine monastery on Thorney Island, now Westminster, in honour of St. Peter. The latter establishment is said to have been miraculously consecrated by St. Peter himself. The so-called "dagger" in the City arms is really the sword (accommodated to one of the quarters of the shield representing St. George's Cross) with which St. Paul as a Roman citizen was beheaded, A.D. 64. The vulgar notion that it represents the weapon with which Sir William Walworth slew the rebel leader Wat Tyler, is untenable on historical grounds. The sword is the Apostle's proper attribute in Christian Art.

291. **St. Anthony of Padua** (June 30th) is represented in Christian Art in the habit of a Franciscan friar, and with a flame of fire in his hand or breast, symbolical of his deep religious fervour. He is said to have preached to the fishes in preference to some obstinate unbelievers upon whom he could not make any impression, which incident will generally be found illustrated in churches dedicated to his honour. It has always been usual among the citizens of Padua to speak of St. Anthony as *Il Santo*, the Saint, without adding any other name. This is because when he died the Franciscans were so fearful of the citizens laying claim to his body in order to bury it in their church, that they endeavoured to keep his death a secret; but we are told that the very children of the city, "being divinely instigated thereto, ran

about the streets crying with a loud voice, *Il Santo è morto! Il Santo è morto!*" (Died 1231.)

292. **St. Phocas of Sinope** (July 3rd) is the patron of gardeners. He lived by cultivating a garden, the produce of which, after supplying his own needs, he gave to the poor. He is represented in Christian Art in the dress and with the implements of a gardener. (Beheaded 303.)

293. **St. Alexis** (July 17th) belonged to one of the first families of Rome. From his youth he devoted himself to the service of God, and under his rich silk garments wore a hair shirt. When his parents chose a beautiful bride for him, he, not daring to disobey their wishes, disappeared on the bridal morn. "Behold," said the bride, "he came into my chamber, and gave me this ring of gold, and this girdle of precious stones, and this veil of purple, and then he bade me farewell, and I know not whither he has gone." Whereupon the entire household went into mourning for him. Meantime he put on a pilgrim's dress and journeyed into Mesopotamia, where he ministered to the sick, and lived in great poverty and humility. After long years he returned to his father, who, not knowing him, ordered him to be taken in out of pity, and the servants put him in a hole under the stairs. Presently, when it was revealed to his father in a dream who he was, he looked in upon him, but, alas! too late; for Alexis had died of neglect and want. Hence he is the patron of pilgrims and beggars. The church dedicated to him at Rome stands on the site of his father's mansion. Pictures of St. Alexis are frequently seen in hospitals and refuges for the poor. He is represented always in ragged attire. (Died 400.)

294. **SS. Justa and Rufina** (July 19th), patronesses of

Seville, were two poor sisters, daughters of a potter. In the city of Seville they sold earthenware, and gave all they could to the poor. One day some idolatrous women went to their shop to buy pots for heathen uses, but the sisters refused to sell them the pots they desired, whereupon the women broke up all their earthenware. The sisters retaliating by breaking an image of Venus, they were martyred, Justa on the rack and Rufina strangled, A.D. 304. In Christian Art they are represented with earthen pots beside them.

295. **St. Bonaventura** (July 14th), Cardinal and Bishop of Albano, is often represented in Christian Art with his cardinal's hat lying at his feet or hanging on the bough of a tree. This is because when the two nuncios of Pope Gregory IX. brought him the red hat, they found him in the convent garden washing the plate from which he had just dined, and he requested them to put it down on the ground, or leave it hanging on a tree, until he could take it in his hands. His attributes are a book, on account of his great learning, and the pyx or Sacramental cup, from the incident related in the legend, that since he considered himself unworthy to receive the Sacrament, it was presented to him by an angel. (Died 1274.)

296. **St. Vincent de Paul** (July 19th) is greatly revered in France for the many good works that he performed. He it was who established foundling hospitals for deserted children, the celebrated La Madeleine Hospital at Paris for abandoned women, and the lay order of the Sisters of Charity. Effigies of him are extremely popular throughout the country. He appears in the habit of a Franciscan friar, with an infant either in his arms or at his feet, and not unfrequently with a sister of mercy kneeling by his side. (Died 1660.)

297. **St. Margaret** (July 20th) is the chosen type of female innocence and virtue, and the special patroness of women in childbirth. This is because, when led out to be beheaded, she thanked God that the end of her travail had come, and prayed that in memory of her miraculous deliverance out of the womb of the dragon, women in labour who invoked her might find help through her sufferings. For, according to the legend, after the Governor of Antioch had cast her into a dungeon, the devil came and tempted her in the form of a dragon, but as she made the sign of the Cross he fled; then returning, he swallowed her up, and the next moment burst; or, as another account says, he suffered her to quit his maw. Hence, the saint is usually represented in Christian Art with a dragon at her feet, with the end of a cross thrust between his teeth. In this character she appears on the Corporation seal of Lynn Regis, *i.e.*, King's Lynn, as patroness of that ancient borough. The garland of pearls generally worn round her neck is in allusion to her name, which among Oriental nations signifies a pearl. (Beheaded 306.)

298. **St. Victor of Marseilles** (July 21st) was a Roman soldier martyred in the Diocletian persecution, because when commanded to offer incense to Jupiter, he broke the idol and overturned the altar. For this he was crushed by a millstone and then beheaded, A.D. 303. He is represented in the Roman military dress, with a millstone beside him.

299. **St. Mary Magdalen** (July 22nd) is the patroness of frail and penitent women, because she threw herself at the feet of our Lord, weeping bitterly for her sins. Her attribute in Christian Art is the alabaster box of precious ointment which she poured upon the head of our Lord

during His Passion; sometimes this takes the form of a cup with a cover, according to the fancy of the artist. (Died 68.)

300. **St. Christina** (July 24th) patroness of Bolsena, in the Venetian States, is represented in Christian Art with a millstone, the instrument of her martyrdom, A.D. 295.

301. **St. Christopher** (July 25th) was originally called Offero, but when he forswore Satan and confessed Christ, he changed his name to Christoffero. He was a man of colossal build and strength, and his image will often be met with in out-of-the-way Continental places hewn out of a rock, or in the side of a church, of gigantic proportions. Persons who look upon such a figure of the saint are believed to be exempt from the perils of earthquake, tempest, and fire for that day; since, at the time of his martyrdom, he said that those who remembered him and trusted in God should not suffer death by earthquake, tempest, or fire. St. Christopher is depicted in Christian Art as wading across a swollen stream bearing the infant Christ on his shoulders, and a pilgrim's staff in his hand, in allusion to an incident in the legend. (Beheaded 364.)

302. **St. James the Greater** (July 25th) is universally regarded as the patron of pilgrims to the Holy Land, because after establishing the Christian religion in Spain, he returned to Judæa on a pilgrimage and was there beheaded. In this character he is represented in Christian Art in the garb of a pilgrim, with staff, gourd, and scallop-shell. The church of St. James the Greater, on Garlic Hill, Upper Thames Street, has an effigy of the saint, nicknamed by Cockneys, "Old Jemmy Garlic," habited as a pilgrim, on the top of the clock; while the scallop-shell serves to mark the parish boundaries. The scallop-shell is the recognized symbol of all pilgrims to

the Holy Land, inasmuch as it abounds on the shores of Palestine. When returning to his own country, the pilgrim always displayed the scallop-shell in his hat, to show that he had carried out his pious intention. Particularly is the scallop-shell an attribute of St. James the Greater, pursuant to the account in the legend, that, when his body was miraculously conveyed to Compostella, in Spain, the marble slab on which it rested was covered with scallop-shells (*see* 449). St. James, or according to the Spanish form of his name, St. Iago, is also the great military patron of Spain. His mission to defend the Christian Church against the Infidel was however reserved until after his death. In the course of the celebrated battle of Clavijo he suddenly appeared on a milk-white charger, waving aloft a white standard, and leading the Christians to victory. This manifestation was in response to the soldiers' invocation of his name, " Sant Iago !" being the battle-cry of that day. Hence the name of the ancient city (Santiago) which contains the cathedral founded in his honour. (Beheaded 44.)

303. **St. Pantaleon of Nicomedia** (July 27th) is represented in Christian Art bound to an olive tree, with a nail driven through his body. This was the manner in which he suffered martyrdom. Instead of the palm he bears in his hand an olive, because, according to the legend, when the tree on which he suffered had its roots bathed with his blood, it brought forth leaves and fruit. As a skilled physician who went about healing the sick without fee or reward. St. Pantaleon is patron of all physicians. (Martyred 303.)

304. **St. Ignatius Loyola** (July 31st), the founder of the Jesuits, or Society of Jesus, is distinguished in Christian

Art by the monogram of the order, I H S; sometimes surrounded by a glory in the sky; sometimes on a tablet borne by angels. In effigies of the saint, the heart crowned with thorns, symbolical of the Sacred Heart of Jesus, is his peculiar attribute; being also the device of the order. (Died 1556.)

305. **St. Lawrence** (August 10th) was roasted alive on a gridiron; therefore his attribute in Christian Art is the instrument of his martyrdom. The church dedicated to him in Gresham Street, City, has a gridiron for a vane, while that at Norwich shows not only the gridiron but the saint stretched upon it. Again, the palace convent of the Escurial, in Spain, was built by Philip II. in the form of a gridiron; the palace buildings comprising the handle, and the rest divided into courts so arranged as to compose the bars. Miniature gridirons of wood, metal, stone, and paint, are also in evidence all over the structure. It was dedicated to St. Lawrence because the battle of Quintin was fought and won on the feast of St. Lawrence. Not everyone knows that Philip II. built the Escurial in order to recompense the monks of the Order of St. Jerome, whose convent he had been obliged to bombard during the siege of Quintin. St. Lawrence is commonly said to be the patron saint of lazy people, because he was too lazy to turn himself over on the gridiron. The Golden Legend, it should be added, is *not* responsible for this not very witty statement. In addition to the gridiron hanging from his girdle, or lying by his side, the saint is represented at times in a deacon's dress, with tongues of fire embroidered upon it, in allusion to his martyrdom. Where the gridiron is omitted he has a plate of gold or silver, or it may be a money-bag in his hand, because the treasures of the Church were in his keeping. (Martyred 258.)

306. **St. Clare** (August 12th) the foundress of the Minoresses, or Grey Sisters, has for her attribute in Christian Art the pyx, containing the Host, in allusion to the miraculous dispersion of the Saracens by its means. The legend states that when the Emperor Frederic was ravaging the shores of the Adriatic, she comforted her nuns with the declaration that God would not permit him to invade their convent. Full of faith, she placed the pyx of ivory and silver on the threshold, and kneeling down with the sisterhood, sang, "Thou hast rebuked the heathen, Thou hast destroyed the wicked, Thou hast put out their name for ever and ever." In consequence whereof, says the legend, the barbarian left them in peace. (Died 1253.)

307. **St. Hippolytus** (August 13th) is regarded as the patron of horses, because he suffered martyrdom by being bound by the feet to the tails of two wild horses. This is how he is usually represented in Christian Art. Occasionally we find him having a bunch of keys hanging from his girdle, as the gaoler of St. Lawrence. (Martyred 252.)

308. **St. Roche** (August 16th) devoted his whole life to the service of those who fell victims to the plague; consequently his intercession is invoked by the pious in times of pestilence. In votive pictures, which are common in Italian churches, St. Roche and St. Sebastian (*see* 255) usually appear together. St. Roche was himself stricken down in the desert by the plague, and in that dread situation, though cut off from all human kind, was miraculously fed every day by a dog bringing him a loaf of bread. This explains why the saint is represented with a dog beside him; also why he raises his pilgrim's habit on one side, for the plague-spot is distinctly seen on his thigh. When the plague was devastating the city of Constance, in the year 1414, a young

monk who had travelled much in France, reminded the council convened there at the time to put down the heresy of John Huss and his followers, of the saint through whose intercession many persons had been saved from the plague. Accordingly the council caused an effigy of St. Roche to be borne in solemn procession through the city, and the pestilence was forthwith stayed. (Died in prison 1327.)

309. **St. Helena** (August 18th), the mother of Constantine the Great, is represented in Christian Art with a crown on her head as empress, and embracing the Cross, because it is to her that modern Christians are indebted for the finding of the True Cross. She is called "Stabularia," on account of the church which she built on the spot at Bethlehem where our Lord was born. The Jews, however, give her this name because, as they say, she was originally the daughter of an innkeeper. (Died 328.)

310. **St. Bernard of Clairvaux** (August 20th) has for his attributes in Christian Art a demon fettered to his feet, or to a rock beside him, in token of his success in putting down heresy, and writing materials, in allusion to his homilies in praise of the Virgin. (Died 1153.)

311. **St. Bartholomew** (August 24th) is represented in Christian Art with a flaying-knife, because he was flayed alive. In olden times, before the dissolution of the monasteries, little knives were distributed to the people at Croyland Abbey as a memento of the Apostle on his anniversary. (Martyred 71.)

312. **St. Dominic** (August 24th), the founder of the Dominican Order of Preaching Friars, has several attributes in Christian Art. The lily in his hand symbolizes the purity

of his life, and the book his great learning. The dog beside him, holding a flaming torch in his mouth, and the star which appears either on his forehead or over his head, are thus accounted for in the legend. A short time before the saint was born his mother dreamed that she had brought forth a black and white dog carrying a lighted torch in its mouth. Then, when his godmother held him in her arms at the font, she beheld a star of extraordinary magnitude descend from heaven and settle on his brow. These portents readily gave rise to the belief that the infant was destined to shed a lustre upon the world ; moreover, the character of the dog afterwards suggested to Dominic the peculiar habit—white tunic and scapulary and black hood and cloak—of the Order that he instituted. (Died 1221.)

313. **St. Augustine, Bishop of Hippo** (August 28th), is regarded as the patron of theologians, on account of his numerous writings in the interests of the Church. His proper attribute in Christian Art is a flaming heart, symbolical of the ardour of his piety. Sometimes it is a heart transfixed by a sword, to express the poignancy of his repentance for having delayed his conversion until a comparatively late period of his life, in spite of the prayers of St. Monica, his mother. Occasionally he is seen with nothing more than a pen and a book. (Died 430.)

314. **St. John the Baptist** (August 29th) is represented in Christian Art at all times in a coat of sheep-skins, in allusion to his life in the wilderness. (Beheaded 31.)

315. **St. Giles** (September 1st) had royal blood in his veins, but he abjured the world and betook himself to a wilderness near the Rhône. There the king discovered him one day while pursuing a wounded hind that had taken

refuge in the cave of the recluse. From this incident St. Giles is generally represented in Christian Art with a hind pierced by an arrow beside him. Of the one hundred and forty-six churches in England dedicated to him, all, or nearly all, were originally situated on the outskirts of the town, in allusion to his love of solitude. In London we have those of St. Giles-in-the-Fields, St. Giles, Cripplegate, and St. Giles, Camberwell. He is the patron of beggars, cripples, and lepers, on account of the many pious offices that he rendered such sufferers before he forsook the world. Leper hospitals have invariably been dedicated to St. Giles. (Died 541.)

316. **St. Rosalia** (September 4th) is the patroness of Palermo, and of Sicilian mariners, by whom she is highly venerated. Her grotto in the mountain on the west side of the Bay is now a place of pilgrimage, and her statue on Mount Pellegrino is visible from the sea. Twice she saved the city from the plague by her intercession. In Christian Art she is generally represented clad in ragged, loose attire, recumbent in a cavern. (Died 1160.)

317. **St. Adrian** (September 8th) had his limbs struck off on a blacksmith's anvil, and was afterwards beheaded. His attributes in Christian Art are an anvil and a sword, or an axe. While in prison awaiting execution all women were denied access to him, but Natalia, his wife, accomplished her object by cutting off her hair and presenting herself in male attire. Though she survived him a short time, she, too, laid down her life for the Faith; her festival is kept on the same day as is that of her husband. (Died 290.)

318. **St. Euphemia** (September 16th) is represented in Christian Art attired in a plain, dark brown mantle, such as

was worn by the Greek philosophers in token of their renunciation of worldly pleasures; and with a lion by her side, because when she was cast to the lions, they merely licked her feet. (Died 307.)

319. **St. Januarius** (September 19th) was thrown into a fiery furnace, but came out of it unharmed. For this reason he is the patron of Naples, and protector of the city against eruptions of Mount Vesuvius. He is represented in Christian Art in episcopal robes, as Bishop of Benevento, and with Vesuvius in the background. (Beheaded 305.)

320. **St. Eustace** (September 20th) was a Roman captain of guards, passionately fond of the chase. One day, after bringing a stag to bay, he discovered that it had a crucifix with the dead Redeemer upon it between its horns. This caused him to reflect upon the new Faith of which he had heard so much, the consequence being that on the very next day he was baptized. His martyrdom was not long delayed, for on refusing to offer incense to the false gods when celebrating the victories of Trajan, he was shut inside the brazen bull. In Christian Art he is represented as a Roman soldier, and his attributes are either a stag with a crucifix, or a brazen bull. (Martyred 118.)

321. **St. Matthew** (September 21st) was originally a publican, or tax-gatherer, in the service of the Romans. In this character he is represented in Christian Art with a purse or money-bag. Occasionally we find him seated at a desk, with money spread out before him. As the Evangelist, he appears with book, pen, and inkhorn, and generally an angel standing by dictating the Gospel to him. He was put to death at Naddabar with a halberd, but in what year is not stated.

322. **St. Maurice** (September 22nd), as commander of the famous Thebain Legion, massacred on the shores of Lake Geneva by the Emperor Maximin, because they refused to offer sacrifices to the gods, is the patron of foot-soldiers. This Thebain Legion consisted of 6,666 Christians, and was so called because levied in the Thebaid to assist the Emperor in his invasion of Gaul. An Austrian by birth, the saint is patron of Austria; and is represented in Christian Art in full armour, bearing either the Austrian standard or leaning on the shield of his country. (Martyred 286.)

323. **St. Thecla** (September 23rd) is represented in Christian Art in a mantle of dark brown or grey, the plain colours generally affected by Greek philosophers and others who forsook the world, and with wild beasts around her. The legend states that she was exposed to the lions in the amphitheatre at Antioch, but these refused to touch her. (Martyred first century.)

324. **SS. Cyprian and Justina** (September 26th) suffered martyrdom together at Antioch in the year 304. Justina was a virgin renowned for her chastity. In vain did Cyprian, the magician, resort to his various artifices to subdue her. At length, finding that his demons were no less foiled by the virtue of this maiden than himself, he worshipped the God of Justina, and by so doing obtained her hand in marriage. With her he was shortly afterwards thrown into a cauldron of boiling pitch, but by a miracle they escaped unharmed. Eventually they were beheaded. St. Cyprian is represented in Christian Art in the habit of a Greek bishop, trampling on his magical books. Justina has in her hand the palm of martyrdom, and at her feet a unicorn, the emblem of chastity, because, according to the fable, such an animal was not to be

captured save by a virgin whose chastity was proof against every temptation.

325. **SS. Cosmo and Damian** (September 27th) are the patrons of physicians and those who attend the sick. The most noted physicians of their age, these brothers gave their services to rich and poor alike, without fee or gratuity; all they did was for charity and the love of God. By their intercession, it is said, the Emperor Justinian recovered from a dangerous illness, and afterwards built a superb church in their honour. They are represented in Christian Art together, in the habit of mediæval physicians, viz., a scarlet robe trimmed with fur, red hose, and red cap. Each holds a box of ointment in one hand, and a lancet, or, in some cases, a pestle and mortar in the other. Their statues, executed by Michael Angelo, are conspicuous objects in the Medici Chapel at Florence, because, as physicians, they were the special patrons of the noble house of Medici, now extinct. (Beheaded 301.)

326. **St. Michael the Archangel** (September 29th), Prince of the Heavenly Host, is regarded as the patron and protector of the Christian Church, because he remained faithful to God, and defeated Lucifer and his apostate angels in the great battle waged in Heaven, as related in the Apocalypse xii. 7. He is represented in Christian Art as a beautiful young man, winged, clad in armour, and with sword and shield combating the dragon (*see* 86, 268.)

327. **St. Jerome** (September 30th), the founder of monachism in the West, is erroneously represented in Christian Art in cardinal's robes, for cardinals were not instituted until three centuries after his death. This is done, however, to invest him with becoming dignity as one of the

great fathers of the Church. His attributes are a miniature church held in his hand, and an open book. Sometimes he is accompanied by a lion, in allusion to his life in the wilderness. He is the patron of scholars and students, more particularly of theology, on account of his writings, notably his translation of the Scriptures, known as the Latin Vulgate. (Died 420.)

328. **St. Francis d'Assisi** (October 4th), the founder of the Franciscan Order of Preaching Friars (*see* 31), has for his attributes in Christian Art a lamb and a lily, the emblems of meekness and purity, and the stigmata, or five wounds of the crucified Christ. We are told in the legend that it was manifested to him in his cell that he should be transformed into a resemblance to Christ, "not by the martyrdom of the flesh, but by the might and fire of Divine love." When the vision had passed away, he discovered that in his hands, feet, and side he carried the wounds of the Redeemer. (Died 1226.)

329. **St. Justina of Padua** (October 7th) was a virgin of royal birth in the city which claims her patronage. She is represented in Christian Art crowned as a princess, and with a sword transfixing her bosom, in accordance with her martyrdom, A.D. 303.

330. **St. Bridget** (October 8th) is regarded as the patroness of fallen women, not because she was at any time of her life unchaste, but from the fact that Henry VIII.'s palace of Bridewell, *i.e.*, beside the well of St. Bride or Bridget, was converted into a House of Correction for refractory females. She is represented in Christian Art with a lamp in one hand, typical of heavenly light and wisdom,

and a cross in the other, as the foundress of the first community of religious women in Ireland, or, indeed, in the Western World. Her long white veil is such a one as was always worn by early converts. The oak which appears in the background is in allusion to her cell among the grove of oaks at Kildare, literally "the cell or place of the oak." (Died 500.)

331. **St. Denys** (October 9th) is the patron of France, where he preached the Gospel, and in whose capital city he suffered martyrdom. The legend expressly states that after he was beheaded he rose and carried his head off in his hand to the summit of Mont Mars (now Montmartre), the angels singing hymns by the way. When, in the fulness of time, King Dagobert I. removed his relics to the famous Abbey of St. Denys, founded by him in his honour, the saint thus became the patron of the French monarchy, and his name the battle-cry of the French armies. Moreover, the *oriflamme*, or sacred banner of France, had its origin in being consecrated on his tomb. In Christian Art St. Denys is represented carrying his head in his hand. Occasionally, too, we find him with his mitred head on his shoulders, and another, a bared one, in his hand. This is to show that he is making an offering of his head to the Church. (Martyred 272.)

332. **St. Theresa** (October 17), the patroness of Spain, is represented in Christian Art kneeling in prayer, with an angel a short distance above piercing her heart with a flame-tipped arrow, in token of the Divine love with which she was animated. The Carmelite Convent which she founded at her birthplace, Avila, in Castile, is now her shrine. The nuns, it may be added, never occupy the choir-stalls in the chapel, but sit on the steps, because, as they say, the angels

were accustomed to sit there whenever the saint attended Mass. (Died 1582.)

333. **St. Luke** (October 18th) is the patron of painters, in accordance with the tradition that he painted a portrait of the Virgin. This may have arisen from the discovery in the Catacombs of a rude drawing of the Virgin thus inscribed: "One of seven painted by Luca." We know, however, that the life of the Virgin in connection with the Infant Saviour is treated with much greater minuteness in St. Luke's Gospel than in that of any other Evangelist; hence the assumption that he painted her portrait can be readily condoned. In Christian Art St. Luke is represented with an easel and painting materials. Beside him is usually an ox, symbolical of sacrifice; in other words, that in St. Luke's Gospel we have the fullest description of the Sacrifice of Christ. At Charlton Fair in former times nearly all the visitors from Greenwich and Deptford bore a pair of horns on their heads, while every booth had a pair of horns displayed on its front. This was in allusion to the saint, on whose day the fair was held. (Died 70.)

334. **St. Ursula** (October 21st) is the patroness of young girls, more particularly school-girls, and the promoters of all institutions designed for the education of her sex, on account of her great learning. The legend of St. Ursula and her 11,000 virgins has been greatly modified in modern times. It is suggested that instead of ten companions, each with a retinue of a thousand virgins, she had but one companion, named Undecimilla, and that this name was originally mistaken for *undecim millia*, or 11,000. Whatever may have been the real facts, it is certain that the church dedicated to St. Ursula at Cologne contains more tombs of virgins than can properly be accommodated.

The revenues of this church, which are considerable, belong to an abbess and six canonesses, who, to do honour to the saint must all be countesses. In Christian Art St. Ursula wears a crown, as princess; has an arrow in her hand, the attribute of her martyrdom; and carries a pilgrim's staff, surmounted by a white banner with a red cross, the Christian standard of victory. (Martyred 453.)

335. **St. Romain** (October 23rd) is regarded as the apostle of Normandy, because he established the Christian religion in that province. As Bishop of Rouen during his lifetime, that city was naturally placed under his special patronage after his death. According to the legend, when the Seine overflowed its banks and threatened to destroy Rouen, he commanded the waters to recede; but no sooner had they done so than from the mud and slime there arose a dragon, which inspired all the inhabitants round about with terror. By the help of a murderer, however, the good bishop eventually vanquished it. Hence it was that until the Revolution the Chapter of Rouen possessed the privilege of pardoning once a year a criminal condemned to death. This dragon legend forms the subject of illustration on one of the windows of Rouen Cathedral. (Died 639.)

336. **SS. Crispin and Crispianus** (October 25th) are patrons of Soissons, in France, where, after preaching the Gospel throughout the country, they suffered martyrdom. They are everywhere regarded as patrons of the shoemaking craft, because they supported themselves by mending shoes during the whole of their Christian mission. In Christian Art they are represented with the palm in one hand, and an awl or shoemaker's knife in the other. (Martyred 287.)

337. **SS. Simon and Jude** (October 28th) have for

their attributes in Christian Art a saw and a halberd, the respective instruments of their martyrdom, A.D. 80.

338. **St. Hubert** (November 3rd), Bishop of Maestrecht and Liège, is represented in Christian Art in episcopal robes, with mitre and crosier, and a stag lying upon a book held in his left hand. He is honoured as apostle of the Ardennes and Brabant, into which provinces he carried the Gospel, and whence, by his zeal, the last remnants of idolatry were destroyed. The account of his conversion is similar to that given of St. Eustace (*see* 320). Though professedly a Christian, he was addicted to neglecting his religious duties for the sake of following the chase. One day during Holy Week, when all good Christians were supposed to be at their devotions, he encountered a stag having a crucifix between its horns, at the same time as he heard a voice admonishing him to repent of his misspent life. Thereupon he retired from the world, took orders, and was subsequently made bishop of that part of France which he converted to the service of God. Under the circumstances nothing was more natural than that, in an age when every vocation had its protecting saint, St. Hubert should have been chosen the patron of hunters. (Died 727.)

339. **St. Winifrid** (November 3rd) is the patroness of virgins, because she was beheaded for refusing to marry Prince Caradoc. According to the legend, her tears falling on the ground gave rise to the famous St. Winifrid's Well, at Holywell, Flintshire, where she suffered, the waters of which well still retain their miraculous powers. Like St. Denys she is generally represented in Christian Art carrying her head in her hands. (Beheaded seventh century.)

340. **St. Charles Borromeo** (November 4th), we are

told, when the pestilence was ravaging Milan, went three times barefooted round the city in his cardinal's robes, and with a halter round his neck, humbly offering himself a sacrifice for the people in order to minister the Sacraments to the dying; yet neither he nor any one of the twenty-eight voluntary priests who accompanied him caught the infection. In commemoration of this incident he is usually represented in Christian Art as a cardinal, barefooted, and with the halter round his neck, his right hand giving the benediction. A colossal statue of him in this character was set up on the borders of Lago Maggiore in the year 1696. (Died 1584.)

341. **St. Leonard** (November 6th) is the patron of prisoners, captives, and slaves, whom he visited, interceded for, and ransomed. In many of the churches dedicated to him, more especially in France, the fetters of released captives may yet be seen. Such fetters are his peculiar attributes. Since the Benedictines claim him as a member of their Order, he is often represented in the black and white tunic and girdle, but more frequently in the dress of a deacon, the highest dignity that he would accept. (Died 559.)

342. **St. Martin** (November 11th) is the patron of vintners, and incidentally of drunkards, for two reasons. In the first place, when the emperor who had invited him to a banquet wished to do him a great honour by offering him the wine-cup before he drank himself, the saint instantly handed it to a poor priest who was standing behind him; "thus showing that he accounted the least of the servants of God before the greatest rulers of the earth." Secondly, November 11th, or Martinmas Day, was originally the Vinalia, or Feast of Bacchus, among the Romans. When,

therefore, the Christian Church merged Bacchus into St. Martin, those who were employed in the vineyards came to look upon the saint as their patron; while drunkards were recommended to invoke him to save them from their besetting sin. The story of St. Martin dividing his cloak with a beggar is familiar to everyone. The Hall of the Vintners' Company, in Thames Street, contains a carved representation of their patron saint and the beggar. St. Martin is the patron of Tours, of which city he became bishop. (Died 397.)

343. **St. Edmund**, King and Martyr (November 20th), was slain by the Danes with arrows in the church at Thetford, Norfolk, and afterwards beheaded. He is represented in Christian Art with an arrow in his hand, and often with a grey wolf crouching at his side, because, according to the legend, when the Christians were searching for his body they found a grey wolf watching over his severed head. The king was buried in the church of the monastery which received the name of Bury St. Edmunds, in his honour. (Slain 870.)

344. **St. Cecilia** (November 22nd) is said to have excelled in music to such a degree, that, finding all known instruments inadequate to give full expression to that flood of harmony with which her soul was filled, she invented the organ, and consecrated it to the service of God. As the patroness of music and musicians, she is always represented in Christian Art playing some musical instrument. The earlier examples however, show her lying on her right side with a veil drawn closely around her head and a wound in her neck, exactly in the same posture as that in which her body was discovered, after it had been pointed out in a dream to Pope Paschal in the ninth century. As the legend tells us, she was wounded

in the neck and left to bleed to death. Such a representation of the saint forms part of an altar-piece in one of the side chapels at the Brompton Oratory. (Martyred 280.)

345. **St. Clement** (November 23rd) is the patron of tanners, whose trade he himself followed before his conversion. His attribute in Christian Art is an anchor, because he was bound to an anchor and cast into the sea. The church dedicated to him in the Strand had formerly an anchor for a vane; the parish boundaries are still indicated by an anchor, while the beadles have an anchor on their staves and buttons. (Martyred 100.)

346. **St. Felicitas** (November 23rd) is the patroness of male heirs, because her seven sons were martyred one by one before her eyes. She is represented in Christian Art, hooded and veiled, as matron and widow, and with her seven sons around her. (Beheaded 173.)

347. **St. Catherine** (November 25th) and her wheel are inseparable in Christian Art. But the wheel is generally broken, because, after she was bound upon it, by the intervention of Heaven it was shattered, and the flying fragments dealt death to her executioners. Under her feet is seen the turbaned head of the tyrant Maximinus, symbolical of the triumph of Christianity over the Infidel. Instead of the sword, the actual instrument of her martyrdom, a book is placed in her hand, in token of her learning. The crown upon her head bespeaks her royal dignity. As a king's daughter she is patroness of princesses and ladies of noble birth. She is patroness also of students, philosophers, and theologians, because she put to confusion all the rhetoricians and scholars who came to dispute with her from all parts of the empire. (Beheaded 307.)

348. **St. Andrew** (November 30th) is the patron of Scotland, because his bones were brought from Patras, a town in the Peloponnesus, and interred in the cathedral of what is now St. Andrews, co. Fife, in the fourth century. He is represented in Christian Art with a transverse cross and ropes, upon which he was crucified. Hence the term, "St. Andrew's Cross." A statue of the Apostle with his attributes appears on the front of the Royal Caledonian Asylum, Islington. (Martyred 70.)

349. **St. Eloy** (December 1st) is the patron of Noyon, of which city he was made bishop. He is represented in Christian Art either in episcopal robes, holding a book in one hand, and a hammer or tongs in the other; or in a short artisan's dress with hammer and tongs. At his feet, in either case, are anvil, bellows, and other implements of the blacksmith's, locksmith's, or metal-worker's craft. This is in allusion to his former occupation; having been bound apprentice to a goldsmith. Later in life, even after his consecration as bishop, he found time to fabricate the church plate and decorate the shrines of the saints. Therefore he is the patron of goldsmiths and workers in the precious metals generally. Farriers and blacksmiths claim him for their patron on account of the following astounding legend. One day, when a horse was required to be shod, he plunged and kicked so much, that it was said he had the devil in him. St. Eloy was then appealed to, but instead of exorcising the devil he quietly cut off the animal's leg, placed it on an anvil and shod it properly, after which he replaced the leg by merely making the sign of the Cross. This legend is represented in bas-relief on the pedestal of his statue in one of the niches of the exterior of Or-San Michele, Florence. The statue was executed by Nanni di Banco, and dedicated by the Guild of Blacksmiths in the year 1420. (Died 659.)

350. **St. Francis Xavier** (December 3rd), the patron and apostle of the Indies, was one of the earliest Christian missionaries in the Far East. He met his death while attempting to reach China. He is represented in Christian Art with a crucifix. (Died 1553.)

351. **St. Barbara** (December 4th) is invoked against tempest and lightning, and all explosions of firearms and gunpowder, because, according to the legend, after her father had followed her into the mountains and cut off her head for embracing Christianity, a fearful tempest with thunder and lightning arose, and God caused a fire to descend upon him, in which he was utterly consumed. She is also invoked against sudden death; those who are devoted to her believing that they will never die impenitent, or without having first received the Sacraments. For this reason St. Barbara, in Christian Art, differs from every other female saint, by carrying the Sacramental cup and wafer. The tower in which her father confined her is always associated with her in one form or another. Sometimes it is a massy building in the background; at others she is leaning upon it; not infrequently she holds a miniature representation of it in her left hand. The sword in her right hand is the symbol of her martyrdom. When the tower does not appear in her left hand, its place is occupied by a copy of the Gospels. (Beheaded 303.)

352. **St. Nicholas** (December 6th) has several attributes. He is the patron of serfdom, and, therefore, of Russia, because he protected the weak against the strong, the oppressed against the oppressor, the poor against the rich; of travellers, sailors, and merchants, because he on several occasions allayed a tempest at sea when invoked by the mariners; of poor maidens, because, out of compassion for a distressed

nobleman about to sacrifice his three daughters to a life of infamy, he cast three purses of gold through his chamber window under cover of night, to enable the girls to marry honourably; of boys, especially scholars, from the astounding miracle related in the legend, to the effect that he restored to life three school-boys whom a wicked innkeeper had murdered and salted in a tub; of parish clerks, because of scholars, who were formerly styled clerks; and of thieves, for having once prevailed upon a gang of robbers to restore their plunder. In the Middle Ages robbers and thieves always called themselves Knights or Clerks of St. Nicholas. As patron of mariners and seaport cities, St. Nicholas is represented in Christian Art with an anchor by his side, or a ship in the background; of scholars, with three naked boys rising out of a tub; of marriageable girls, by three golden balls embroidered on his cope, or placed on a copy of the Gospels in his hand. In all cases he appears in episcopal robes, with mitre and crosier, and beardless, in allusion to his youth when consecrated Bishop of Myra. (Died 326.)

353. **St. Lucy** (December 13th) is the patroness of the poor, on account of her boundless charity. She is invoked by persons afflicted with diseases of the eye, because, rather than accept the hand in marriage of a lover who desired her for the sake of her beautiful eyes, she plucked them out, and sent them to him with this message: "Here hast thou what thou so much desirest; and for the rest, I beseech thee, leave me now in peace!" Nevertheless, as the legend expressly tells us, her sight was restored to her the next day. Her martyrdom, instigated by her rejected lover, was accomplished by a poignard thrust into her neck. In Christian Art she is generally represented as bearing a dish or platter with two eyes on it. Occasionally, the blood is seen trickling from the wound in her neck. (Martyred 303.)

354. **St. Thomas** (December 21st) was a fisherman; yet his attribute in Christian Art is a builder's square. The reason of this is explained in the following account of the Golden Legend. During the time that Thomas was at Cæsarea, the Lord appeared to him, saying, "The King of the Indies, Gondoforus, hath sent his provost, Abanes, to seek for workmen well versed in architecture, who shall build for him a palace finer than that of the Emperor of Rome. Behold, now, I will send thee to him!" In obedience to this Divine command, Thomas presented himself to Gondoforus, who gave him much silver and gold to build for him the sumptuous palace he coveted during his enforced absence in a distant country. At the end of two years he returned, but instead of a palace he found that Thomas had bestowed all the silver and gold entrusted to him upon the sick and the poor. Thereupon Gondoforus cast him into prison, to await a horrible death. Meantime, the king's brother died, and Gondoforus resolved to build for him a magnificent tomb. But the dead man suddenly appeared to his brother the king, and said, "The man whom thou wouldst torture is a servant of God. Behold! I have been in Paradise, and the angels showed to me a wondrous palace of gold and silver and precious stones, and they said, 'This is the palace that Thomas the Architect hath built for thy brother, King Gondoforus!'" Then the king hastened to deliver Thomas out of prison. And Thomas spoke to him thus: "Knowest thou not that those who would possess heavenly things have little care for the things of this earth? There are in heaven rich palaces without number, which were prepared from the beginning of the world for those who purchase the possession through faith and charity. Thy riches, O king, may prepare the way for thee to such a palace, but they cannot follow thee thither!" This beautiful story is fittingly illustrated on one of the stained-glass windows of Bruges Cathedral, the

gift of the Builders' Company of that city. St. Thomas is the patron of masons and builders for the reason just stated.

355. **St. Stephen** (December 26th) was the earliest Christian martyr. The manner of his death is well symbolized by the stone which appears on his shoulder, and another on the side of his head. The book carried in his left hand refers to the Gospel that he preached just before being stoned. His dress is that of a deacon, because St. Peter himself appointed him to that office during his ministry. (Martyred 35.)

356. **St. John the Evangelist** (December 27th) has for his attribute in Christian Art a Sacramental cup with a winged serpent issuing from it. This is in allusion to the legend that when Aristodemus, the priest of Diana, challenged him to drink a cup of poison, St. John made the sign of the Cross upon it, and then drained its contents, which proved innocuous. In memory of this incident, consecrated wine was formerly sold to the laity on St. John's Day. As Evangelist, St. John is attended by an eagle, because, since that bird soars higher into the heavens than any other, so his soul, in virtue of its singular purity, mounted up to receive the light of Divine Wisdom. (Died 99.)

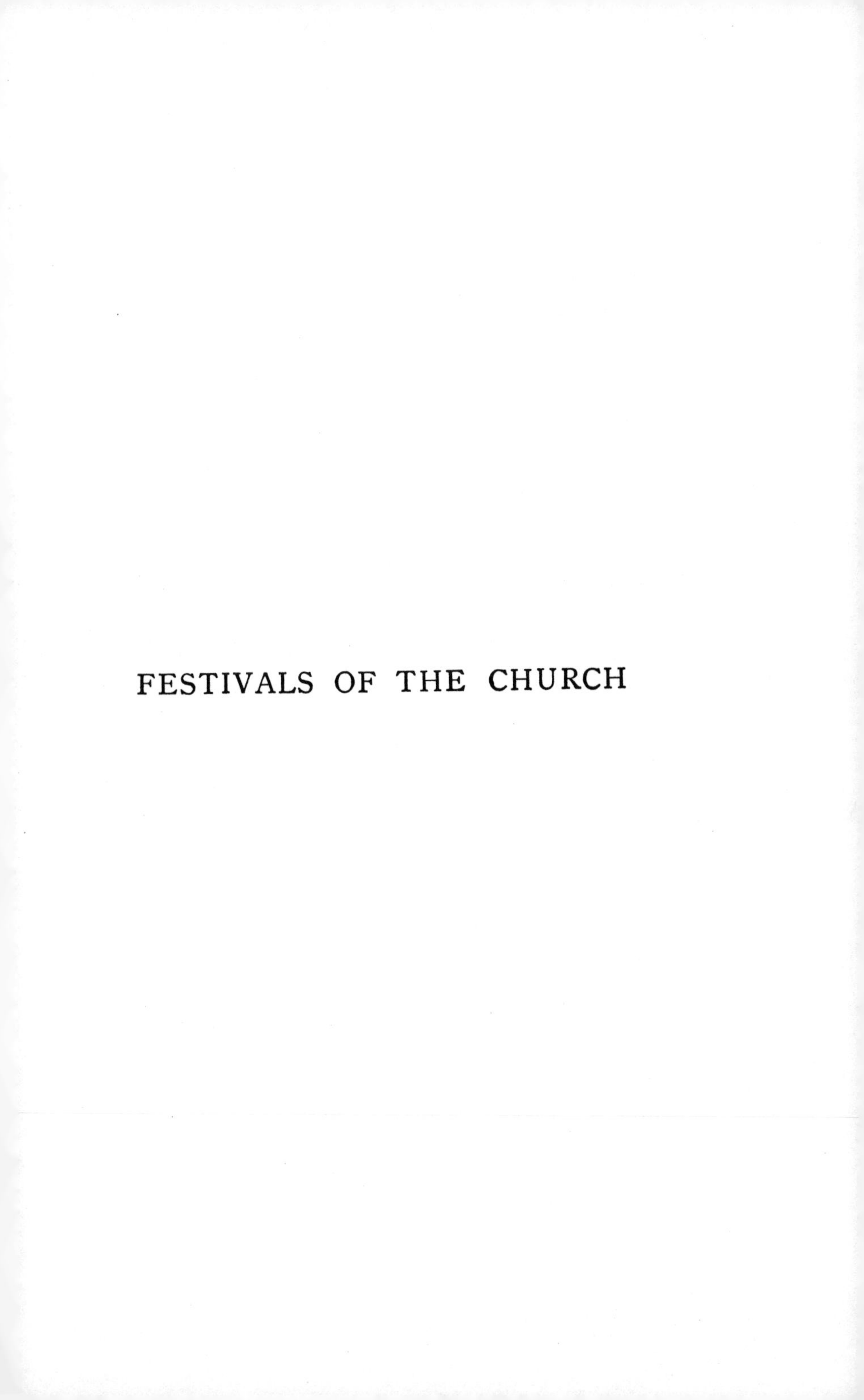

FESTIVALS OF THE CHURCH

FESTIVALS OF THE CHURCH

357. **Annual Festivals** in honour of the saints and martyrs were instituted by Gregory, Bishop of Cæsarea, in the third century, to facilitate the conversion of the pagans, who were unwilling to forego the recreations incidental to the festivals of their gods. This example once set, the institution of **Holy Days**—a term now corrupted into "holidays"—in commemoration of some of the most important events in the history of the Church was easy. In old almanacks such holy days were set forth in red ink, and the rest in black. Hence the expression, **Red-Letter Day.**

358. The first day of the Christian Year commemorates the **Circumcision of our Lord.** It was instituted as a solemn festival in the sixth century, to atone for the excesses committed by the pagans on this day. In accordance with the Jewish custom, the Child Christ was circumcised in the Temple on the eighth day after His Birth, and on the same occasion he received the name of JESUS, as made known to the Virgin by the angel Gabriel (Luke i. 31). Circumcision on the eighth day after the birth of a male child is still enjoined upon all Jews. The Mohammedans have recourse to circumcision too, but it is not performed by them until the child is old enough to make his own profession of faith: "There is no God but God, and Mohammed is the Apostle of God." It was practised by the Arabs ages before the time of Mohammed, having been introduced by the Ishmaelites,

the descendants of the son of Hagar, from whom the Arab al Mostéreba, or naturalized Arabs (in contradistinction to the Arab al Ariba, or pure Arabs), trace their origin. From the Jews, likewise, the Egyptians, Colchians, Phœnicians, and Ethiopians derived the custom, but, as is the case among the Mohammedans to-day, these ancient peoples performed it merely from motives of cleanliness, to promote health, and secure immunity from certain painful diseases to which males in hot climates are subject. It is only among the Jews that circumcision is regarded as a religious rite. Its meaning is explained in Genesis xvii.

359. **The Feast of the Epiphany** (January 6th), so called from the Greek *Epiphaneia*, a showing or appearance, commemorates Christ's manifestation to the Gentiles, represented by the three kings, or Magi, named Gaspar, Melchior, and Balthazar, who, guided by a miraculous star, came to adore Him. It may be mentioned here that the bodies of the Magi repose in Cologne Cathedral, whither they were removed from Milan in 1162, when Frederick Barbarossa laid waste that city.

360. An odd religious observance took place in olden times on January 14th, known as the **Feast of the Ass.** A beautiful girl, seated on an ass with gay trappings, and holding an infant child at her breast, was led through the town to the church, and there placed at the Gospel side of the altar while Mass was being said. This was in commemoration of the Flight into Egypt.

361. In connection with the **Feast of St. Anthony** (January 17th), there is a curious blessing of beasts of all kinds at the church dedicated to that saint at Rome, and possibly elsewhere. Everyone, from the Pope himself to the

peasant, who possesses a horse, mule, ass, or dog, sends it with a small donation to St. Anthony's Church, to be there sprinkled with holy water, and so placed under the special protection of the saint. The life-long solicitude of St. Anthony for the lower animals is a sufficient explanation for the existence of this singular custom.

362. **The Festival of St. Peter's Chair** (January 18th) was instituted as an act of gratitude for the Primacy of St. Peter. Alban Butler, the author of the "Lives of the Saints," informs us that it is of considerable antiquity, being mentioned in a martyrology copied during the lifetime of St. Willibrod, viz., in the year 720. He adds: "Christians justly celebrate the founding of this Mother Church, the centre of Catholic Communion, in thanksgiving to God for His mercies, and to implore His future blessing." On this solemn festival, which is one of the few "functions," as they are called, celebrated in the magnificent church of St. Peter, the Pope is borne on the shoulders of twelve men in his *Sedia Gestatoria*, or Pontifical Chair of State, attired in vestments of gold, and wearing the tiara, or triple crown (*see* 24). On each side of His Holiness is carried a large fan of ostrich feathers, into which are set the eye-like portions of peacocks' feathers, symbolical of vigilance and universal supervision.

363. The ceremony of **Kissing the Pope's Foot** on the Feast of St. Peter has always been a fruitful theme for comment. But this kissing of the foot is an ancient Oriental rite, expressive of esteem and affection. At the present time it is no uncommon thing for a Mohammedan to wash and kiss the feet of a guest who has travelled a long distance to pay him honour. Instances are recorded of the Roman emperors having their feet kissed by their subjects as a mark of homage. The same act of humiliation is performed by

the Pope himself on Maundy Thursday (*see* 378). Did not the penitent Magdalen kiss the feet of our Lord? We read that Cornelius, the centurion, cast himself at the feet of Simon Peter in veneration of the Divine messenger. It would appear that this mode of paying homage to the successors of St. Peter existed from very early times, because it is related of St. Susanna, a virgin who suffered martyrdom in the year 294, that she kissed the feet of Pope Caius, "according to custom." The most powerful princes of the Christian world have paid homage to the Pope by kissing his feet. Yet this homage is not intended for the Pope himself. Since the time of Gregory the Great, so the Rubricists remind us, the Popes have been accustomed to wear the Cross on their sandals, so that the homage might be referred to Christ crucified.

364. On the **Feast of St. Agnes** (January 21st) two chosen lambs are blessed by the priest in the church of St. Peter ad Vincula, at Rome, which stands on the site of the martyrdom of St. Agnes. This has a two-fold significance. In the first place, it commemorates the lamb which appeared by the side of the saint when she manifested herself in a vision to the early Christians (*see* 256). Secondly, it was a custom among the Romans to invoke the blessing of sheep by Pales, the goddess of sheepfolds and pastures; and as the early Christians could not easily be weaned from this pagan observance, the blessing of a lamb on the altar as the symbol of purity and innocence, together with the reading of the Gospel of the Good Shepherd, was permitted in all churches throughout Christendom on St. Agnes' Day. In most cases this lamb, gaily decorated, was first led through the streets by a holiday-making populace. But at the church of St. Agnes, at Rome, two lambs are blessed for a very special purpose. Perhaps it will be

more correct to say that it is the fleeces of these lambs which receive the blessing, since it is from them that the material for the pallium of a Roman Catholic archbishop is provided. After Mass on St. Agnes' Day the sheep are carefully guarded until shearing time, when the wool is woven in old-fashioned style by the nuns of St. Lawrence. On the vigil of the Festival of SS. Peter and Paul, the newly-made pallia are carried on gilded trays to the Altar of the Confession in the magnificent church dedicated to St. Peter, and at the conclusion of the first vespers appointed for that day they are solemnly blessed by the Pope. All night long they are left lying upon the shrine, and on the following day are locked up in a silver coffer close to the relics of St. Peter, where they remain until required for the investiture of new archbishops. It is on account of their deposition on the tomb of the Prince of the Apostles that the pallia, when forwarded to their intended wearers, are said to come "from the body of St. Peter."

365. On **St. Paul's Day** (January 25th) in the olden time, a fat buck and doe were annually presented to the Dean and Chapter in St. Paul's Cathedral, in the presence of the Bishop of London, and a priest from each parish within his diocese. This singular custom had its origin in the obligation incurred by Sir Walter de Band, an Essex knight, in the year 1375, when he obtained permission to enclose twenty acres of the Dean's land, subject to the presentation by him to the clergy of the cathedral of a fat buck and doe every year on the Festival of the Conversion of St. Paul.

366. **The Feast of the Purification** (February 2nd) commemorates the Purification of the Virgin in the Temple on the fortieth day after childbirth, and the presentation of our Lord on the same occasion, in accordance with the

Jewish custom. It is called **Candlemas Day,** because on this day the Catholic Church blesses her candles for the whole year, and invites the congregation to attend Mass with lighted candles in their hands, in memory of the Divine light with which Christ illuminated the whole Church at this presentation, when holy Simeon took Him into his arms, saying: "Lord, now lettest Thou Thy servant depart in peace, according to Thy word; for mine eyes have seen Thy salvation which Thou hast prepared before the face of all people: a light to lighten the Gentiles, and the glory of Thy people Israel." With this meaning the festival was instituted by Pope Gelasius in the fifth century, under the following circumstances, as set forth by Pope Innocent XII. in the course of a sermon: "Why do we in this feast carry candles? Because the Gentiles dedicated the month of February to the infernal gods, and as at the beginning of it Pluto stole Proserpine, and her mother Ceres sought her in the night with lighted candles, so they, at the beginning of this month, walked about the city with lighted candles; because the holy fathers could not extirpate this custom they ordained that Christians should carry about candles in honour of the Blessed Virgin Mary, and thus, what was done before to the honour of Ceres, is now done to the honour of the Virgin." In olden times the people were accustomed to walk with lighted candles through the streets in procession to early Mass on this day. It is in honour of the Purification of the Virgin, too, that Catholic women hold a lighted candle in their hands at their "churching" after childbirth.

367. **The Feast of the Annunciation** (March 25th) was instituted in memory of the day upon which "the angel of the Lord appeared unto Mary" and announced that she was to become the mother of the Son of God. It

will be noticed that it occurs exactly nine months before Christmas Day. The secular term for this festival, **Lady Day,** is obviously a corruption of "Our Lady's Day" or Feast of our Lady.

368. **Shrove Tuesday** received its name from the shriving or confession enjoined upon all devout Catholics in pre-Reformation times as a fitting preparation for the penitential season of Lent (*see* 425).

369. The word **Lent** is an abbreviation of the Old English and Anglo-Saxon term for Spring. As everyone knows, the season of Lent commemorates the miraculous forty days' fast of our Saviour in the desert. Counted from Ash Wednesday to Holy Saturday inclusive, there are forty-six days, but since, with the exception that flesh meat and fish are not allowed at the same meal, the six Sundays do not count, the number of actual fast days is reduced to forty. In olden times the Lenten fast was observed in a very strict manner. Not only was flesh meat forbidden during the whole forty days, but even the things derived from flesh, such as milk, eggs, butter, cheese, and lard, were interdicted for the like period. Consequently they had to be used up on Shrove Tuesday, and were invariably made into pancakes (*see* 425). Fish was the common diet of the people at this season. The historian Froissart tells us that "there were daily delivered to the Germans in the army ten tons of herrings for Lent, and 800 carp, without counting different sorts of fish, which cost the king immense sums." There was, however, a reason for this. He adds: "The fast was encouraged for political purposes, to promote the fisheries and naval service, to the saving and increase of butcher's meat."

370. **Ash Wednesday** ushers in the penitential season of Lent. On this day, in the Roman Catholic Church, the ashes obtained by the burning of the palms used on the Palm Sunday previous, are blessed and distributed by the priest, who makes the sign of the Cross with them on the forehead of every member of the congregation, saying, "Remember, man, thou art but dust, and unto dust thou shalt return." This ceremony commemorates God's curse of Adam after the Fall, and its celebration at the commencement of Lent is appropriate, inasmuch as the Jews in ancient times were accustomed to cover their heads with ashes, and wear garments of sackcloth during a period of mourning and penance. In the Anglican Church, the reading of the curses directed against impenitent sinners takes the place of the distribution of ashes on this day.

371. Every Friday in Lent an impressive service, styled **The Way of the Cross,** takes place in the Roman Catholic churches. Around the walls of the church will be found fourteen pictures representing the progress of our Lord from the judgment hall of Pontius Pilate to Mount Calvary, His Death upon the Cross, and the deposition of His Sacred Body in the sepulchre. These are called "the Stations of the Cross." The priest, attended by the altar and choir-boys, and often followed by members of the congregation, passes from station to station, there to meditate upon a particular incident of Christ's Passion. This devotion originated in the pilgrimages which so many pious people of the olden time undertook to the Holy Land during Lent, in order to walk in the very footsteps of our Saviour, and to pray upon the very spot where He suffered. As it was impossible for every one to make these pilgrimages, the Church authorized the erection or representation of corresponding "Stations" in the churches, and granted to all who

visited them the same Indulgences as were claimed by the pilgrims who went to Jerusalem.

372. **Ember Days,** so called in allusion to the ancient mode of doing penance in sackcloth and ashes, are days set apart for special fasting and prayer in each of the four seasons of the year. They were instituted by Pope Calixtus in the third century, primarily to prepare the clergy for ordination, according to the manner set forth in Acts xiii. 3; and secondly, as a means of supplicating the Divine blessing upon the produce of the earth. The Council of Placentia of 1095 fixed the days uniformly as follows: the Wednesday, Thursday, and Saturday after the first Sunday in Lent, Whit Sunday, September 14th, and December 13th. The weeks in which these days occur are styled **Ember Weeks.**

373. **Passion Sunday,** or the Sunday before Palm Sunday, is so called because it is set apart in the Roman Catholic Church for a general commemoration of the Passion. From the eve of this day until Easter Sunday, all pictures and statues in the churches are covered over, so as to concentrate the attention of the congregation upon the Passion and Death of our Lord. The cloths employed for this purpose are purple, which is the mourning colour of the Church (*see* 379).

374. According to local tradition, the origin of **The Ober-Ammergau Passion Play** was as follows. When, in the year 1633, a deadly plague threatened to depopulate the districts of Partenkirchen, Eschelohe, and Kohlgrub, which are separated from Ammerthal, or the Valley of the Ammer, by a rampart of mountains, the Ammerthalers succeeded for a time in protecting themselves against the

dread contagion; but one day a native who had been working all the summer at Eschelohe, evaded the quarantine, and entered the Ammerthal by a secret path in order to celebrate an annual Church festival with his family. Two days afterwards he was a corpse, and in less than three weeks the plague had carried off eighty-four of the Ammerthalers. Despairing of all human succour, the terrified survivors addressed themselves to God, and registered a solemn vow that if He heard their prayer and removed the scourge, they would represent every ten years "for thankful remembrance and edifying contemplation, and by the help of the Almighty, the sufferings of Jesus, the Saviour of the world." Presumably their prayer was heard, for we are told that "not a single person died of the plague after the vow was made, though many were infected by it." The first representation of the Passion Play, in fulfilment of the vow of these simple villagers took place at Ober-Ammergau in the following year, and it has been repeated every ten years without a single omission.

375. **Palm Sunday** owes its name to the distribution of palms to the congregations in the Roman Catholic churches to commemorate the triumphal entry of our Lord into Jerusalem seated on an ass, while the populace strewed palm branches in His path, crying, "Hosanna to the Son of David!" In olden times, the better to impress this incident upon the minds of the people, a wooden figure of an ass mounted upon wheels, and with an effigy of the Saviour upon it, was drawn through the church, and as the priests walked in front chanting the service, the congregation threw their palm twigs down before it.

376. The commemoration services of **The Passion** commence on Wednesday in Holy Week, because it was on this

day that the Jews at their great council resolved to take the life of our Lord by charging Him with sundry crimes before Pontius Pilate, the Roman governor. This is the reason also why Lent begins on a Wednesday, and why Wednesday as well as Friday is observed as a fast day during Lent and Advent. In olden times Wednesday, like Friday, was a fast day throughout the year.

377. On Wednesday, Thursday, and Friday evenings in Holy Week, a solemn and impressive service is chanted in the Roman Catholic churches. This is called the **Tenebræ**, literally, darkness. On a triangular candlestick, placed at the Epistle side of the high altar, are fifteen candles, seven yellow ones on each side, and a white one on the top. These correspond to the number of psalms recited. As each psalm is concluded one of the yellow candles is extinguished, until the white one alone remains. At the same time, while the *Benedictus* or Canticle of Zachary is sung, the lights on the altar and in the body of the church are also extinguished. Then the white candle is taken down and concealed behind the altar, and a loud rapping on their prayer-books on the part of the congregation takes place. Eventually, after the recital of the fifteenth psalm, the white candle is restored. The extinction of the yellow candles represents the death of the prophets who lived and died before the time of our Lord; and the concealment and reappearance of the white candle His own death, burial, and resurrection. The rapping on the prayer-books is in allusion to the splitting of the rocks and the opening of the tombs at the Crucifixion.

378. **Maundy Thursday** is so called from the *Mandate*, or washing of the feet appointed for the day in imitation of our Lord before the Last Supper. This act of humiliation

is still performed by the Pope, bishops, and superiors of religious houses, as it was also in former times by Christian sovereigns and princes throughout the world (*see* 429). The predecessors of Leo XIII. invariably washed the feet of thirteen bishops, representing the twelve apostles, and the angel who appeared to Gregory the Great while he was performing a special act of charity on behalf of some poor people. After the washing and drying His Holiness reverently kissed the right foot of each bishop, and then waited upon them with his own hands at the supper-table. Instead of the feet of thirteen bishops, the present Pope washes those of twelve poor men, literally beggars. The apron that he wears over his soutane during this ceremony is regarded as a great treasure, and is afterwards made by the Benedictine nuns into palls to cover the chalices for all the convents of their Order. The washing, and kissing of the right foot concluded, His Holiness serves the supper to these twelve beggars in a room adjoining his study. The discovery of a bank-note for a hundred francs under the table-napkin of each doubtless adds a pleasurable zest to his appetite.

379. **Good Friday** is a very solemn day in all the churches of the Roman Catholic Communion. It was anciently styled **Long Friday** on account of the length of the service. The high altar is stripped of all its decorations, and the Eucharist is removed to a side altar, or "Sepulchre," so that visitations to the latter will not interfere with the due observance of the Passion at the chief altar of the church, which the rubrics require to be left without any ornament whatsoever. For the ordinary wax candles and torches, ghastly-looking yellow ones are substituted. At Rome, the nakedness of the Papal throne, and the seats of the cardinals indicate the utter desolation of the Church consequent on

the death of the Saviour. On this occasion only the cardinals appear in robes of purple, which is their mourning colour (*see* 206). Neither they nor the bishops wear their rings. Even the Pope lays his signet aside for the day. The Papal mace and the arms of the Papal guards are carried reversed (*see* 205). All over the city, from Maundy Thursday until after the *Gloria* at Mass on Holy Saturday morning, the bells are silenced. Even in hotels and private houses, what is called a *troccota*, or pair of small wooden clappers, takes the place of the usual handbell rung at meals for the time being.

380. **Holy Saturday** owes its name primarily to the commemoration of the burial of our Lord, and, secondly, to the various holy offices which are performed by the Roman Catholic clergy on this day against the solemn festival of Easter. It has always been the custom of the Church to bless those things which the people make use of in ordinary life; hence fire and water are annually blessed on Holy Saturday. All lights and fires being first put out, a new fire is struck from a flint, and blessed. "This new fire," says St. John Chrysostom, "represents Christ rising to kindle in our hearts a new spiritual fire of His love; the old profane fire of our earthly profane passions being first extinguished in us by His victory over sin. It likewise serves symbolically to put us in mind of our obligation of walking in the newness of a spiritual heavenly life, being now risen with Christ by His grace." The blessing of the baptismal font, the water used for sprinkling, and the Paschal candle are also peculiar to this day (*see* 381).

381. **Easter**, commemorative of the Resurrection of our Lord, is one of the greatest festivals of the year. The term itself has no Christian significance, being derived

from *Eoster*, the goddess of light, or Spring, in whose honour the pagan Saxons celebrated an annual festival at this season (*see* 432). On Easter Sunday the churches are gaily decorated, and the organ, which has been silent during Lent, once more breaks out into solemn harmony. The **Paschal Candle**, on the Gospel side of the high altar is particularly noticeable. This great candle was in ancient times employed to give light during the watchings of the congregants in the church on Easter Eve. From Easter until the end of Paschal-time, or Pentecost, it is always lighted during Mass and Vespers, as an illustrious emblem of Christ, the Light of the World, having risen from the dead. The five grains of frankincense stuck into it symbolically represent His five precious wounds, and the sweet spices brought by the devout women to the sepulchre. It may be mentioned here that the term **Pasch** comes from the French *pasque*, the Latin *paschalis*, the Greek *pascha*, and the Hebrew *Pesach*, or Passover, which festival occurs about the same time as our Easter (*see* 397). As determined by Gregory the Great, the reformer of the Christian Calendar, Easter must be the Sunday which follows the fourteenth day of the Paschal moon; if that fourteenth day be a Sunday, then Easter must be the Sunday following. It is by Easter that all the other movable feasts of the year are determined.

382. As symbols of the Resurrection, **White Lilies** enter largely into the Eastertide decoration of the churches. This is in accordance with a Judæan legend that after the Saviour rose from the tomb, the places whereon He trod were marked by white lilies which sprang up and blossomed in His footsteps.

383. **The Spital Sermon** annually preached at Christ Church, Newgate Street, on Easter Tuesday, in the presence

of the Lord Mayor, the Sheriffs, the Governors of Christ's Hospital, and the Blue-coat boys, is a relic of an ancient custom, pursuant to which the Bishop of London preached a sermon at St. Paul's Cross on Good Friday on the subject of Christ's Passion, and three other divines upheld the doctrine of the Resurrection during Eastertide at the pulpit-cross of the Spital, otherwise the churchyard of St. Mary of the Spittle (now Spitalfields), where the "Blues" had a gallery erected for them. The Spital sermons were afterwards preached at St. Bride's Church, Fleet Street, and then, having been reduced to two, were continued at Christ Church, where only one sermon is now preached. Previous to attending the church the Blue-coat boys generally wait upon the Lord Mayor at the Mansion House to receive certain gratuities.

384. What are called **Rogation Days,** from the Latin *rogare*, to beseech, occur on the three days preceding Ascension Day. These are days of special supplication for pardon of sins, peace, blessings on the fruits of the earth, and protection from the power of the arch enemy of mankind. On these days, in ancient times, the clergy, accompanied by the churchwardens, the school-boys, and a goodly number of the congregation made a perambulation of the parish boundaries, where, at certain prescribed places, prayers were offered up for the good of the harvest and the confusion of the devil. If the parish boasted of a fine oak-tree, the Gospel of the day—or rather of the preceding Sunday, called **Rogation Sunday,** because the Gospel appointed for it teaches us how to ask of God in order that we may receive—was read, and a short sermon was preached under it. On this account the tree received the name of a **Gospel Oak.** At certain other places near the parochial boundaries the school-boys received a whipping, with the

object of fixing them firmly in their minds (*see* 428). In all cases a representation of the Evil One, in the form of a dragon, was carried at the head of the procession, side by side with the image of the patron saint of the parish, and at times also of our Saviour. As often, however, as a pause was made for prayer the dragon was taken to a place quite out of ear-shot, and left there until the procession moved on again. This explains why so many parishes have their dragon localities, such as the "Dragon's Rock," the "Dragon's Well," etc., denoting the places where the dragon was left at prayer-time, or, as may have happened in some cases, where it was kicked, stoned, buffeted, and even pulled to pieces by the processionists at the close of the third day's rogation.

385. **The Feast of the Ascension** is celebrated on the fortieth day after Easter Sunday, in memory of the Ascension of our Lord into Heaven from the summit of Mount Olivet, in the presence of His Mother, and His Apostles, and disciples. Originally the Paschal candle was removed after High Mass on Ascension Day, but it is now allowed to remain in its accustomed place until Whitsuntide (*see* 386).

386. **The Feast of Pentecost**, signifying "the fiftieth day," is synonymous with *Shovuos*, the second great festival of the Jewish ecclesiastical year, in commemoration of the giving of the Law to Moses on Mount Sinai fifty days after the deliverance of the Israelites out of Egypt. By Christians, Pentecost is kept as a great festival in honour of the descent of the Holy Ghost upon the Apostles in the form of fiery tongues. In olden times, the better to impress this incident upon the minds of the people, a dove was let down from the roof of the church in the course of the Mass on this day. Another name for this festival is **Whitsuntide**, so called

because the catechumens who had received the rite of Baptism on the previous day were clothed in white while attending Mass during Pentecost. Hence Whit Sunday is really a corruption of "White Sunday."

387. The annual **Flower Sermon** preached at the church of St. Katherine Cree, Leadenhall Street, on Whit Tuesday evening, was instituted by the Rev. Dr. W. M. Whittemore, the rector, because, as he himself states, he "thought it would be a good opportunity of leading our youthful hearers to a closer contemplation of God's wisdom and love as manifested by the beautiful and fragrant flowers which He scatters around us in such rich profusion." The first flower sermon was preached in the year 1853, and the subject has always been a floral one. On this occasion a beautiful offering of flowers adorns the pulpit, and every member of the congregation is armed with a bouquet. The flowers are afterwards presented to various orphanages.

388. **The Feast of the Holy Trinity**, which occurs on the first Sunday after Whitsuntide, was instituted in honour of the Three Persons in One Godhead by Pope Gregory IV., in the year 828. It is believed to have been introduced into England by St. Thomas à Becket towards the end of the twelfth century.

389. **The Feast of Corpus Christi**, in honour of the Body and Blood of Christ, which, as all Roman Catholics believe, are ever present in the Sacrament of the Holy Eucharist as instituted by our Lord Himself at the Last Supper, is celebrated on the first Thursday after Trinity Sunday in order to reanimate the devotion of the faithful towards that adorable mystery. As such a high festival could not well have been observed during Holy Week, it

was most fittingly transferred to the Thursday within the octave of Trinity Sunday. Corpus Christi Day is a great day of religious processions in Catholic countries, as it was also in England in pre-Reformation times. On the eve of this festival the choristers of Durham Cathedral ascend the tower in their surplices and sing the *Te Deum.* This is to commemorate the miraculous preservation of the tower on Corpus Christi Eve, A. D. 1429, when it was struck by lightning and set on fire; for though the flames raged all night and till the middle of the next day, the tower and its bells remained uninjured. The extinction of the flames was by everyone imputed to the special intervention of St. Cuthbert, whose relics are enshrined in the Cathedral.

390. **Harvest Festivals** are, so far as the Anglican Church is concerned, a latter-day institution. This is strange, seeing that in pre-Reformation times **Lammas Day,** so called from the Anglo-Saxon *hlaf,* a loaf, and *mæsse,* a feast, and which fell on August 1st, was marked by the presentation of a loaf made of new wheat in the churches by every member of the congregation. Previous to the reformation of the Calendar in 1752, Lammas-tide ushered in the second quarter of the year. Since then the term has fallen into total disuse. Different peoples have different seasons for harvest thanksgiving. When the Jews inhabited Palestine the festival of Pentecost embraced a thanksgiving for a bountiful harvest; but as the wheat is not gathered in Northern Europe at the time of Pentecost, flowers take the place of the first-fruits in the synagogues. The Druids had their harvest festival on November 1st; the Chinese and Japanese have theirs at the year's close; while in America November 24th is everywhere observed as **Thanksgiving Day** for the blessings of the year in general and the bounties of the harvest in particular. This "Thanksgiving

Day" is a legacy of the Puritans, who abolished Christmas out of their hatred of the prelacy.

391. **The Feast of the Holy Rosary** (October 1st) was instituted by Pope Pius IV., in thanksgiving for the Christian victory over the Turks at Lepanto, which was believed to have been due to the special intercession of the Virgin in response to the prayers of the Rosarians to this end. The original title of the annual commemoration was "The Feast of St. Mary of Victory," but Pope Gregory XIII. afterwards changed it to "The Feast of the Holy Rosary." It was St. Dominic who established the devotion of the Rosary, out of his intense veneration for the Blessed Virgin. Chaplets of beads for counting prayers and pious ejaculations had been in use centuries before his time among the Benedictines and the followers of Mohammed, both of whom derived them from the Egyptian anchorites. St. Dominic was responsible only for the arrangement of the chaplet in its present form, and the meditations upon the life of our Saviour in association with His Blessed Mother as set forth in the prayer-books. This devotion became so popular among the poorer classes, particularly women, that it is said he made more converts by its means than by all his preaching. The term **Rosary** had its origin in the rose—a flower specially dedicated to the Virgin—with which each individual bead was anciently impressed.

392. On October 16th every year what is known as **The Lion Sermon** is preached at the church of St. Katherine Cree, Leadenhall Street. This is in commemoration of the miraculous deliverance of Sir John Gayer, an opulent City merchant, and erstwhile Lord Mayor, from the jaws of a lion in an Arabian desert, two centuries and a half ago. By some means this good knight missed his caravan,

and while in search of it, a huge lion stalked up to him. Perfectly defenceless, he gave himself up for lost, and on bended knee offered up his soul in prayer to God. To his intense astonishment, the huge animal "eyed him, and gently walked away." Shortly afterwards Sir John rejoined his caravan none the worse for his extraordinary adventure; yet so fully impressed was he with the peril he had passed through, and the Divine interposition on his behalf, that he resolved to make an adequate provision for an annual thanksgiving sermon at the church of his "beloved Aldgate," in which his mortal remains now rest. He also founded some almshouses at Plymouth, his native place. The foregoing particulars may be gleaned from the brass tablet which has been placed within the last year or two in the chancel of St. Katherine Cree church.

393. **The Feast of All Saints** (November 1st) was instituted by Pope Boniface in the seventh century, to commemorate the conversion of the Roman Pantheon into a Christian church, and its dedication to the Virgin and all the martyrs. This festival was for many years kept on May 1st, but after the institution of "All Souls' Day" (November 2nd), it was transferred to the day preceding that solemn commemoration. The alternative designation for "All Saints' Day," is **All Hallows' Day,** conformably to the Anglo-Saxon *haligan*, holy. On this day Anglicans, as well as Roman Catholics, honour all the saints, and especially those who have no fixed days appointed to them throughout the year.

394. **All Souls' Day** (November 2nd) is a day set apart by the Roman Catholic Church for the remembrance of all the faithful departed, and the offering up of special prayers for the release of the suffering souls in purgatory. This

solemn commemoration was instituted by St. Odo, Abbot of Cluny, in consequence of what was told him by a pilgrim returning from the Holy Land. The pilgrim having been compelled in the course of his voyage to land on a rocky island, whose sole inhabitant was a hermit, was assured by the latter that there existed among the cliffs an opening into the infernal regions, whence huge flames ascended, and the groans of the suffering souls could be distinctly heard. Moved by compassion for these poor souls, St. Odo appointed the day following, which was November 2nd, for a special Mass and commemorative service for the dead, a pious observance which was repeated on each anniversary as long as he lived. It is worthy of note in this connection, that the Chinese have in their seventh month what is called a "Feast of All Souls," upon which they offer up prayers for the deceased relatives; while the anniversaries of the dead were observed with peculiar solemnity by the Greeks, Romans, and Druids. The visitation by all classes in Paris of the beautiful cemetery of Père la Chaise on All Saints' Day is a trait which goes far towards redeeming the frivolities of the gay Parisians.

395. **The Festival of the Nativity**, or **Christmas**, literally the Feast of Christ, was not always celebrated on December 25th; but as soon as the Feast of the Annunciation was instituted it became fixed, as we now have it (*see* 367). It is customary for every Roman Catholic priest to say three Masses on this day, in honour of the three births of our Lord, viz.: His *eternal* birth in the bosom of the Father; His *temporal* birth in the stable at Bethlehem; and His *spiritual* birth in the hearts of the just. The **Crib** in the churches was first introduced by the Franciscan Friars in the thirteenth century (*see* 242).

JEWISH FASTS AND FESTIVALS

JEWISH FASTS AND FESTIVALS

396. There is much to admire in the Jewish people. Admittedly wanderers on the face of the globe, they have preserved their national characteristics, their ancient festivals, rites, and ceremonies, in spite of persecutions and the onward march of Time. Though forming only a comparatively insignificant population in the Christian countries which they inhabit, they are unswerving in the observance of the Sabbath on their own particular day of the week; and notwithstanding their natural addiction for money-getting, cheerfully lay their occupations aside whenever the Mosaic Law requires them to do so. Even devout Roman Catholics resident in a Protestant country consider their duty sufficiently discharged by hearing Mass on what is called a Day of Obligation, and then quietly pursue their ordinary business. The reason of this religious unanimity of the Jews lies in the fact that they are a distinct race or nation, and not merely the scattered members of a particular creed. We find much the same thing, though in a lesser degree, among the Scotsmen, who, no matter in what remote part of the world they may be, make high holiday on New Year's Day, and pay due honour to their patron saint on the Festival of St. Andrew. The festivals of the Jewish ecclesiastical year were instituted by Moses during the forty years' sojourning in the desert, in order to keep alive the sentiment of their common nationality among the Israelites wherever the Tabernacle of the Lord should be

set up. Thus, when the Jews resided in the Holy Land, it was incumbent upon all males to go up to Jerusalem three times every year, there to make their offerings in the Temple on the Feasts of the Passover, of Pentecost, and of Tabernacles respectively.

397. The first festival of the Jewish ecclesiastical year is also one of the most important. This, the **Festival of the Passover,** occurs in the first month (*Nisan*) corresponding to portions of March and April of the Christian year. In Biblical times all males were bound to go up to Jerusalem to keep the Passover and make their offerings to God in the Temple. The Paschal lamb was slain on the fourteenth day of *Nisan*, in commemoration of the lamb which God commanded the Israelites to slay when about to deliver them out of the land of bondage, and whose blood they sprinkled on the doorposts of their houses, to protect them from the Destroying Angel. The open selection of a lamb for sacrifice by the Israelites had a meaning all its own. As the lamb was a sacred animal in the eyes of the Egyptians, it indicated that they (the Israelites) *dared* to do that which during the whole 210 years of their captivity had been impossible; in other words, that their deliverance was at hand. Since the destruction of the Temple, sacrifice among the Jews has been abolished; but various symbolical observances there are which serve to commemorate the great event. Commencing on the fourteenth day of *Nisan*, the Festival of *Pesach*, or Passover, lasts eight days. During the whole of this period the Jews are forbidden to eat anything leaven, or even to have anything leaven in their houses. Hence Passover is also known as **The Feast of Unleavened Bread.** To ensure the removal of every kind of fermented food, such as bread, beer, etc., the master of the house is in duty bound to make a strict search through-

out the house on the eve of the fourteenth of *Nisan.* This is therefore called **The Eve of Searching for Leaven.** What is known to Christians as **Passover Bread** constitutes the Jewish staff of life during *Pesach.* This is because on the night of the departure of the Israelites out of the land of bondage, the anxiety of the Egyptians to send them away was so great that they had not time to bake their bread. Their kneading troughs being already bound up with their clothes upon their shoulders, they were obliged to remove their dough before it was leavened, and out of this dough they afterwards baked unleavened bread; for as we read, "it was not leavened." The eve of the Passover (that is to say, the fourteenth day of *Nisan*, for the Passover proper does not commence until the evening of the fourteenth) bears the name also of **The Fast of the First-born,** because it is the duty of the first-born male, above the age of thirteen, of every Jewish family to fast on this day, in commemoration of the deliverance of the first-born of the Israelites from the Destroying Angel. The first two and the last two days of the festival are kept by all Jews as strictly as the Sabbath; but on the four intervening days urgent business may be attended to. On the first two evenings of the festival the household table must be set out with (1), a dish containing part of the shank-bone of a lamb roasted, symbolical of the Paschal offering; (2), a dish containing a roasted egg, the symbol of the generation of the human race, the usual festival sacrifice; (3), a dish containing a mixture of chopped apples, almonds, etc., in allusion to the mortar used by the Israelites in Egypt; (4), a cup of vinegar or salt water, and the green tops of the horse-radish, which, like the chopped apples, etc., are to remind the present generation of the bitter oppression suffered by their forefathers in the land of bondage (*see* 141). The members of the household having then taken their places, the head of the family recites the "Sanctification of the Festival," followed by the history of the deliverance out of Egypt. The evening meal is next partaken, and the service concludes with a solemn chant of hymns in praise and glorification of God. On the eve of the second evening of *Pesach*, the **Counting of the Omer** commences, and is continued for forty-nine days (*see* 399). This is in remembrance of the offering of an omer (a Hebrew measure equal to half a gallon) of the newly-reaped barley, as commanded in the Bible, in the Temple, when the Israelites dwelt in Palestine. The seventh day of the festival is marked by the recital of that portion of Exodus which describes the passage over the Red Sea by the Israelites, in commemoration of that event, which took place on the seventh day of the Passover. The song chanted by Moses and the children of Israel on that occasion is likewise read.

398. The second month (*Iyar*) of the Jewish ecclesiastical year contains three minor fast days, viz., the first Monday, the first Thursday, and the second Monday. The object of these fasts is to atone for sins unknowingly committed, or for the neglect of any of the religious exercises enjoined upon all Jews during the Festival of *Pesach* or Passover. The fourteenth day of *Iyar* was, during the Biblical era, observed as **The Second Passover** by such as were unable to keep the festival in its proper season owing to sickness or unavoidable absence on a journey. The eighteenth day of *Iyar*, corresponding with the thirty-third day of the omer (*see* 397), is a minor festival kept by school children, and generally described as **The Scholars' Feast.** This commemorates the sudden cessation of a plague on the thirty-third day of the omer, which, in addition to a large proportion of the general inhabitants

of Palestine, carried off many thousands of the Rabbi's pupils.

399. The second of the three great festivals of the Jewish ecclesiastical year occurs on the sixth and seventh days of the third month (*Sivan*), which includes parts of May and June. It is called in Hebrew *Shovuos*, but more generally **The Feast of Pentecost,** from the Greek *pentekoste*, the fiftieth day; since it commemorates the giving of the Law to Moses on Mount Sinai fifty days after the deliverance of the Israelites out of Egypt. It was on the sixth day of *Sivan* that God spoke the Decalogue from the top of Mount Sinai, consequently one of the names for this festival is **The Time of Giving the Law.** It is called also **The Feast of Weeks,** because it marks the completion of seven weeks, counted from the second day of *Pesach* or Passover. On that day the Jews of Palestine presented their omer of newly-reaped barley in the Temple, and counted forty-nine days from it; until on the fifteenth day they celebrated the Feast of Pentecost. This counting of the omer is still observed by the modern Jews (*see* 397). Two other names for this great festival are **The Day of First Ripe Fruits,** because the first ears of ripe wheat were offered in the Temple at Jerusalem; and **The Harvest Festival,** or the period of the wheat harvest in the East. As, among the Western nations, the Festival of Pentecost does not occur during the wheat harvest, but when the flowers are in full bloom, the scattered races of the Jewish people decorate their synagogues with flowers and shrubs, grateful to the eye and fragrant with many perfumes. Strict Jews consider themselves in duty bound to stay up during the first night of the festival to read portions of the Law and excerpta from the prophets. The three days preceding *Shovuos*, or Pentecost, are styled **The Three Days of Setting**

Bounds, in allusion to the Divine command to Moses to set bounds round Mount Sinai before the giving of the Ten Commandments.

400. The seventeenth day of the fourth month (*Tammuz*) of the Jewish ecclesiastical year is **The Black Fast,** or **Fast of Tammuz.** From sunrise until nightfall on this day no food may be taken, on account of the grievous calamities which befell the Jewish nation on the seventeenth of *Tammuz*. After withstanding a siege of two years' duration, the walls of Jerusalem gave way before the attacks of Nebuchadnezzar, King of Babylon; the Jewish king was taken prisoner, and after witnessing the slaughter of his two sons, both his eyes were put out. Many years later, again on the seventeenth of *Tammuz*, the city of Jerusalem fell into the hands of the Emperor Titus, at the head of a Roman army, and a wholesale massacre of its inhabitants took place. Moreover, it was on this day that Moses descended from Mount Sinai, and seeing the Israelites worshipping the golden calf, he, in his anger, broke the two Tables of the Law at the foot of the Mount. In punishment for their idolatry Moses, in the name of God, commanded the sons of Levi to pass through the camp, sword in hand, and slay all the wrongdoers, sparing neither friend nor brother. The number who fell on that day, we read, was about 3,000. Truly such a mournful day is fittingly commemorated by a strict fast. For the Jews find comfort in the words of the prophet Zechariah (viii. 19), that their days of sorrow shall be turned to gladness: "Thus saith the Lord of hosts; The fast of the fourth month, and the fast of the fifth, and the fast of the seventh, and the fast of the tenth, shall be to the house of Judah joy and gladness, and cheerful feasts."

401. The fifth month (*Av*) of the ecclesiastical year con-

tains the most mournful day in the Hebrew calendar. On the ninth day of *Av* the destruction of Jerusalem, commenced respectively by Nebuchadnezzar and Titus, on the seventeenth of *Tammuz* was completed. By the former victorious monarch the kingdom of Judah was carried into its ever-memorable Babylonian captivity; by the latter its dispersion over the face of the earth was accomplished. In commemoration of these events the descendants of the Israelites observe the day with fasting and sorrow. The fast called **The Fast of Av** is of longer duration than that which occurs in *Tammuz*, viz., from sunset on the eighth until nightfall on the ninth day. The synagogues present a scene of desolation. All the usual ornaments are removed, the Ark is stripped of its curtain, the light of day is excluded, and in its place two or three candles emit a feeble light. Instead of in their allotted places, the worshippers are seated on the ground, and the service is chanted in a low and mournful key. In addition to the Book of Lamentations, special dirges, descriptive of the sufferings of their ancestors, and the woe and destruction that fell upon the city are recited. The fifteenth day of *Av* is observed as a minor festival in remembrance of the reconciliation of the Israelites and the Benjamites, which took place on this day, after two sanguinary battles had been fought between them. The circumstances which occasioned their warfare are related in Judges xix. and xx.

402. The sixth month (*Alul*) is the only one out of the twelve that contains neither fast nor feast. Nevertheless, it is regarded as a month of preparation for the New Year and other important days which follow closely upon it. On all the days except the Sabbath the ram's horn is sounded in the synagogues to give warning; and during the fourth week, which immediately precedes the

New Year, special propitiatory prayers are offered up (*see* 403).

403. The seventh month (*Tishri*) of the Jewish ecclesiastical year is the first month of the civil year. As two great festivals in addition to the solemn Day of Atonement occur therein, this is considered by far the most important month of the whole twelve. The first and second days of *Tishri* constitute the **Festival of the New Year**; or, as it is properly expressed in the Hebrew tongue, **The Head of the Year.** It has also three other names: **The Day of Memorial,** because the Jews believe that all their sins committed during the past year are on these days remembered by God; **The Day of Judgment,** for the sins of His people being remembered by God, they are naturally reviewed and subjected to His judgment on these days; and **The Day of Sounding the Horn,** on account of the ram's horn being sounded several times during the service in the synagogues as a solemn warning that the Day of Atonement is drawing near. The use of the ram's horn at this season is appropriate, since, according to tradition, it was on the first day of *Tishri* that a ram was offered up instead of Isaac on Mount Moriah. The first ten days of *Tishri* are called **The Ten Days of Penitence,** and also **The Days of Awe**; they are spent by all good Jews in serious meditation and solemn preparation for the sacred Day of Atonement. The third day of *Tishri* is a fast day, called **The Fast of Gedaliah.** This is in memory of the good Gedaliah, the son of Ahikam, governor of the humbler classes left by Nebuchadnezzar to cultivate the soil and tend the vineyards after the major portion of the inhabitants of Judah were carried into captivity to Babylon. His rule in the Holy Land only extended over seven months, for he was treacherously murdered by Ishmael, son of Nethaniah,

of the royal seed, who coveted the supreme power in Palestine. The Sabbath between the New Year and the Day of Atonement is styled **The Sabbath of Repentance.** The dread **Day of Atonement** is at once the most solemn day of the whole Jewish year; it is the Sabbath of Sabbaths. From sunset on the ninth of *Tishri* until nightfall on the tenth a strict fast is enjoined upon all Jews without exception. In contradistinction to the Black Fast of *Tammuz*, and on account of the purity of heart with which it should be embraced, it generally bears the name of **The White Fast.** Its conclusion is announced by the sounding of the *Shofor*, or ram's horn, on the termination of the sacred days' observances in the synagogues, where all the congregants are expected to assemble from sunrise until nightfall on this dread day. The third and last of the important festivals commanded in the Bible—**The Feast of Tabernacles,** or, in Hebrew, *Succous*—commences on the fifteenth of *Tishri*, and continues for nine days. This is kept in commemoration of the Israelites who dwelt in portable booths or tabernacles (*taberna*, a hut), formed of branches of trees and covered with leaves, during their forty years' wandering in search of the promised land. Even at the present day strict Jews build for themselves temporary tabernacles roofed with leaves, and though they may not entirely dwell, they at least take their meals in them during the festival. In accordance with the Biblical command they also take branches of the palm, the myrtle, of the willow of the brook, together with the fruit of the citron, and rejoice with them before the Lord. These various branches are tastefully bound together, and with them and the citron in their hands they recite the hymn of praise, and afterwards walk round the synagogue in procession chanting the hosanna. The ceremony in the synagogues on the seventh day of the festival is very impressive. This particular day is styled

The Great Hosanna, from the prayers uniformly recited throughout the whole Jewish world. The seven scrolls of the Law are taken out, and the palm-bearing worshippers walk seven times round the synagogue chanting the hosannas. Then, towards the conclusion of the service, the leaves are beaten off the willow branches in remembrance of the ceremonial in the Temple, when the Jews with joyful song strewed the altar with the willow twigs which they had used during the festival. The eighth day of *Succous* is styled **The Eighth Day of Solemn Assembly**, special prayers being offered in the synagogues supplicating God to send both wind and rain in due season. The ninth and concluding day of the festival is called the **The Rejoicing of the Law.** On each Sabbath throughout the year a portion of the Law is read in the synagogues, but on this particular day the last portion of Deuteronomy, narrating the death and burial of Moses, is read, and at once a return is made to the creation in Genesis.

404. The eighth month (*Cheshvan* or *Marcheshvan*) of the Jewish ecclesiastical year, corresponding to portions of October and November of the Christian year, contains three minor fasts similar to those which occur in *Iyar*, and for a similar intention, viz., to make amends for any sins committed or religious duties neglected in the course of the preceding festival (*see* 398).

405. **The Festival of Chanukah**, or Dedication, commences on the twenty-fifth day of the ninth month (*Kislive*) of the Jewish ecclesiastical year, and continues for eight days. This is in solemn commemoration of and thanksgiving for the purification of the Temple on this day by Judas Maccabæus, after it had been polluted by Antiochus Epiphanes, King of Syria, about the year B.C. 170.

The Scripture relates that when the perpetual lamp was about to be relit, it was discovered that but one flask of holy oil, sufficient for that day, only remained, but by a miracle wrought by God, the oil lasted for eight days, by which time a further supply was forthcoming. In memory of this miracle at the re-dedication of the Temple, the modern descendants of the people of Jerusalem employ in their synagogues and houses on the first night of the festival one light, on the second two lights, on the third three, and so on until the end of the festival.

406. The tenth day of the tenth month (*Tivise*) of the Jewish ecclesiastical year is observed as a fast, in sorrowful remembrance of the siege of Jerusalem, commenced by King Nebuchadnezzar on this day. This is one of the fasts referred to by the prophet Zechariah (*see* 400).

407. On the fifteenth day of the eleventh month (*Sh'vat*) of the Jewish ecclesiastical year, corresponding to parts of our January and February, what is called **The New Year Festival for the Trees** occurs, because just about this time the sap begins to rise in the trees. In Palestine the rigours of the winter are now past, the weather is commencing to get warmer, the spring is at hand, and it behoves mankind to be grateful to God for having been spared through the winter months to enjoy the prospect of the approaching season of fruit and flowers. On the last Sabbath of this month, if it is an ordinary year, that portion of Exodus which relates to the children of Israel who were numbered being commanded to give "every man a ransom for his soul unto the Lord," to the amount of a half shekel, the same to be devoted to the service of the Tabernacle, is read. For this reason the Sabbath is called **The Day of the Section of the Shekels.** When the year is intercalary, this Sabbath

occurs on the first day of *Adar*, or the month following. The collection in all the synagogues which, in commemoration of the offering of the half shekel of the Israelites, is made for the poor, does not, however, take place until the first night of *Purim* (*see* 408).

408. The twelfth month (*Adar*) of the Jewish ecclesiastical year contains, on the thirteenth day, what is called **The Fast of Esther**, and on the fourteenth day, **The Festival of Purim.** The origin of both these observances is set forth in the Book of Esther. Briefly stated, when Ahasuerus, King of Persia, put away his wife Vashti, and took in her place Esther, a Jewish maiden who had been brought up by her cousin Mordecai, Haman, the king's minister, conceived such a deadly hatred against the Jewish population in Persia, consequent on the sudden advancement of Mordecai, and because he would not bow down to him, that he resolved to put all the Jews to death. Unfortunately, the king was very weak-minded, and granted his minister everything he asked of him. The latter, therefore, cast lots to determine in what month he should carry out his cruel design. The lot fell upon *Adar*, so on the thirteenth of that month Haman sent messengers into all parts of the kingdom to put the Jews of all ages to the sword, sparing none, not even children. In this extremity, Mordecai begged Queen Esther to intercede for her own people. Now, according to olden custom in Persia, any person whatsoever who ventured into the king's presence without a previous intimation of the king's desire to see him or her, was at once put to death, unless the king held out to him or her his golden sceptre as a token of his favour. Knowing this, the queen, nevertheless, undertook to endanger her own life for her people. But, first of all, she commanded all the Jews residing in Shushan, the Persian capital, to fast for three days. She fasted herself,

also, during this period. Then, attired in her royal robes, she approached the king, who immediately held out to her his golden sceptre, whereupon the queen pleaded her cause so earnestly and so eloquently that the king ordered Haman and his ten sons to be hanged, and gave all the Jews full liberty to defend themselves against their enemies. The slaughter of their enemies by the Jews of Shushan took place on the fourteenth day of *Adar*, which is known as **The Feast of Purim**, or of casting lots; and is regarded as a day of rejoicing for their miraculous deliverance. On the night and morning of this day, the *Megillah*, a parchment scroll upon which the Book of Esther is written, is read in the synagogues. The fifteenth day is also a day of rejoicing, of giving presents to one another, and alms to the poor. This is styled **The Purim of Shushan**, for the reason already stated. **The Fast of Esther**, therefore, on the eve of this festival, in remembrance of the three days' abstinence imposed on her people by the queen is a suitable preparation for the rejoicings which follow upon it. The Sabbath preceding *Purim* is called **The Sabbath of Remembrance**, because Haman, having been descended from the tribe of Amalek, that portion of Deuteronomy (xxv. 17-19), which begins, "Remember what Amalek did unto thee by the way, when ye were come forth out of Egypt," is read in the synagogues. The last Sabbath of *Adar*, which is the one just before the new moon of *Nisan*, bears the name of **The Sabbath of the Month**, *i.e.*, of the month *Nisan*. On this Sabbath the twelfth chapter of Exodus, which according to the Divine command fixes *Nisan* to be the beginning of months, or the first month of the year, is read in the synagogues.

SECULAR OBSERVANCES

SECULAR OBSERVANCES

409. **New Year's Day** is described by Lord Chesterfield as "a time when the kindest and warmest wishes are exchanged without the least meaning, and the most lying day in the whole year." Whatever amount of truth may underlie this cynical assertion, the universal interchange of good wishes on the threshold of another year can at least boast of a hoary antiquity. The ancient Romans spent the day in paying visits to wish one another "a happy New Year." The bestowing of **New Year's Gifts** was also a popular observance. As the magistrates entered upon their office on this day, they were accustomed to receive presents in token of congratulation. In course of time, however, such presents were not only regularly looked for, but even demanded as a right by those in high places. Each New Year's Day the emperor exacted a tribute from his subjects of a pound of gold as **Strena**—a term which, like the custom, was originally introduced by King Tatius, who received branches of vervain gathered in the sacred grove of Strenua, the goddess of strength, as a good omen, on the first day of the year, B.C. 747. Hence, in ancient times, New Year's gifts commonly bore the name of *Strenæ*. In all countries where the New Year is the principal festival in the Calendar, New Year's gifts are an institution. In China and Japan the people set out to pay visits and make presents to their friends with the dawn. Even the poorest in Scotland exchange sips of hot spiced ale, and make offerings of cakes,

buns, and shortbread to their neighbours when ushering in the New Year on the stroke of midnight. On New Year's Eve the children in France place their shoes in the fender before going to bed, fully expecting them to be filled with dainties by the morning. New Year's Day is in Paris a great day of gift-making for young and old. There was a time, too, when New Year's gifts were much more common in England than they are now, but that was when the year commenced on March 25th instead of January 1st. As ours was the last of the countries of Christendom to adopt the reformed Calendar, this perhaps accounts for our reluctance to put our hands in our pockets for our neighbours' behoof so soon after Christmas, which among ourselves has always been looked upon as the proper season for gift-making. When the year was reckoned from Lady Day, there was a sufficient interval to admit of presents being made at both seasons. The usual New Year's gifts in former times were gloves. Judges and other public officers frequently received presents of gloves on New Year's Day as a bribe. The characteristic letter of Sir Thomas More to a certain Mrs. Croaker in acknowledgment of a pair of gloves containing two angels has been quoted again and again. "It would be against good manners," wrote the honest Lord Chancellor, "to forsake a gentlewoman's New Year's gift, and I accept the gloves; their *lining* you will be pleased to bestow elsewhere." By the "lining" was meant the money in the palm, for which a snug little pocket was usually provided.

410. **The Wassail Bowl**, which in olden times was so greatly in request during the festive season, was identical with the Grace Cup of the Greeks and Romans, as mentioned by Plautus. It was known both to the Gauls and the ancient Britons. The pledging of Vortigern by Rowena, *Wass heil,*

"To your health!" cannot, therefore, be accepted as the origin of the drinking of healths (*see* 146).

411. On **New Year's Day** at Queen's College, Oxford, the bursar of the college presents each and all the members with a threaded needle, saying, "Take this, and use thrift." The meaning of this odd custom lies in the fact that the Latin words for needle and thread (*aiguille et fil*) form a sort of pun upon the name of Robert de Eglesfield, the founder of the college in the year 1340. It was called Queen's College in compliment to Queen Philippa, consort of Edward III., whose confessor he was.

412. **Twelfth Day** is so called on account of the number of days counted from Christmas Day. On this day formerly masques were always performed at Court, and in the great halls of the Inns of Court, to mark the termination of the Christmas festivities. It is styled **Old Christmas Day** because, previous to the re-arrangement of the Calendar in 1752, Christmas Day fell on what is now January 6th. This is why, in the Treasury accounts, where the Old Style still obtains, the Christmas dividends are not considered due until Twelfth Day; nor the Midsummer dividends until July 5th. Similarly, the financial year of the Chancellor of the Exchequer does not commence until April 5th, which, according to the Old Style, was Lady Day.

413. As the **Twelfth Cake** can be traced back to a period much older than Christianity, the vulgar opinion that it was instituted as a memorial of the offerings of the three kings to the infant Christ at Bethlehem on the Feast of the Epiphany is incorrect. During the last days of the Roman Saturnalia, the members of each household drew lots to determine who should be King of Saturnalia—a personage

corresponding to the Lord of Misrule in more modern times —and exercise temporary authority, by means of a bean inserted in a large plum cake. This was called an Election of King by Beans. In many cases a pea was also inserted for the Queen, and the characters of King and Queen were supposed to be maintained with mock majesty by those who drew the slices containing the bean and pea until midnight. The northern nations made no provision for a queen, but whosoever drew the bean was arrayed in fanciful robes and invested with the direction of the mummeries that wound up the Yule-tide merry-makings. When Mary, Queen of Scots, assisted at the cutting of the Twelfth Cake on Twelfth Day, 1563, at Holyrood Palace, her maid, Mary Fleming, had the good fortune to draw the bean, and forthwith that person was dressed in her royal mistress's robes for the remainder of the day. To such an importance did this social diversion formerly attain in France, that the expression, *Il a trouvé la fève au gâteau!* ("He has found the bean in the cake") is now popularly applied to anyone who has had exceptional good luck. In Rome, the children hang up their stockings to be filled with good things overnight on going to bed, as is the custom in England and elsewhere on Christmas Eve.

414. January 7th is still known in some of the rural districts as **Distaff's Day.** A still older name for it was **Rock Day,** the word *rock* expressing the Anglo-Saxon for a distaff. It was on this day that, the Christmas festivities having been brought to an end on Twelfth Night, the spinning maids were expected to return to their distaffs. But they were rarely suffered to do so unchallenged. As the rustics did not return to their labours until Plough Monday (*see* 415), or the day after that, and as they did not relish the idea of their sweethearts having a shorter holiday

than themselves, they invariably set fire to the flax and tow, or carried off the distaffs. In retaliation, the maids poured pailsful of water upon them; and so the first day of their so-called work was really spent as a sort of winding-up day of the Christmas sports.

415. On **Plough Monday,** which was the first Monday after Twelfth Day, the ploughmen and other rustic labourers were supposed to return to their labours in the field, but they did not really do so until the day following. In the days when all England was Roman Catholic, they made a judicious compromise between levity and hard work by attending the parish church in a body, and there offering lighted candles before the high altar by way of calling down a blessing on the labours of the year. This was the manner in which they passed the morning; but as their pockets, after the indulgence of such a long holiday, must have been pretty well drained, they made a procession through the villages, dragging their plough after them, to beg money for the purpose of keeping the candles alight during the remainder of the day. When the Reformation put out the lights in the churches, it did not succeed in abolishing the ploughman's festival. Instead of begging money for candles, the holiday makers now clamoured for beer money, and if they failed to obtain it, they promptly ploughed up the road in front of the house.

416. **Handsel Monday,** the first Monday in the New Year, is still kept as a holiday by the peasantry in the northern counties. On this day the farmers call their labourers together and give them a feast. They also make them presents, usually of money, to buy their wives or children some new garments. In Scotland a **Handsel** is equivalent to a New Year's gift. Postmen, scavengers, and others

always look for their annual perquisites on Handsel Monday, rather than on Boxing Day, as is the case among ourselves.

417. **Mallard Day** (January 14th) is observed at All Souls' College, Oxford, with sundry merry-makings, chief among which is the eating of the largest and finest mallard the cook can procure. This is because when digging the foundations of the college buildings, in the year 1437, the workmen discovered a splendid mallard in a drain, and Henry Chicheley looked upon it as a sure token of the future prosperity of his good work. Mallard Day, it need scarcely be added, is the foundation day of the college.

418. The celebrated **Feast of Lanterns**, which occurs towards the close of the New Year's festivities in China, viz., on the fifteenth day of the first moon, perpetuates an incident in the life of a famous mandarin. Whilst walking one night on the shore of a beautiful lake, his daughter fell in and was drowned. As soon as the mandarin heard the sad news, he hastened to the spot with his entire household, everyone carrying a lantern. Attracted by such a vast illumination, all the inhabitants of the country round about appeared on the scene also, bearing lanterns and torches. The search proved unavailing, for the body was not recovered until some time afterwards. On the anniversary of the accident, the mandarin caused fires to be lighted on that part of the lake-side where the damsel was alleged to have fallen in, and a solemn illuminated procession was made to the spot by all his friends, relatives, dependents, and neighbours, there to offer up prayers for the repose of her soul. This ceremony was repeated year after year, until by slow degrees the solemn character of its origin was forgotten, everyone making it an occasion for feasting and rejoicing.

419. **St. Blaise's Day** (February 3rd) was anciently the festival of the wool-combers in honour of their patron saint (*see* 259). At Bradford and other centres of the woollen industry, a grand procession of Bishop Blaise and Jason of the Golden Fleece, in which the masters, masters' sons, apprentices, wool-combers, dyers, shepherdesses, and shepherds took part, was held once every seven years. No meaning, however, could be assigned for the fires which were lighted on all the hill-tops on this day, except that the people harboured a notion that they must be honouring the saint by making a blaze on St. Blaise's Day.

420. **St. Valentine's Day** was originally a church festival instituted in memory of the good Bishop Valentine, who suffered martyrdom at Rome, February 14th, A.D. 278. Now as this was the day on which the Roman youths were wont to make a choice of sweethearts by drawing the names of young women from a box—a custom derived from the old notion that birds begin to couple on February 14th—the pagan observance was engrafted on to the Christian festival; with this difference, that for the names of the women those of certain female saints were substituted. The saint thus drawn by chance as patron for the ensuing year was called a "valentine." But ere long, as might have been expected from the first, the fair daughters of Eve still inhabiting this mundane sphere began to supersede those already translated beyond the skies. A present of a scarf or other article of female finery was the usual intimation to the fair one of the issue of the drawing. When, therefore, we at the present day prefer what is called a "useful valentine" to the old-fashioned paper valentine, we are only reverting to the custom of the gallants of ancient Rome. The poetical epistles, which in this prosaic age are rapidly dying out, first came into existence during the age of chivalry.

421. On **St. David's Day** (March 1st) the Welsh people wear a piece of leek in their hats in commemoration of the signal victory won by their ancestors over the Saxon invaders on this day in the year 540. As often happened in the early days of British history, owing to the want of a uniformity of costume on the part of the combatants on either side, friends could rarely be distinguished from foes in the heat of battle. Knowing this, St. David, the Welsh archbishop (*see* 264), ordered his countrymen to wear a piece of leek in their caps so that they might recognize one another. This precaution contributed in no small degree to their success in repulsing the enemy, and from that day forth the leek came to be regarded as their national emblem.

422. **St. Patrick's Day** (March 17th) was formerly the annual holiday of the Running Footmen and Sedan Chairmen, who were almost without exception Irishmen. On this day the Irish all the world over wear a sprig of shamrock or trefoil in their hats in honour of their patron saint, who employed it when preaching the Gospel to the Irish people as an illustration of the Trinity. This was the origin of the shamrock as the Irish national emblem (*see* 2). It is a fact little known that the trefoil was accredited with peculiar virtues in the cure of disease by the ancient inhabitants of the country.

423. **The Carnival,** a term composed of the two Italian words, *carne*, flesh, and *vale*, farewell, expresses a season of feasting and merrymaking, in preparation for the fasting and religious exercises enjoined upon all good Catholics during Lent. As Selden observes: "What the Church debars one day she gives us leave to take out in another. First we fast, then we feast; first there is a carnival, then a Lent." The

licence which pervades all classes of society at this time is traceable to the early Christians of Rome, who could not forget, neither were they to be entirely weaned from, their ancient pagan festivals (*see* 467). The carnivals at Rome, Naples, and Milan have been celebrated from time immemorial, but none more so than those of Venice, which were freely encouraged in the days of the Republic by the Senate in order to divert the minds of the people from the burden of government, else life would have been well-nigh intolerable to them. Even now the Venetian Carnival retains much of its ancient character. In France the Carnival is restricted to the three days preceding Ash Wednesday; then all is sedate until Mi-Carême, or the Thursday of mid-Lent, when the people break out again into revelry for that day only. On the last day, as in Venice and elsewhere, prize oxen are led through the streets, obviously to remind the people to eat their fill of flesh meat while there is yet time. On the following day (Ash Wednesday) people carry round the French villages and small towns an effigy something like a Guy Fawkes, and collect money, as they say, for the burial of good living. Then, after some insane mummeries, they bury it. Something of the same kind was formerly in vogue amongst ourselves. Taylor, the Water Poet, alludes to it.

424. **Collop Monday** was the name given in the olden time to the day before Shrove Tuesday, because on this day the people were accustomed to cut up their flesh meat into collops or steaks for salting and hanging up until the end of Lent. As this was the last day on which, except on Sundays, flesh meat was allowed to be eaten during Lent in pre-Reformation times, collops, eggs, and bread formed the usual dinner dish on this occasion (*see* 369). What were called **Bacchus Verses**, being verses in praise or dispraise of Bacchus,

were formerly written by the Eton boys and fastened on the college doors on Collop Monday. This custom sprang out of the ancient festival in honour of Bacchus, which was held by the Romans on this day.

425. The **Pancakes** eaten on Shrove or Pancake Tuesday had originally a double significance. Before the Reformation in England, the fish diet imposed upon all devout Catholics on Ash Wednesday and afterwards during Lent, Sundays only excepted, was considerately led up to by a dinner fare of collops on the Monday (*see* 424), and pancakes on the Tuesday, "thus showing," says an old author, "by a practical lesson that rebellious man is better introduced than driven to mortification, although a very necessary and indeed a universal observance." The object of the pancakes in preference to any other substitute for flesh meat was really to use up all the eggs, grease, lard, dripping, etc., which were forbidden on Ash Wednesday and after (*see* 369). Such pancakes, therefore, as the monks could not consume among themselves were distributed to the poor who mustered at the monastery gates. In private families, when the fare was ready for serving up, the apprentices and other members of the household were summoned to the meal by ringing a bell. There was yet another good reason for eating pancakes on the eve of the Lenten fast. This was because they by their very nature afforded a tolerable stay to the appetite during the long hours of waiting to be "shrived" in church. The church bell which called the people to the confession or shriving bore the name of the **Pancake Bell**, not merely because it began to ring about the time when they would be sitting down to the meal, but because the bell-ringer was traditionally supposed to be entitled to a pancake from each family for reminding them of their duty. In some parishes,

e.g., at Bromley in Kent, the Pancake Bell is still rung on Shrove Tuesday.

426. **Shrove Tuesday** was formerly a great day for English schoolboys. In view of the fasts and vigils to be observed during Lent, they expected to have one day of unrestrained liberty. This day was generally begun by locking the master out of school. If they admitted him at all it was only under a promise that he would participate in the Shrovetide sports. As **Cock-fighting** (*see* 251) was the recognised sport of the day, they then produced their gamecocks. The school was turned for the nonce into a cockpit, the master was appointed director, and great was the glee of the youngsters at seeing the birds fight. Another sport peculiar to the day was **Cock-throwing.** This consisted in imprisoning a cock in an earthen vessel so that its head and tail were exposed, the game being to break the vessel with a well-aimed cudgel from a few yards' distance. If the bird was struck on the head it was, of course, killed. A penny was payable to the master by each boy; this payment was styled "Cock-penny." Sometimes the bird was merely tied by one of its legs to a stake and literally beaten to death. Cock-throwing originated among the ancients, who regarded the cock as the emblem of impiety and parricide. Both the Greeks and Romans were addicted to carrying out capital sentences upon animals for the sake of example. When a parricide was put to death for his crime, a cock was generally sewn up in a sack with him. The cock-throwing at Shrovetide, then, was intended to inculcate a horror of parricide among schoolboys, but whether it had the desired effect is questionable. In the afternoon the boys went abroad **Lent-crocking.** For this purpose they collected all the old pans and kettles they could find, and made a noise outside the door of every

house they came to, until they were given a penny or more to go away. This practice they must have learnt from their elders, who were accustomed to show their resentment at an ill-assorted marriage in a very animated manner (*see* 194). Beating down the gilt basin at the end of a barber's pole also entered largely into the "alarums and excursions" of the scholars during their Shrovetide saturnalia. **Thrashing the Fat Hen** was in times past a popular diversion of the English peasantry on Shrove Tuesday. The bird was generally tied on a man's back, and the object of his fellows, who were blindfolded, was to thrash the hen with boughs by the sound of the bells fastened on the man's arms as he shifted his position. The fun consisted largely in the men thrashing one another instead of the hen, as the bearer adroitly ducked himself. When they had had enough of this kind of sport, the bird was boiled with bacon and pancakes, and all the party sat down to the feast. As the men's sweethearts stood by enjoying the fun, it is reasonable to conjecture that this hen-thrashing was originally devised for their amusement as a modification of the cock-throwing, peculiar to the day. Moreover, the fowl being a delicacy to the labourer, it was, perhaps, given to him by the farmer for sport and food.

427. In several of the English counties, **Simnel Cakes** are eaten on Mid-Lent Sunday in commemoration of the banquet given by Joseph to his brethren, the subject of which forms the first lesson of the day; and of the feeding of the five thousand in the wilderness with the five barley loaves and a few fishes, which is the Gospel appointed for the day. The word *simnel* is but slightly altered from the German *semmel*, a manchet loaf or roll. Children and domestics in service, when visiting their parents on this Sunday, according to a time-honoured custom, always take

with them such a cake as a present; while furmity is the standing dish served up at table. The designation **Mothering Sunday**, given to Mid-Lent Sunday, is, however, of much older date than most people imagine. It was primarily descended from the ancient Romans, who held a festival of the Hilaria, or "Mother of the Gods," on the Ides of March, the people making offerings in the temple, which became the property of the priests. After the establishment of Christianity the same festival was appropriated by the Church, and styled Mothering Sunday, because the faithful were expected to make offerings to the "Mother Church" on the afternoon of this day.

428. **Beating the Bounds** on Holy Thursday is a custom still observed in many English parishes. In olden times, when maps were scarce, it was universal, not only on this day, but also on the three days before the Festival of the Ascension. These days were called **Ganging Days** from the ganging or going round the parishes, and also Rogation Days, being the three days following Rogation Sunday (*see* 384). The object of perambulating the parish boundaries was two-fold. In the first place, it was considered necessary to impart a correct knowledge of the parish limits to the people, who, probably, had never seen a map in their lives; secondly, in pursuance of the character of the Rogation Days, the clergy instituted a religious procession to call down the Divine blessing on the fruits of the earth. The religious part of this observance originated in the fifth century, when Mamercus, Bishop of Vienna, instituted special prayers and fasting and processions on these days, after frequent earthquakes had destroyed the greater part of the vegetation in the district. The secular perambulation was, however, derived from the *Terminalia* of the Romans, being a festival celebrated on February 22nd, in honour of Terminus, the

god or guardian of boundaries and landmarks. To this god on such occasions they offered cakes and wine while assembling for the purpose of sport at the boundaries. In modern times, when the religious procession was discontinued, the parish school-children accompanied the clergy and parish officers through their respective parishes from end to end, carrying willow wands, with which they struck or beat the boundaries as they were pointed to them. By this means they were taught to define the limits of their parish; the more especially, when, as frequently happened, they received a flogging with their own willow wands at such places.

429. **Washing the Feet of Poor Men** on Maundy Thursday, in imitation of Christ, Who washed the feet of His disciples on the eve of His Passion, is now no longer performed by royal personages, as of old, the Empress of Austria alone excepted. By her the *Fusswaschung* is still observed with due solemnity. William of Orange was the first English sovereign who shirked this onerous duty. True, it was for many years afterwards continued by the Royal Almoner; but nowadays the gift of certain sums of money to as many poor people as the monarch can boast of years is considered much more pleasant, not to say more in accordance with the spirit of the times, so that the historic washing of the feet has quite passed out of memory. Even the royal maund, or gift of food and clothing delivered in a maund, the Saxon term for an alms-basket, has been diverted into a money equivalent. Occasion may be taken here to state that the name of **Maundy Thursday** was not derived, as so many suppose, from this maund, or alms-basket, but from *Maundé*, the French for the first word in the phrase, *Mandatum novum do vobis*, spoken by Christ during the ceremony which preceded the Last Supper. This washing of the feet is regularly

performed by the Pope at Rome on Maundy Thursday (*see* 378).

430. **The Hot Cross Buns** peculiar to Good Friday are nothing more than the cakes which the pagan Saxons ate in honour of Eoster, the goddess of light, at the annual festival of Spring. These had on their surface, singularly enough, a Greek cross, exactly like our Good Friday buns, and as the clergy found it impossible to wean the converts to Christianity from their pagan practices, they, with that keen foresight which has characterized the Church in all ages, distributed similar cakes made from the dough whence the consecrated Host was taken, to the communicants after Mass on Easter Sunday. In France and some other Catholic countries, such blessed bread is still given in the churches to those communicants who have a long journey home before they can break their fast; as also to such as, from any impediment, are unable to receive the Communion. This observance obtains throughout the year; but what is an equivalent for the blessed bread takes the form in this country of Good Friday buns, and has no longer an ecclesiastical significance. Having now disposed of the buns themselves, it still remains for us to account for the cross upon them. More than sixteen hundred years before the Christian era, Cecrops, one of the early kings of Greece, we read, offered up the sacred Cross Bread, composed of fine wheat and honey, to the divinity; just as the Egyptians had done centuries before to their female divinity, the queen of heaven, the Moon. Among the Mexicans and Peruvians a similar custom prevailed at stated periods of the year, as it still does in China. But the sacred bread of the ancient Egyptians had imprinted upon it originally, instead of a cross, a pair of horns, because it was eaten before the sacrificial altar whenever an ox was offered to the gods. From this circum-

stance, the bread-loaf was called *bous*, which, in one of its oblique cases, is *boun*, and so, by an easy transition, we derive the name of **Bun**. In course of time, however, the horns gave place to an equilateral cross, for no other reason, than that it was the more readily broken into four pieces. Like the Greeks, the Romans partook of the cross-bread on the occasions of public sacrifice, such bread being usually purchased at the doors of the temple and taken in with them, —a custom alluded to by St. Paul in I. Corinthians, x., 28. At Herculaneum a couple of small loaves, about five inches in diameter, and plainly marked with a cross, were brought to light many years ago. Moreover, on one ancient piece of sculpture now preserved in the Museo Borbonic at Rome, representing the miracle of the five barley loaves, the Greek cross appears on each of the loaves. To trace the origin of the Good Friday buns, therefore, is tantamount to going back to the remotest ages of pagan history. The Holy Eucharist in the Greek Church has a cross imprinted upon it.

431. **The Tansy Cake,** or **Tansy Pudding,** formerly eaten at Easter, was a Christian adaptation of the bitter herbs which entered into the paschal feast of the Jews, as a reminder of the bitter oppression suffered by their ancestors in the land of bondage (*see* 397). A **Gammon of Bacon** was also eaten by our forefathers at Eastertide, to show their abhorrence of their Jewish neighbours for crucifying Christ.

432. **Easter Eggs,** or, as they are sometimes called, **Pasch Eggs,** are nowhere so popular as in Russia, where the people present them to their friends, saying, "Christ is risen!" to which the recipients reply, "He is, indeed!" The same pious custom was formerly universal in England and France. The coloured eggs of sugar are still displayed

in the confectioners' windows, it is true, and, to a certain extent, they are doubtless purchased for presentation, but their meaning is known only to a few. Ever since the time of the ancient Egyptians the egg has been regarded as the symbol of re-creation. This idea originated among the subjects of the Pharaohs from their close observance of the habits of the scarab, or sacred beetle, which buried its balls in dung in the grave it had dug for itself, in the hope, as they thought, of a speedy resurrection. It never occurred to them that the pellets contained eggs, which, in the fulness of time, were brought to maturity by the warmth of the sun. When the insect appeared once more amongst them, they were content to believe it was the original one they had seen bury itself on the same spot, now brought to life again by the Sun God. So the beetle was reverenced by them as a sacred thing, because it gave them hope of a similar resurrection of their mummified bodies (*see* 46). By the Jews the egg was looked upon as the symbol of the duration of the human race and of their successive generation; it entered into all the mysterious ceremonies called apocalyptic, and occupied a prominent position on the household table during the paschal season (*see* 220, 397). In accordance with the traditions of the Magi, or Persians, the world was hatched from an egg in the beginning at that season of the year which corresponds with the vernal equinox; for which reason eggs are popularly presented as New Year's gifts by the modern Persians at this time (*see* 409). It was from this custom that the northern nations came to regard the paschal eggs as emblematical of creation, or the re-creation of Spring at the vernal equinox. When Christianity usurped the pagan rites and observances of the Saxons, the paschal eggs were invested with a new significance, namely, that of the Resurrection of Christ; and they were coloured red in allusion to the blood shed for the salvation of men. The curious **Ball**

Play in Church, of which we read during the Middle Ages, took its rise from the paschal egg that was thrown from one to the other of the choristers in the nave of the church while an anthem was being sung, during the Eastertide festival (*see* 186). As the egg was often missed, and allowed to break on the ground, a ball was in course of time substituted. In some parts of Scotland, hard-boiled eggs, dyed purple, are rolled or thrown about, and finally eaten, as often as Eastertide comes round. In the rural districts of France, children make a round of all the houses and farms begging for red eggs on Easter Day.

433. **Easter Cards** were first introduced by the Americans as substitutes for the pasch eggs. Our transatlantic cousins are an extremely practical people, as all the world knows. Instead of spending both money and time for the purpose of presenting the eggs, they consider a pretty card sent through the post sufficient to meet all requirements.

434. A singular custom which survived in many parts of the country, particularly at Chester, down to comparatively recent times, was the **Lifting at Eastertide.** On the Monday the young men lifted the women, and on setting them down again demanded a kiss; while on the Tuesday the lifting and kissing fell to the share of the women. All which was intended to typify the Resurrection of Christ at this season. Another singular custom peculiar to Eastertide was the **Hocking,** *i.e.*, parties of men and women reciprocally stopping the way against foot passengers with a rope, and pulling them along until they had purchased their release with a donation. This **Hock Tuesday Money,** as it was called, was handed over to the landlord, who entertained all his tenants at a sumptuous feast on Hock Tuesday proper, being the second Tuesday after Easter week, in commemo-

ration of the expulsion of the Danes, and the death of Hardicanute on this day.

435. The origin of **All Fools' Day,** or more correctly speaking, **Auld Fools' Day,** has exercised the minds of not a few antiquaries in vain. The great stumbling block in the path of their investigations is, and has always been, the singular circumstance that the Hindoos make fools of one another precisely in the same manner as we do ourselves, on March 31st, which is the last day of their important festival of the *Huli.* Yet it does not appear to have dawned upon these usually astute inquirers that, since the *Huli* corresponds in character, though not in point of time, with the Roman Saturnalia and the Feast of Fools of the Middle Ages, the Hindoos bring their great Spring festival to an end by burlesquing the once universal custom of making presents and paying visits at the vernal equinox, which among the nations of antiquity, and indeed throughout all the western nations until a century or two ago, marked the commencement of the year (*see* 409). Analogous though the European fooling on April 1st is with that of the Hindoos on March 31st, the former was certainly never taken from the latter. For the true origin of April Fools' Day we must look to France, which took the lead among the nations of Christendom in commencing the New Year on January 1st instead of March 25th. This change was effected as long ago as 1564, nearly two centuries before England made up its mind to follow suit. We have seen already how the French have lost nothing of the old Roman fashion in the matter of paying visits and bestowing gifts on New Year's Day. This being so it was often found necessary, in a deeply religious age, to pospone the customary New Year's observance to the *octave* of the actual festival, simply because March 25th chanced to occur in Passion week, at times

even on Good Friday itself. Consequently, it was on April 1st, rather than March 25th that the New Year's gifts and congratulatory visits were made. When, however, after the adoption of the Reformed Calendar in 1564, the New Year's Day was carried back to January 1st, only pretended presents and mock ceremonial visits were made on April 1st, with a view of making fools of those who had forgotten the change of date. The persons thus imposed upon were, and are still, called *Poissons d'Avril*, or **April Fish**, *i.e.*, a mackerel, which like a fool or booby, is easily caught. In England generally the common expression is an April Fool; in Scotland it is a "Gowk," the native appellation for a foolish person. Germany and Spain also have their fools on April 1st.

436. The lavish display of primroses on April 19th, which on this account bears the name of **Primrose Day**, is a pleasant custom destined to keep alive the memory of Benjamin Disraeli, Earl of Beaconsfield, who died on this date in 1881. It originated in the beautiful wreath of primroses which Her Majesty the Queen caused to be laid on the coffin of the great Minister, inscribed with the words in her own handwriting: "His favourite flower."

437. A ludicrous custom, discontinued only within the last few years, was the **Freemen's March** at Alnwick, Northumberland, on St. Mark's Day, April 23rd. Those who claimed the freedom of the town on this day were conducted in solemn procession on horseback, dressed in white, and with swords hanging by their sides, by the bailiff to what was called the Freemen's Well, a large dirty pool on the borders of the common. Arrived there, they dismounted, and deliberately walked through the pool, emerging on the opposite side begrimed with mud and dripping with water.

This decidedly unpleasant duty was imposed upon them by King John as a punishment for the filthy condition of their roads when he paid a visit to Alnwick on St. Mark's Eve, in the year 1209.

438. **St. George's Day** (April 23rd), was in bygone times an occasion of public rejoicing and solemn pageantry at Leicester, in honour of the saint and his triumph over the dragon of the legend. St. George's horse, richly caparisoned, always stood at one end of St. George's Chapel, in St. Martin's Church; and **The Riding of the George**, as it was called, by the Mayor, followed by all the town dignitaries through the streets, was an observance invested with all the importance of a Lord Mayor's Show.

439. **The May-day Festival** of rural England is a relic of the *Maiama*, a festival in honour of Maia, the mother of Mercury, held annually at Ostia, a town about sixteen miles from Rome, on the first day of the month named after her. Instituted by Claudius as a separate festival, it was eventually grafted upon the *Floralia*, or feast of Flora, which was held on April 27th and lasted several days. The latter was essentially a festival for the Roman women, who ran races night and day in the amphitheatre, the winners of the prizes being crowned with flowers. Flora was a courtesan who left all her fortune to the people of Rome, but feeling ashamed of her profession they made her the goddess of flowers. The May-day festival at Ostia was a very different thing. There the sexes were equally represented, and all who came decorated themselves with garlands. The doors of the houses were adorned with branches laden with fruit and flowers; but not content with this, many of the Roman gallants caused entire trees to be brought from the adjacent forest and set up in front of the

houses of their mistresses. Perhaps, if the truth were known, Ostia was the place where most of the mistresses of the gilded youth of Rome resided; certainly the festival was more than once abolished on account of the licentiousness of the games. To put a stop to such a wholesale destruction of fine straight trees, it was ordered that a tall shaft or pole, ornamented with garlands, should suffice. Here then we have the true origin of the **Maypole.** From a charter of 1207 we learn that a maypole was allowed to be set up before the houses of the nobility. The **Milkmaid's Festival** on May 1st arose out of the old English custom of bringing home the maypole over-night by a yoke of oxen adorned with flowers, attended by boys blowing cows' horns or hollow canes, and milkmaids wearing garlands, which they afterwards hung up in the churches. The milch cow and the huge garlands borne on the heads of the milkmaids, were at one time familiar objects in the London streets. The fiddlers and clarionet players who accompanied them were the successors of the more ancient horn-blowers, but both milkmaids and musicians in their turn gave place to the chimney sweepers. Two very good reasons are assigned for the **Chimney Sweepers' Holiday** on May 1st. To commence with, the Morris Dancers who went round from house to house soliciting pence on this day, generally blacked their faces to make them pass for Moors (*see* 457). As we know, the term **Morris Dance** is simply a corruption of Moorish dance, or dance of the Moriscoes, which John of Gaunt introduced into this country after his return from Spain. Five men and a boy took part in it, and as the latter—who was the clown of the set—wore a helmet much too large for him, called a *morion*, he received the name of "Mad Morion," which became perverted into **Maid Marian,** when in due time the popular ballads of Robin Hood stimulated the people to impersonate the various characters that made up the court of the merry monarch of Sherwood Forest. Owing to the fact that the celebrated outlaw died on May 1st, the festival came generally to be dedicated to him. This explains why so many places in different parts of England and Scotland bear such names as "Robin Hood's Hill," "Robin Hood's Bay," etc.; it was there where the Robin Hood games were held. Dr. Owen Pugh, the Welsh archæologist, thinks that our **Jack in the Green** was intended to represent Meloas, King of Somersetshire, who disguised himself in green boughs and laid in ambush for Guenever, the wife of King Arthur, as she was returning from a hunting expedition. He is, however, much more likely to have been derived from the trees which, as we have already seen, were set up outside the houses at Ostia during the May-day festival. Like the **Rush-bearing** of bygone days, the beautiful ceremony of **Crowning the May Queen** formed part and parcel of the Ostian games; while the **Well Dressing**, which is still to be met with in some parts of England and France, came from the *Fontinalia* of the Romans, being religious festivals in honour of the nymphs of wells and fountains. To return to the chimney sweepers' holiday. Almost everyone has heard how Mrs. Montague, the foundress of the celebrated Blue-Stocking Club, in 1780, treated all the London chimney sweepers to a roast beef and plum-pudding dinner, and a present of a new shilling, on the lawn of her house in Hill Street, Portman Square, on May 1st, as long as she lived. This kindly act on her part was in commemoration of the providential recovery of a little boy belonging to her husband's family, who had been kidnapped by some chimney sweepers to be made use of as a "climbing boy." The story goes that one May-day morning, after the sweeps had been sent for to cleanse the chimneys of her town mansion, the tiny urchin whose business it was to ascend the flues, was discovered to be none other than the long-lost relative.

440. In the north of England May-day is often called **Beltine Day,** although the ancient observance peculiar to the evening of this day has long since died out. This was one of the days when the Druids lighted bonfires on the hill-tops in honour of the sun. The Irish still use the expression *La Bheltine,* the day of Bel's fire; from *La,* a day, *Bel,* the sun-god (Baal), and *tenie,* fire. The fires which in some parts of Ireland, the Isle of Man, and the Scottish Highlands are kindled in the fields on festive occasions are traces of this Druidical worship (*see* 446).

441. On **Royal Oak Day,** also called **Oak Apple Day,** the people formerly wore oak leaves or oak apples in their hats to commemorate the manner in which the partisans of Charles II. welcomed the king's return to England on his birthday, May 29th, 1651; in allusion to his concealment in an oak tree near Boscobel House, Shropshire, after his defeat by Cromwell at the battle of Worcester on September 3rd previous. It was from this incident that publicans affected the sign of the Royal Oak during the Restoration period.

442. **The Godiva Procession** at Coventry is occasionally revived to keep alive the memory of Lady Godiva, the wife of Leofric, Earl of Chester, who, on Trinity Friday, 1057, rode naked through the streets in order to obtain from her lord, on behalf of the citizens, a restitution of rights and privileges. A bust of "Peeping Tom" adorns the corner house where that inquisitive tailor, as tradition states, was struck blind while trying to steal a peep at the fair equestrienne through the shutters as she passed by.

443. One of the annual solemnities of Venice in bygone times was the **Marriage of the Adriatic** on the Festival of the Ascension. This was instituted in the year 1177 by Pope Alexander III. in commemoration of the signal victory of the Venetians over the hostile fleet of Frederick Barbarossa at Istria. Giving the Doge a ring from his own finger, the Pontiff desired him to cast a similar one into the Adriatic on Ascension Day each year and so espouse the sea, promising him that his bride would be as dutiful to him as is a wife to her husband. Hence, from time immemorial, Venice has borne the style of **The Bride of the Sea.** The inaugural ceremony was performed on Ascension Day, 1177, amid great rejoicings. The Bicentaur or Gondola of State, magnificently appointed, and manned by forty-two rowers, after leaving the Piazza San Mark under a salute of guns, proceeded slowly towards the Isle of Lido. Immediately in its wake, gondolas, barges, sailing vessels, and galleys, occupied by persons of rank, with minstrels and other attendants, made for the same destination. Arrived there the Doge, after pouring holy water into the sea, took the ring from his finger and dropped it on the bosom of the Adriatic, saying, "We espouse thee, O sea, in token of our just and perpetual dominion." A solemn Mass in the church of St. Nicholas on the Isle of Lido, and a sumptuous banquet at the ducal palace brought this perennial function to an end (*see* 444).

444. An analogous ceremony to that anciently performed by the Doge of Venice (*see* 443), takes place every three years at Cork. This is officially known as **Throwing the Dart.** By virtue of a clause in the City's charter, the Mayor of Cork is constituted Admiral of the Port, but he must triennially claim jurisdiction over it by throwing a dart into the sea. The dart employed is generally made of mahogany

tipped and winged with bronze. Attended by a numerous retinue, the civic functionary steams in his gaily-decorated barge to the outer limits of the port, and there performs the ceremony; which being concluded, he departs to the City Hall, there to preside over a grand banquet.

445. The Whitsuntide merry-makings of the olden time traced their origin from the *Agapai*, or Love Feasts of the early Christians, and the *Drinklean*, an annual festival of the tenants and vassals of the lord of the fee, which occurred about this time. They were called **Whitsun Ales** because, as at an ordinary **Church Ale**, the churchwardens laid in a stock of malt, which they brewed into beer, and sold it to the holiday-makers for refreshment in the church porch, or, more frequently, in the churchyard. The proceeds of such sales, as well as those from sundry games, were given to the poor, for whom the parish rates made no provision. As old Aubrey says: "There were no rates for the poor in my grandfather's days; but for Kingston St. Michael (no small parish) the church ale of Whitsuntide did the business." It would appear, also, that the tree nearest the church door had affixed to it a banner, beneath which comely maidens were stationed with contribution boxes for the same laudable object. At the church-house close by, spits, crooks, and other utensils for cooking provisions were provided, and there the housekeepers met and made merry, while without the young folk indulged in dancing, bowls, shooting at butts, and other amusements, "the ancients sitting by and looking gravely on."

446. **The Midsummer Marching Watch,** or grand illuminated march-past of the Watch, which in the olden times drew such a vast concourse of sightseers to London and other cities on the Vigil of the Nativity of St. John the

Baptist (June 24th), was a Christian survival of the pagan celebration of the return of the summer solstice, but transferred from Midsummer Day to St. John's Eve, because that saint, though not the Light, was sent into the world to give testimony of the Light. This mid-day of the year was specially set apart by the Druids for the worship of the sun, in prospect of reaping a good harvest. All night long the festival was kept up by solemn chants, processions, and sacrifices, and piling up of huge bonfires. In many parts of Ireland, even nowadays, the people dance around bonfires on St. John's Eve, as they say, "in honour of the sun." Elsewhere, firebrands are carried about, wheels with straw twisted around them are set on fire and then rolled downhill, and fireworks are discharged, ostensibly to purify the air; but which practices have undoubtedly a pagan origin (*see* 440).

447. An imposing spectacle, known as **The Procession of the Minstrels,** annually took place at Chester on the Nativity of St. John the Baptist, until the year 1756, when it was abolished. It originated as follows:—At Chester Fair, as elsewhere, the temporary exemption of criminals and debtors from arrest, which the display of a glove gave faithful promise of (*see* 210), naturally attracted a vast concourse of lawless and ruffianly people to the place. It was during one of these Chester Fairs that Ranulph de Blundeville, Earl of Chester, found himself besieged in his castle at Rhuddlan by the yet unsubjugated Welsh. When the news reached the ears of John Lacy, Constable of Chester, he at once called together all the minstrels who chanced to be at the fair, and with their assistance collected a great number of disorderly people. These he armed with the readiest weapons to hand, and with the minstrels sent them off under the command of Hugh Dutton, in the hope of

effecting the relief of the besieged earl. The result was even better than he anticipated. When this savage-looking horde reached Rhuddlan, the Welsh mistook them at a distance for the regular army, and without waiting to test their discipline or the efficiency of their weapons, raised the siege and fled. Whereupon, out of gratitude for the service which the minstrels had rendered him, the earl placed them under the jurisdiction of their captain for ever. This was why the minstrels were required to appear once a year before the lord of Dutton at Chester. Their place of assembly was Eastgate Street, where the earl or his heir gave them a cordial greeting. Then the banners were unfurled, and, with spirited music, they marched through the city. In more modern times, when genuine minstrels were no longer to be found, the civic authorities satisfied the public demand for an annual show in a manner that was in all respects praiseworthy.

448. The prognostication that if it rains on **St. Swithin's Day** (July 15th) it will rain for forty days in succession, has been very ably controverted by the Rev. John Earle, Professor of Anglo-Saxon at Oxford University. According to the popular tradition, the saint made a dying request that he might be buried just outside the church porch, exposed to the drippings from the eaves overhead, and so that the worshippers might regularly walk over his grave. Subsequently, however, steps were taken by the clergy to remove the body of the good bishop within the cathedral (Winchester), but a heavy downpour of rain necessitated a postponement of the attempt day after day for thirty-nine successive days, until, on the fortieth, they resolved to abandon it altogether. Now, by the publication of a facsimile and translation of a Saxon MS., the earliest account of St. Swithin's life extant, Professor Earle "has done the State

some service" by proving, in the most conclusive manner, that the weather on the occasion of the disinterment of the deceased bishop was favourable for the attempt; that no phenomenon of any kind took place; and that, therefore, the elements did not conspire to frustrate the removal of the body into the church. The most reliable explanation of the vulgar belief concerning St. Swithin's Day which gave rise to the tradition is, as Professor Earle suggests, that in one particular year, about the time of this feast, the rainy constellations of Præsepe and Avelli arose cosmically, and caused rain to fall for more than a month together. There are similar "rainy saints' days" in France, Belgium, and Germany.

449. As often as July 25th comes round, the denizens of towns and cities are reminded, if they ever bestow a thought on such things, that it is the Feast of St. James the Greater, the patron saint of Spain. "**Please remember the Grotto!**" is the persistent plaint of children of tender years who, scallop-shell in hand, opportune the passers-by to contribute "only a halfpenny" towards the cost of illuminating the miniature grotto erected by them on the inner side of the street-pavement. Because, in lieu of scallop-shells, the grotto is more generally composed of oyster-shells, many Londoners entertain a hazy idea that it must have something to do with the commencement of the oyster season, since the close time for the sale and capture of English oysters expires on the eve of old St. James's Day, which was August 4th. How much they are mistaken in this view will be seen from the statement that it was formerly the custom in this country and elsewhere for persons to set up a grotto of scallop-shells on this day, as a hint to the pious who could not make a pilgrimage to the famous shrine at Compostella, that they might show their reverence to the

saint equally well by bestowing alms on their poorer neighbours (*see* 302).

450. The well-known proverb relative to **Oyster-Opening Day,** "Whoever eats oysters on St. James's Day will never want money," admits of a ready explanation. As oysters are, of course, dearer on the opening day of the season than afterwards, this statement was originally published by the oyster-sellers in order to induce the town-folk to indulge in them to an extravagant degree, and hence to push business.

451. **Doggett's Coat and Badge,** annually rowed for on the Thames between London Bridge and Chelsea by six young watermen, whose apprenticeship comes to an end on that day, viz., on August 1st, are provided out of a fund left for the purpose by Thomas Doggett, a famous actor and zealous Whig, to commemorate "the happy accession to the throne" of George I. on August 1st, 1714. The much-prized livery was first competed for in the year 1716. Since Doggett's death, in 1721, the race has been regularly organized by the Fishmongers' Company.

452. **Michaelmas Day** (September 29th) is the day on which, from time out of mind, civic and municipal rulers have been elected to office all over the country. This is because our ancestors recognized an analogy between their chief magistrates and titular protecting angels, in so far as the former presided over and protected the people. No better day, therefore, could have been hit upon for their **Mayor-choosing Day,** as it is often styled, than the Festival of St. Michael the Archangel, guardian and protector of the Christian Church (*see* 326).

453. **The Michaelmas Goose** is a dish without which no well-ordered dinner-table on September 29th would be complete. The story goes that Queen Elizabeth was having goose for dinner on Michaelmas Day when the news of the total defeat of the Spanish Armada was brought to her; in remembrance of which she resolved always to eat goose on that day. There is, however, a little discrepancy here. Considering that the Armada was literally swept off the seas between July 21st and 25th, it is most unlikely that the good tidings must have required two months and four days to reach England. At all events, a goose was regularly served up for dinner long, long before Queen Elizabeth made her appearance in the world. The custom arose out of the practice of the rural tenantry bringing a stubble-goose to their landlords when paying their rent, or to make them lenient if on occasion an excuse had to be tendered in place of the money. At this particular time of the year geese were plentiful and at their best, owing to the benefits they derived from stubble feeding. And since the landlords received many more such presents than they could themselves consume, they forthwith passed them over to their friends or acquaintances. In this way the Michaelmas goose became a standing dinner-dish.

454. Almost everyone has heard of the **Dog-Whipping at Hull**, which took place on October 10th, the eve of the annual fair. To trace the origin of this now obsolete custom we must go back to the time when the monasteries provided not only the education but also the daily food of the poor. The Carmelites and the Dominicans were particularly strong in "the good old town of Hull" before the Reformation; Whitefriar-gate and Blackfriar-gate still remind us of their old haunts. As it had always been the practice of the friars to provide a liberal allowance of food and drink for the poor wayfarers who were attracted to the town during

the fair, it happened in one particular year that while they were busying themselves with the necessary preparations, a stray dog wandered into the larder, and snatching up a joint of meat, made off with it as fast as his legs could carry him. Although the cooks did not immediately discover their loss, the thief could not well pass out of the monastery gates without arousing the suspicions of the hungry mortals that lingered around; so giving chase, they succeeded at last in making him relinquish his booty. After that, whenever a dog showed himself outside the monastery while the preparations for the poor men's banquet were going forward, he was beaten off with whips, and boys considered it fine sport to chase him all over the town. This grew into such a settled custom that every dog that ventured abroad on October 10th was sure to receive a drubbing at the hands of the town boys. The introduction of the new police put a stop to this time-honoured practice once and for all.

455. **St. Crispin's Day** (October 25th) is still observed as a holiday by the majority of shoemakers in large towns and cities in honour of their patron saint (*see* 336). In France and Flanders the shoemakers of the Middle Ages kept the day with religious ceremonies, enlivened with miracle plays. In England and France, pursuant to a royal proclamation, it was kept as a general holiday, because the battle of Agincourt was fought and won on St. Crispin's Day, 1415. This accounts for the shoemakers' festival surviving after every other trade festival had been suffered to die out. The chief feature of the day was the procession, in which various well-known personages were represented by shoemakers. St. Crispin and the monarch then occupying the throne were the usual objects of attraction. The processions at Edinburgh and Stirling were noted for being somewhat elaborate. At the former place the mock king

was dressed in a very fair imitation of the royal robes, while at the latter both Houses of Parliament followed the pseudo-monarch, as well as officers and men-at-arms without number. In London, during the Mayoralty of Sir Simon Eyre, who had once been a shoemaker, an imitation king of the City followed very closely upon the heels of the imitation monarch in the shoemakers' annual procession, and ever afterwards the Lord Mayor was generally represented. The procession over, a dinner invariably took palce, and the day closed with a dance, led off by the workman who had played the part of king. Although such shows have long ago fallen into abeyance, there are few shoemakers who are not addicted to "keeping Crispin" on October 25th.

456. The mystic rites which take place on the domestic hearth throughout the three kingdoms, but more particularly in the West of Scotland, on what is called **Hallowe'en,** are a relic of paganism. This is the season when superstitious influences prevail. On this night the spirits of the dead are supposed to wander abroad for a brief space, and divinations are practised, out of the belief that such spirits have the power of foreshadowing the future to their relatives still in the flesh. From the nuts requisitioned for this purpose, the Vigil of Allhallows bears the name in the North of England of **Crack-nut Night.** On first thoughts the apples would seem to have nothing whatever to do with the festival further than to afford the young folk some harmless necessary amusement. But stay! By the pagan Saxons November 1st was dedicated to a goddess who presided over fruits and seeds. This festival—which some writers trace to an Oriental source—was called *La Maes Abhal*, or "Day of the Apple Fruit," a designation easily corrupted into "Lamb's Wool," which expressed a drink of roasted apples, sugar, and ale, popularly indulged in on the

evening of this day. So that the apples employed for divination and sport are well in season. Curiously enough, November 1st was also the great autumn festival of the sun, in thanksgiving for the harvest of the Druids. It was from them that our forefathers derived the superstitious notions peculiar to this season. As we know, the Druids believed in the doctrine of the transmigration of souls. Every year, according to their teaching, on the eve of the harvest thanksgiving, *Saman*, the Lord of Death, called together the souls that had been assigned within the last twelve months to occupy the bodies of animals to final judgment. The punishment of the wicked souls might, however, be greatly commuted by charms and magic, by sacrifices offered to Baal by their living relatives, and by presents made to the priests for intercession on their behalf. Fatted calves and black sheep were the usual sacrifices on this occasion. Here, then, we have an explanation of the house to house collection in the remote districts of Ireland of bread, cakes, butter, cheese, and eggs; the slaughter of the fatted calf and the black sheep; the baking of the griddle cakes, and the presentation of lighted candles in honour of St. Colomb Kill, which is a Christian substitute for *Saman*, on the Vigil of Allhallows Day. Long before the institution of All Souls' Day (*see* 394) the ancient Irish prayed to *Saman*, in front of their lighted candles, for the souls of their departed relatives. Even now fires are lighted on the hill-tops and in the fields as on Beltine Day (*see* 440).

457. It is a mistake to suppose that the effigies which are carried through the streets on **Guy Fawkes' Day** were unheard of before the diabolical attempt to blow up both Houses of Parliament on November 5th, 1605; the only thing new about them was the designation "Guy." Throughout the preceding reign the anniversary of the

accession of Queen Elizabeth on November 17th had been celebrated by parading an effigy of the Pope during the daytime, and throwing it into a bonfire after nightfall. In Queen Anne's time an effigy of the Pretender afforded similar sport to the exultant Protestants. In these days of religious toleration November 17th is allowed to pass by without any manifestations of popular rejoicing, but Guy Fawkes' Day continues to be celebrated with its wonted spirit. Many of the masqueraders who attend the guys black their faces, in imitation of the May-day Morris Dancers, who did so to make them pass for Moors (*see* 439). Hampstead Heath is an appropriate locale for the bonfire carnival on Guy Fawkes' Night, inasmuch as it was there—on **Parliament Hill**—where the fellow conspirators of the redoubtable Guy waited to see the explosion that never came. Hence its name.

458. When one considers the vast wealth and commercial importance, the ancient rights and privileges, and the traditions of the City of London—the oldest existing Corporation in the world—the public interest in that hardy annual the **Lord Mayor's Show** is a matter for small surprise. Let us just consider for a moment who and what the Lord Mayor of London really is. He is at once the representative of the Sovereign within the City. A few days after his election to the Chief Magistracy by the Livery on Michaelmas Day (*see* 452) he is formally presented to the Lord Chancellor, acting on behalf of the Queen outside the City, in the House of Lords; and the primary object of the civic procession on November 9th is the formal introduction of the Chief Magistrate to Her Majesty's judges at the Royal Palace of Justice. Now that the Law Courts have been transferred to within a stone's throw of the Temple Bar memorial, the procession to Westminster is no longer neces-

sary, albeit the original route has only been modified to the extent of making a divergence at Charing Cross. The secondary object of the Lord Mayor's Show is to afford the citizens an opportunity of making themselves acquainted with the personality of their new ruler. In olden times, when photographs and illustrated newspapers were unheard of, the populace had no means of knowing what their rulers, princes, heroes, and other celebrities were like except by attending a processional function of this kind (*see* 242). Prior to the year 1851, members of the Royal Family, and even the Sovereign exercised the courtesy to knock at the gate of Temple Bar as often as they desired to enter the City in state; whereupon the Lord Mayor would deliver up the keys into the royal hands in person. The earliest intimation of a death in the Royal Family is always sent to the Lord Mayor of London by a special messenger; moreover, he is the only one of Her Majesty's subjects who possesses the passport to the Tower of London. This passport is changed quarterly. As the representative of the Queen, he attends in his robes of state to open the Central Criminal Court at the Old Bailey. Within the clearly-defined limitations of the City, therefore, he may be said to reign as absolute king. The senate over which he presides at Guildhall is typical of that which sways the destinies of a vast empire at Westminster. The Court of Aldermen constitutes his House of Lords, and the Court of Common Council his House of Commons. In his person the Lord Chancellor and the Speaker are combined. For him a palatial residence, a private chaplain, a mace-bearer, a sword-bearer, and custodians of the gold chain and seals of office are provided. He is addressed as "The Right Honourable the Lord Mayor," because he ranks as and wears the robes of an earl. Is it a matter for surprise, then, that the inhabitants of such an ancient city, famous for its affluence, independence, power, and hospitality, should desire to pay him honour at his inauguration, to manifest their appreciation of his many years' faithful service in the Council Chamber that have gone before? In days of old, when the procession to Westminster was by water, the new Lord Mayor was greeted on his return with congratulatory speeches, composed for the occasion by the civic poet laureate, who received an annual stipend for such services. The last City poet was Elkanah Settle, who died in 1724. As showing the importance which still attaches to the outgoing from office of the Lord Mayor, it may be observed that on November 7th, which is the eve of the expiration of his Mayoralty, his lordship leaves his card at Buckingham Palace, Marlborough House, York House, Clarence House, Gloucester House, and the Prime Minister's official residence in Downing Street. On the day following he formally inducts the Lord Mayor-elect to the civic chair by presenting him with the mace, sword, chain, and seals of office (*see* 5, 77).

459. An annual diversion called the **Stamford Bull Running** took place in the streets of Stamford, Lincolnshire, on November 13th, down to a recent period. Punctually at eleven o'clock in the morning, on the ringing of St. Mary's Church bell—the streets having previously been barricaded and cleared of children and infirm persons—a bull was turned loose, and chased through the town, over the bridge, into the river; allowed to swim ashore, and then chased again, until both pursuers and pursued were tired out, when the animal was slaughtered, and its flesh was sold at such a cheap rate that all could have bull-beef for supper that night. According to local tradition, this popular sport was instituted by William, Earl de Warren (*temp.* King John), who, while standing on the battlements of his castle, saw a couple of

bulls fighting in the meadow beneath. Presently, when some butchers succeeded in parting them, one of the animals ran into the town, and created such a confusion among the inhabitants, that the Earl, who followed on horseback on purpose to see the fun, declared he would give the meadow in which the fight began to the town, provided the butchers found a bull to be annually run through the streets on November 13th "for ever after." One great point in favour of this tradition is that the town-folk of Stamford still exercise certain rights over what is known as "the Bull Meadow."

460. **Almanack Day**, on November 22nd, was formerly a very busy day at Stationers' Hall, when the publication of almanacks of all kinds was a sight to see. The Stationers' Company still publish a few almanacks, but they no longer possess the exclusive monopoly of this species of publication. The fact that they regularly send a copy of each of their almanacks as a present to the Archbishop of Canterbury is perhaps very little known. The custom originated in the following manner. At the time when Dr. Tenison was Archbishop, a near relative of his, who was Master of the Stationers' Company, one Lord Mayor's Day, while awaiting his lordship's return from Westminster Hall in the civic state barge at Westminster Stairs, thought he would improve the occasion by slipping over to Lambeth Palace to pay his kinsman there a flying visit. On his arrival, the Archbishop entertained him and his fellow aldermen with a pint of wine apiece, and the watermen with hot spiced ale, with bread and cheese. This grew into a settled custom year by year until the Mayoral procession by water was abolished, the Stationers' Company always acknowledging the hospitality on this occasion by presenting the Archbishop with copies of their several almanacks as soon as published.

461. **St. Andrew's Day** (November 30th) is a great day of reunion among Scotsmen wherever they may be. In London, every Scotsman worthy the name makes a point of attending the national concert at St. James's Hall on the evening of this day (*see* 348).

462. The secular observances formerly in vogue on **St. Nicholas' Day** (December 6th) have either died out altogether or been transferred to another date. In very few places indeed do the children now hang up their stockings on St. Nicholas' Eve in the hope of having them filled with sweetmeats by their patron saint over-night; Christmas Eve, New Year's Eve, and Twelfth Night are the occasions when such gifts are more usually looked for in different parts of Europe (*see* 409, 413, 468). In former times, too, both in England and abroad, convent boarders placed their silk stockings at the chamber door of the Abbess, or Mother Superior, labelled, "To Great St. Nicholas;" and the next morning never failed to receive their share of good things out of the bounty of their patron saint. This was a religious adaptation of the secular custom of young women praying to St. Nicholas to provide them with good husbands and a marriage dowry (*see* 352). The mediæval practice of choosing a **Boy-Bishop** from the choir-boys on this day was tolerated by the clergy, who had not the slightest fear of the Faith of the people being endangered by such mummeries. He was arrayed in full canonicals, and his authority lasted until Innocents' Day (December 28th). If he died in the meantime he was interred with all the honours due to a bishop; as appears from the piece of sculpture representing a boy, in episcopal robes and mitre, trampling upon a lion-headed and dragon-tailed monster, on the north side of the nave of Salisbury Cathedral. The origin of this singular custom is ascribed to the youth of the saint at the time when

he became Bishop of Myra, and the fact that he is the patron saint of boys (*see* 352). Instead of being entirely abolished at the Reformation, it was merely secularised into the **Ad Montem,** *i.e.*, "To the Mount," of the Eton boys, or in other words, the **Eton Montem,** which survived until the year 1874. Old Etonians will remember that the procession to Salt Hill was somewhat military in character, and that certain boys, called Salt-bearers, preceded them in fancy costumes, to levy contributions from the passers-by. These contributions were supposed to be devoted to the maintenance of their captain at college, and all who gave received a pinch of salt in return. Of course, the actual amount thus raised was insignificant, not at all to be compared with that which fell to the lot of the Boy-Bishop in more ancient times. As salt enters so conspicuously into the ceremonies of the Church, its meaning in the juvenile procession was clear; and doubtless from this the ancient college custom of **Salting in a Freshman,** before he was entitled to join the rest in their games and amusements, took its rise.

463. On **St. Thomas's Day** in the country women and girls go the rounds of the district collecting money for the purpose of enabling them to lay in a store of good things against Christmas. This is called in some parts "a-gooding," in others "mumping," in others, "doleing." In Warwickshire it is "corning," because originally a large bag was carried to receive contributions of corn from the farmers. Sprigs of evergreen are in every case left at the houses in return for such presents. These acknowledgments are a relic of paganism. It was the custom of the Druids to send their young students from house to house with sprigs of holly and mistletoe, a few days before the approach of the great winter festival, as a peace-offering (*see* 464). What is called the **Vessel Cup** is still carried about by carol

singers from house to house in the north of England, between St. Thomas's Day and Christmas Day. The term is clearly a corruption of "Wassail Cup," from the cup originally borne by one of the party as a reminder of the festivities of the approaching season. In the absence of such a cup, a small box decorated with holly, within which two dolls, representing the Virgin and Child, are seen under a glass cover, now bears the name of the Vessel Cup. This idea is of course borrowed from the Crib set up in the Roman Catholic churches at this season. Like the country folk above mentioned, these carol singers invariably give a twig from the Vessel Cup in return for the gratuity bestowed upon them.

464. Of all the festivals of the year, religious as well as secular, **Christmas** is at once the most important. During the dead season, when Nature sleeps beneath its snowy mantle; when the harvest has been gathered in, and tillage-time has not yet come round; when the days are shortest, and the nights long and dreary; when the scattered members of the family are for the nonce re-assembled round the glowing hearth: this is the season for mirth and jollity in cottage and in hall. It needed not the institution of a new religion to instil feelings of peace and goodwill into the minds of men at such a time. On the contrary, each and all the practices which mark the close of the Christian year have been derived most directly from pagan sources. The holly, box, ivy, laurel, and bay, which enter so largely into our **Christmas-tide Church Decorations** adorned not only the temples and private houses of the Romans during their Saturnalia, but also the rude huts of the ancient Britons at their great winter festival, which occurred at the same period. Mention has already been made (*see* 463) of the sprigs of holly and mistletoe which the Druids sent round to the

people a few days prior to the great event. Though intended as a peace-offering, they were really a reminder to deck their dwellings with evergreens, so that the sylvan spirits might repair to them, and in this way shelter their inmates from frost and wintry blasts until the milder season of spring had renewed their natural foliage. We know how greatly the **Mistletoe** was venerated by the Druids; partly because they ascribed peculiar medicinal virtues to it, and partly because it was found on the stalwart oak, the favourite tree of their god *Tutanes*, or *Bel;* corresponding to the Phœnician sun-god *Baal*, who was worshipped under so many different names by the nations of antiquity. On stated days they cut the sacred plant with a golden knife, and distributed it among the people; but on December 21st, when the sun resumed its upward course, in addition to the usual ceremonies, two white bulls were sacrificed in the thickest part of the grove, and huge fires were lighted in honour of that bright luminary whose festival was now inaugurated. In the early days of Christianity the clergy made the most strenuous attempts to prevent the decoration of the churches with evergreens, but all to no avail. All they could do was to prevent the mistletoe from being employed in combination with them. The white and everlasting flowers which have latterly come into general use for adorning the principal parts of the church, are emblems of purity and everlasting woe. For the social custom of **Kissing under the Mistletoe** we are indebted to Scandinavian mythology. Baldur, the Apollo of the North, and the favourite of the gods, was hated by Loki; but as nothing that sprang from fire, earth, air, or water, could harm him, the wicked spirit accomplished the death of Baldur by means of a mistletoe dart. As some reparation for this injury the plant was afterwards dedicated to Frigg, Baldur's mother, so long as it did not touch earth, Loki's empire. In her hands it became the emblem of love, for everyone who passed under it received a kiss to show that it was no longer the instrument of enmity and death. This is why the mistletoe is suspended in our houses during the season when amity, peace, and good-feeling abound.

465. **The Burning of the Yule Log** had a Scandinavian rather than a Druidical origin. Although a counterpart of the Midsummer fires lighted out of doors in all parts of the country at the festival of the summer solstice (*see* 446), the Scandinavian nations gave the name of *Yuul* to their great winter festival, at which immense bonfires were enkindled in honour of their god Thor. The bringing in from the woods and placing on the hearth of the baronial hall the ponderous block was a time-honoured observance on Christmas Eve.

466. **Bringing in the Boar's Head** was formerly an elaborate ceremonial during the Christmas Day repast at all the mansions of the wealthy. This was a survival of the Middle Ages, when a whole boar, richly gilded, was served up at table by way of brawn. The time-honoured custom still obtains, if nowhere else, at Queen's College, Oxford, in memory of an incident connected with the history of that establishment. One day, while walking in Shotover Forest, absorbed in the study of his Aristotle, a young collegian was suddenly made aware of the presence of a wild boar, in consequence of the animal making a rush at him open-mouthed. With extraordinary presence of mind he made no more to do of it than to exclaim "Græcum est," and thrust the philosopher's ethics down his assailant's throat; then, having effectually choked the monster, went on his way rejoicing. At least so runs the story.

467. **The Christmas Mummeries** of a bygone day,

which were brought to an end on Twelfth Night, all traced their being, like the modern Carnival (*see* 423) to the **Roman Saturnalia**, a festival said to have been instituted B.C. 497, to commemorate the equality which prevailed on the earth in the golden reign of Saturn. Whatever its origin, the Saturnalia was unquestionably a season of remarkable licence. Slaves were freed for the time being, and even waited upon by their masters. Everyone had full liberty to speak his mind. Work was stopped, the schools were closed, and war was temporarily suspended. Gifts were exchanged by all classes, who went about in masks and fantastic attire, while feasting and debauchery marked the hour. To check the mischievous tendencies of these excitements, which suffered no abatement during the first centuries of Christianity, the clergy invented plays, farces, and pantomimes, founded upon mythological subjects and popular legends, and these they performed in the churches during the holiday season, hoping thereby to divert the people from the more dangerous amusements out of doors. The Easter and Whitsuntide plays were of a different kind, being essentially religious in character; but even these contained a modicum of buffoonery, suited to the coarse tastes of the age. As for the Christmastide entertainments, they were burlesques of the most extravagant order. So outrageously did even the highest dignitaries of the Church disport themselves with their congregations, that the season soon received the name of **The Feast of Fools.** About the same time similar buffooneries were introduced at Court and in the castles of the nobility, all the retainers taking part therein under the direction of "the Lord of Misrule," a personage corresponding to the "Abbot of Misrule" in the monasteries and churches. In the sixteenth century these displays became more refined, and thenceforward received the name of **Masques,** from the large masks still worn by some of the performers. They were really the private theatricals of the nobility, answering the same purpose as the drawing-room plays and acting charades of the present time. How much the Court masque had in common with the modern Christmas pantomime is shown in another place (*see* 230).

468. The custom of making presents at Christmas time was derived from the Romans, who made gifts to one another during the Saturnalia (*see* 467). They are called **Christmas Boxes** from the alms-boxes formerly placed in the churches to receive the donations of the congregation for the benefit of the poor on Christmas morning. As the alms were not doled out until the following day, December 26th came to be known as **Boxing Day.** On the same occasion watchmen, scavengers, and others made the rounds of the parish collecting perquisites (*see* 416, 469). The early Christians presented their children with toys, fruits, and clothing on Christmas morning, under the pretence that they had been dropped through the roof by the Christ-Child while passing over the houses during the night. A similar deception is practised in Germany, where "Kriss Kringle" has almost entirely usurped the place of St. Nicholas in the minds of the little folk. In Holland and Belgium it is still **Santa Klaus** who is supposed to fill the stockings and shoes with good things over-night, though why he should do this on Christmas Eve rather than St. Nicholas' Eve, as of old, surpasses understanding. True, there may be a few out-of-the-way places where the original date is still observed. Years ago it was the custom in Friesland to send round to all the houses on St. Nicholas' Eve a fellow dressed in imitation episcopal robes and mitre to impersonate the saint, inquiring whether the children had been good or bad, and promising them toys or a rod, as the

case might be, against the morning. An adaptation of this custom still lingers in many German villages, where on Christmas Eve, one "Knecht Rupert," in high buskins and an enormous flaxen wig, brings the children their presents if good, or a rod if disobedient, according to instructions received from their parents. In some places he is called "Pelsnichol," or Nicholas with the fur, from the fur cap and coat trimmed with fur that he wears. It should be mentioned in this place that our **Father Christmas**, represented as an old man with snow-white beard and locks, is taken from the Priapus of Virgil and Petronius, who held in his capacious bosom all manner of fruits and dainties.

469. **The Christmas Waits** were originally Court pages, and afterwards town musicians, who, to show that they dispensed the Lord Mayor's music, wore his cognizance on a badge on their arms. At a later period, the civic watchmen employed to call out the successive hours of the night took upon themselves the doubtful pleasure of serenading the sleeping inhabitants with joyful song at the approach of Christmas. These performances certainly enhanced their prospects of receiving a gratuity when Boxing Day came round (*see* 468). Last of all, when the watchmen were displaced by the police in 1829, private musicians embraced the opportunity of earning a little money in the character of waits. The reader will scarcely require to be informed that the hymns rendered on such occasions had their origin, like the **Christmas Carols**, in the "Gloria in excelsis Deo," sung by the angels in the hearing of the shepherds at the birth of the Saviour. If there is one country more than another where the people enter thoroughly into the spirit of the Nativity, it is Holland. In nearly every Dutch town, at two o'clock on Christmas morning, the young men assemble in the market-place, singing the "Gloria,"

and various other appropriate hymns. One of them carries a large artificial star, within which is a lighted candle, aloft on a pole. This is supposed to represent the star that guided the steps of the three kings to the stable at Bethlehem. The effect of the solitary light in the surrounding darkness is very marked. Their devotions ended, the whole party make a parade through the town to the house of some opulent inhabitant, where a supper is spread before them.

470. **The Christmas Tree** was introduced into England by the Prince Consort shortly after his marriage with Queen Victoria. In America it is much more popular than among ourselves, having been introduced over there long ago by the German and Dutch emigrants. That it should be peculiar to Germany is strange, seeing that its origin carries us back to a period long anterior to Christianity. It is a well-known fact that the palm-tree puts forth a branch every month; wherefore the ancient Egyptians employed a spray of the palm, having twelve shoots upon it, at the time of the winter solstice as a symbol of the completed year.

471. **The Christmas Candles** which in some remote parts of the country are still burned from the early dawn until the close of day, lest some evil should befall the house during the ensuing year, are a survival of the monstre Yule candle which in former times shed its light upon the festive board at this season. Although an accompaniment of the Yule log, the candle had a totally different significance. Whereas the former claimed a pagan origin, the latter was a sign of the Light that came into the world, as prophesied by John the Baptist. The lighting of the tiny coloured candles on the Christmas tree (*see* 470) has the like meaning. It was the presentation of these candles by the tallow

chandlers to their regular customers at Christmas time that made other tradesmen follow suit with a Christmas box (*see* 468).

472. **The Roast Beef of Old England** still enters most conspicuously into our Christmas dinner fare. It will doubtless be news to many to learn that the object of serving it up at this season was really to remind our forefathers of the bulls sacrificed by the Druids when the sacred mistletoe was cut (*see* 464). The **Christmas Pudding** is supposed to be emblematical of the rich offerings made by the three kings to the Infant in the stable at Bethlehem. The **Mince Pies** are all that are left to us of the immense Christmas pie of forced meat and sweet materials, formerly placed upon the festive board in the shape of a cratch or cradle, emblematical of the manger in which our Saviour was laid. When the large pie first gave place to a multitude of smaller ones, they were made coffin-shaped instead of round as nowadays, the better to realize the idea of the manger.

473. **The Pantomime on Boxing Day** is a time-honoured institution. It was on December 26th, 1717, that John Rich produced the first English pantomime, "Harlequin Executed," at the Lincoln's Inn Fields Theatre, and from that time to the present King Pantomime has regularly followed close upon the heels of Father Christmas. Pantomimes are said to be "invented" rather than written nowadays. Here again we note the analogy between the pantomime and the Court masque. A masque produced upon a scale of unparalleled splendour at Whitehall on Shrove Tuesday, 1663, was announced as "invented" by Inigo Jones and Thomas Carew, the Cavalier poet (*see* 230).

474. **Innocents' Day** (December 28th) was formerly regarded as the most unlucky day of the whole year. To instil into their minds a horror of Herod's Massacre of the Innocents on this day, children were soundly whipped in their beds before rising by their parents. This was an ecclesiastical idea. Being undeserving of such punishment, the young folk were thus taught to suffer pain, like the Innocents, for Christ's sake.

475. A strange superstition prevails in many English families in connection with the **Christmas Holly.** Before midnight on New Year's Eve every vestige of holly must be removed, or ill-luck will be sure to fall upon the house. The inference to be drawn from this is that the New Year must be entered upon in all seriousness, with nothing to put them in mind of the late festivities. According to old-established rule, the holly should not be taken down until after Twelfth Night.

INDEX

INDEX

NOTE.—*The references here are to pages, those in the Contents are to articles.*